THE
EVERYTHING.
INDIAN SLOW COOKER
COOKBOOK

Dear Reader,

Growing up in an Indian family among the vibrant spices and aromatic kitchen, Indian food never came across as complicated to me. But many years and a move around the globe later I was dumbfounded by the perception that Indian cuisine holds. It has often been perceived to be a little complex. Although thanks to globalization and thousands of talented Indian cooks, Indian cuisine is gaining a well-deserved popularity today. Garam masala and turmeric are sneaking into many new kitchens slowly, but many busy cooks like us are facing yet another dilemma: how to cook a good wholesome meal for the family while also taking care of the thousand other things throughout the day.

   With this book I have tried to make Indian food simple enough to be cooked in a slow cooker. Here you will find recipes from all across India. Be it chole masala from Punjab, pav bhaji from the streets of Maharashtra, or Goan shrimp from the beautiful beaches of Goa, you can whip it all up without a fuss in your slow cooker, right in your kitchen. I have tried to bring to you a wide variety of Indian recipes suitable for every occasion, with simple steps to follow.

   I hope the dishes in this book help tingle your taste buds and warm your heart.

Prerna Singh

Welcome to the EVERYTHING Series!

These handy, accessible books give you all you need to tackle a difficult project, gain a new hobby, comprehend a fascinating topic, prepare for an exam, or even brush up on something you learned back in school but have since forgotten.

You can choose to read an Everything® book from cover to cover or just pick out the information you want from our four useful boxes: e-questions, e-facts, e-alerts, and e-ssentials.

We give you everything you need to know on the subject, but throw in a lot of fun stuff along the way, too.

We now have more than 400 Everything® books in print, spanning such wide-ranging categories as weddings, pregnancy, cooking, music instruction, foreign language, crafts, pets, New Age, and so much more. When you're done reading them all, you can finally say you know Everything®!

QUESTION

Answers to
common questions

FACT

Important snippets
of information

ALERT

Urgent
warnings

ESSENTIAL

Quick
handy tips

PUBLISHER Karen Cooper

MANAGING EDITOR, EVERYTHING® SERIES Lisa Laing

COPY CHIEF Casey Ebert

ASSISTANT PRODUCTION EDITOR Melanie Cordova

ACQUISITIONS EDITOR Kate Powers

SENIOR DEVELOPMENT EDITOR Brett Palana-Shanahan

EDITORIAL ASSISTANT Matthew Kane

EVERYTHING® SERIES COVER DESIGNER Erin Alexander

LAYOUT DESIGNERS Erin Dawson, Michelle Roy Kelly, Elisabeth Lariviere

Visit the entire Everything® series at *www.everything.com*

THE EVERYTHING

INDIAN SLOW COOKER COOKBOOK

Prerna Singh

Aadamsmedia
Avon, Massachusetts

AASHVI, this is for you!
Love,
Maa

———————————

An Everything® Series Book.
Everything® and everything.com® are registered trademarks of F+W Media, Inc.

Published by Adams Media, a division of F+W Media, Inc.
57 Littlefield Street, Avon, MA 02322 U.S.A.
www.adamsmedia.com

Contains material adapted and abridged from *The Everything® Indian Cookbook* by Monica Bhide, copyright © 2004 by F+W Media, Inc, ISBN 10: 1-59337-042-3, ISBN 13: 978-1-59667-042-8; *The Everything® Vegetarian Slow Cooker Cookbook* by Amy Snyder and Justin Snyder, copyright © 2012 by F+W Media, Inc., ISBN 10: 1-4405-2858-6, ISBN 13: 978-1-4405-2858-3; *The Everything® Healthy Slow Cooker* by Rachel Rappaport with B. E. Horton, MS, RD, copyright © 2010 by F+W Media, Inc., ISBN 10: 1-4405-0231-5, ISBN 13: 978-1-4405-0231-6; and *The Everything® Slow Cooker Cookbook, 2nd Edition* by Pamela Rice Hahn, copyright © 2009 by F+W Media, Inc., ISBN 10: 1-59869-977-6, ISBN 13: 978-1-59869-977-7.

ISBN 10: 1-4405-4168-X
ISBN 13: 978-1-4405-4168-1
eISBN 10: 1-4405-4169-8
eISBN 13: 978-1-4405-4169-8

Printed in the United States of America.

10 9 8 7 6 5 4 3 2 1

Always follow safety and commonsense cooking protocol while using kitchen utensils, operating ovens and stoves, and handling uncooked food. If children are assisting in the preparation of any recipe, they should always be supervised by an adult.

Many of the designations used by manufacturers and sellers to distinguish their products are claimed as trademarks. Where those designations appear in this book and Adams Media was aware of a trademark claim, the designations have been printed with initial capital letters.

This book is available at quantity discounts for bulk purchases.
For information, please call 1-800-289-0963.

Contents

Introduction 9

1 Basics of Indian Cooking 11

Essential Techniques 12

Essential Ingredients 14

Cooking with Spices 15

Basic Indian Spice Pantry 17

Grinding and Storage Guidelines 18

Tools 18

Masaledani 19

Adapting Recipes for Your Slow Cooker 23

Don't Be Afraid to Take Shortcuts or Improvise 24

2 Basic Sauces and Spice Mixes 26

3 Indian Slow Cooker Foundation Recipes 36

4 Appetizers 44

5 Soups and Stews 62

6   Lentils and More. 83

7   Vegetarian 109

8   Poultry 139

9   Beef, Pork, Goat, and Lamb. 161

10   Fish 183

11   Rice 204

12   Desserts 237

13   Chutney and Raita Dips 258

14   Beverages. 275

15   Basic Breads of India 286

Glossary 293

Index. 297

Acknowledgments

There's a huge list of people who have helped me get here with this book. I do not think a "Thank you" would help me express how grateful I am to each and every one of them, but I will try.

To my gorgeous little family for being the wind beneath my wings. My husband Abhishek for all his love, support, and belief in me. My daughter Aashvi for inspiring me to do better every day and being my biggest stress buster. To both the mothers in my life, mummy (my mom) and mumma (my mother-in-law) for teaching me all the cooking that I know today and for helping me understand the value of a good and healthy kitchen. To my father, father-in-law, and brother Abhinav for cheering me every step of the way.

To all my friends in the blogging world and beyond for their support, especially Kulsum, Rose, and Kankana for graciously sharing their recipes for this cookbook. To each and every one of the readers of IndianSimmer. com.

And last but definitely not the least, to the whole team of Adams Media and especially Kate Powers for being there with me all along the way. I cannot thank you enough, no matter how hard I try. *Thank you, Sukriya, Dhanyawad* from the bottom of my heart!

Introduction

ONE OF THE ANCIENT civilizations known to man, India is home to more than a billion people. Its people live in several regions, follow different religions, speak different languages, and to an extent dress differently, too. But all of this, when it comes together and works together harmoniously, is what makes India. Just like its rich and varied culture, Indian food is as varied as it can get. The region of the country defines it crop, and crops define the cuisine of that region—which turns out to be endless in number and diversity. Followers of several religious beliefs have also played a big role in the evolution of Indian cuisine. In addition, the multitude of invaders throughout the country's history has greatly influenced Indian cuisine: the Mughals, Turks, Europeans, and Portuguese all left their mark. With its extensive use of spices and herbs, Indian cuisine is widely accepted around the world. But there is much more history behind this rich cuisine.

Through the course of time, Indian cuisine has kept evolving. Every event and era left an impression on it, and so has modernization. With today's globalization and modern lifestyle, the cuisine is reaching another height of popularity. There was a time when Indian food meant alien flavors and unknown spices to foreign pallets. But today, tandoori chicken and naan are far from alien words anymore. Indians have reached every corner of the world, and so has Indian food. Haldi and Garam Masala have entered kitchens around the globe, and these flavors are getting more and more familiar.

But with liking the cuisine comes the issue of time crunch. Everyone is on the run today. People are busy going places as they try to keep up with our fast-moving world. But at the same time, every responsible person wants good home-cooked food for their family, including the Indian food lover. But who has time to sit and slowly reduce kheer (rice pudding) or make a perfectly cooked pork roast while juggling so many roles? The invention of the slow cooker has made home-cooked dishes a reality for busy people like you and me.

Dum pukht is a centuries-old cooking practice followed by Indian cooks and chefs. Slow cooking follows the same science of dum pukht by slowly cooking food in minimal liquid, trapping steam inside the cooking vessel, which helps food cook in its own juices. This cooking process greatly enhances the flavor of food while using comparatively less spices. And the best part is that the food can be cooked while you are on the go. Just add the ingredients together in the slow cooker; and when you come back, your house is filled with aroma, and the slow cooker is filled with a home-cooked meal waiting for you.

The Everything Indian Slow Cooker Cookbook® is a collection of 300 such Indian recipes that will help you make your favorite Indian dish right at home in your slow cooker.

CHAPTER 1

Basics of Indian Cooking

There is nothing like the taste, smell, and flavor of an Indian kitchen. Between the spicy bite of curry powder and the sweetness of a mango, Indian is among the most flavorful styles of cooking in the world today. The aroma of spices combining together to make the flavor come alive, the mouthwatering fragrance of the day's meals simmering together, the spicy taste of a freshly prepared dish—all of these things make Indian cuisine a favorite among foodies. And the best part? It's not as hard as you think to have your kitchen filled with the delicious smells and flavors of India.

Essential Techniques

Indian cooking and cuisine are often perceived as complicated. It's true that there are several complicated flavors and some not-so-common techniques used in Indian cooking, but once you know the basics, Indian cooking will turn out to be one of the simplest things you have ever tried to do. In this chapter, you will learn some basics of Indian cuisine and some commonly used techniques in the Indian kitchen. Even though you will be using a slow cooker for these recipes, it's important that you learn the ins and outs of Indian cooking and cuisine.

It is important to understand a few simple cooking techniques before you begin your journey into the world of Indian cooking. These techniques can be used individually in recipes, but more often they are used in unison. By understanding the principles behind each technique, you can ensure the success of your recipes.

Dum (Steaming)

Dum refers to cooking the food in its own steam. You will notice that many recipes direct you to cover the cooking pot with a lid and reduce the heat to complete the cooking process. This is the modern-day version of dum—it helps the dish retain its aroma and helps the flavors seep in. In olden days, the lid of a cooking pot was sealed to the pot using wheat flour dough, thus ensuring that the steam would not escape. This pot was then placed on hot charcoals, and the dish was allowed to cook.

Tadka or Baghar (Tempering)

Tempering is the process of seasoning a dish with hot oil infused with spices. This can be done at the beginning of the recipe or at the end, depending upon the dish. It involves heating the oil until it is almost smoking, reducing the heat, and then adding the spices. The spices begin to sizzle and change color, indicating that they are cooked; then either more ingredients are added or the tempered oil is poured over a completed dish.

There are a couple of things to keep in mind with this process. When you add spices to hot oil, they will sizzle and splatter, so be prepared to remove the skillet from the heat immediately or have the additional ingredients on hand so you can add them quickly. Do not add any water to this seasoning;

this will cause the oil to lose its flavor and potency. Also note that when you are adding spices to the heated oil, you should add them one at a time. Begin with the whole spices, then add the herbs, and then the powdered spices. Add each spice one at a time.

Bhunao (Sautéing)

Bhunao is the most commonly used cooking technique in Indian cooking. This technique requires sautéing ingredients over medium to high heat while constantly stirring. In the recipes where sautéing is required, you can add a bit of water to the ingredients to keep them from sticking to the pan. This technique allows the ingredients to release their true flavors. To ensure that the ingredients are fully cooked, continue to sauté until the fat begins to separate from the spice mixture or the masala that is being cooked.

Tandoori Cooking (Grilling)

Traditionally, roasting in the Indian kitchen was done in clay ovens called *tandoors*. All the recipes in this book that call for any kind of tandoori cooking have been modified to suit your grill or oven. Just remember, if a recipe calls for a dish to be marinated prior to grilling, make sure to follow the recipe's directions as to how long it should be marinated to ensure that the marinade is able to exude its flavors. Discard any remaining marinade per the recipe directions.

ALERT

Safety is important when you are deep-frying, so please take appropriate precautions when using hot oil. Make sure the deep fryer or wok is not easily accessible to children.

Talina (Deep-Frying)

Another key cooking technique used in Indian food is deep-frying. Traditionally, a deep vessel, similar to the Chinese wok, is used to heat the oil. You can use a deep fryer if you wish. Although some people like to reuse oil used for deep-frying, it is best to use fresh oil each time you deep-fry. The key to deep-frying is to let the oil return to frying temperature between fried batches. Also, do not use large quantities of oil to deep-fry—the quantity should be just enough to immerse the ingredients, usually about 1 or 2 inches of oil is enough.

Essential Ingredients

It's important to become familiar with the common ingredients in Indian cooking, their usage, and their necessity in the cuisine. Once you have mastered these basic ingredients, you can begin to improvise on the recipes.

Basic Spices and Spice Mixes

Spices are used in Indian cooking to provide a myriad of flavors. They can be used whole, ground, toasted, rarely raw, individually, or as mixes. Chapter 2 introduces you to some basic spice mixtures that are used throughout the book. You should prepare these mixes as needed (not in advance) to ensure that you get the best flavor each time.

Many Indian grocery stores now sell some of these spice mixes premade. These can be a real time saver if you are in a pinch. If you buy premade mixes, be sure to check the manufactured dates on the packages. Spices are covered in more detail later in this chapter.

Ginger-Garlic Paste

A mixture of minced ginger and garlic, this paste is used in many recipes in this book. This book provides a recipe for you to prepare this at home. Again, if you are in a pinch, you can buy premade Ginger-Garlic Paste at your local Indian grocer. This paste keeps for months if refrigerated. Ginger-Garlic Paste cooks quickly and can burn, so watch it carefully when you cook with it.

Oils

Traditionally, Indian cooking uses ghee, or clarified butter, as a cooking medium. Most of the recipes in this book can be prepared using any light vegetable oil of your choice. Ghee is used in some dishes to provide a unique nutty flavor to the dish. In some eastern Indian states, mustard oil is used as a cooking medium. This oil is very pungent and should be heated to a smoking point before using (to reduce its bitterness).

Olive oil is not used in traditional Indian cooking because it causes the spices to lose their individual flavors. Also, many Indian dishes require cooking at a very high heat, and olive oil tends to burn easily.

Souring Agents

Indian dishes have a balance of many flavors—hot, sour, sweet, salty, spicy—all in one recipe. Common souring agents are tamarind, lemon or lime juice, vinegar, tomatoes, and even yogurt. Tamarind and lemon juice can generally be substituted for each other in the recipes here, except in the recipe for Tamarind Chutney (Chapter 13). When a dried (as opposed to wet) souring agent is needed, amchoor, or dried mango powder, is often used.

Tenderizers

Traditional Indian cooking uses raw papaya and yogurt as meat tenderizers. In this book you will find the use of one additional tenderizer, pineapple.

Thickening Agents

You will notice the use of yogurt, chickpea flour, onions, and nut pastes in a number of recipes. These are traditionally used as thickening agents. They add a lot of body to sauces in Indian dishes.

Cooking with Spices

Using spices in Indian cooking is a 3,000-year-old tradition. Ancient Indian texts focused primarily on three characteristics of spices—their medicinal properties, their ability to act as food preservatives, and their ability to season food. Ayurveda, the ancient Indian art of healing, teaches that food plays an essential part in one's health and sense of well-being. For food specifically, these texts say that you should have sweet, tangy, salty, and hot all in the same meal or at least in the day; this helps balance out your sense of taste. Spices provide all of these flavors.

Combining Spices

Spices also add depth and complexity to food. They can be added individually or in mixes. Use the spice mix recipes provided in this book or create your own. There really is no single right spice mixture—if it tastes good to you, it is the right mix! Many Indian grocery stores sell premade spice mixes that can be a real time saver if you are in a bind.

The secret to making perfect Indian dishes is in the spices. Understanding the flavors that they provide, at what point in the cooking process to add them, and in what order to add them is at the heart of Indian cuisine. Most spices need to be cooked to help release their flavors. There are a few spices that can be used raw. Raw green cardamom or cloves, for instance, are often used as a garnish.

Guidelines for Preparing Spices

If you are using oil or ghee (clarified butter) to cook your spices, ensure that the oil is hot before you add the spice. Hot oil has the ability to retain the flavor of the spice. If your oil is too cold, the spice will not release its flavor. Ghee, which is often used in India, has the ability to be heated to very high temperatures. It also retains spice flavors a lot better than oils.

If you need to roast spices, first make sure that you use a totally dry skillet—no oil or water. Second, ensure that the skillet is hot before you add the spices. Spices cook very quickly and can easily burn, so you must constantly stir and be ready to remove them from the heat as soon as they brown and you can smell their fragrance.

Be careful when making substitutions. Coriander powder, for instance, cannot be substituted for fresh coriander, or cilantro, and saffron cannot be substituted for turmeric. If you are unsure about a spice, check the glossary of this book for more information. You can use ground spices for whole spices in some cases, but just remember that whole spices have a much stronger flavor. Taste to adjust seasoning as necessary, being careful not to overspice.

As you begin to gain an understanding of spices, their flavors and characteristics, and begin to cook some of the recipes in this book, follow this piece of advice: Stick to the recommended steps and spice quantities the first time. As you gain more experience with the spices and are able to determine how to balance the amount of spices to add to a dish, you can improvise as you like.

Finally, make sure that you have all the spices ready to go before you start cooking. In many recipes the spices need to be added in quick succession, and you will not have time to go looking for them in the middle of the cooking process. Remember, spices tend to burn easily, so having them at the ready will make the process easier. If your spices do burn, toss them away and begin again. There is nothing worse than the taste of burned spices!

Basic Indian Spice Pantry

Every Indian spice pantry needs to have the bare essentials to start cooking Indian meals. Make sure your shelves are always stocked with the following spices:

- Salt
- Red chili (whole and powder)
- Turmeric
- Coriander (whole and powder)
- Cumin seeds
- Mustard seeds
- Bay leaves
- Cinnamon
- Cloves
- Black peppercorns
- Asafetida
- Green and black cardamom
- Carom seeds (also called *ajowan* or *ajwain*)
- Mango powder
- Tamarind pulp
- Dried fenugreek leaves

Grinding and Storage Guidelines

Make sure that your spices are fresh—this is the golden rule of Indian cooking. Replace your spices at least once a year. How should you test freshness? Use your nose. If you open a package of spices and cannot smell the aroma, the spices have lost their potency and should not be used. Even for the mixed masala or spice mixtures, you will notice a difference in smell (and flavor!) if you prepare them fresh when you need them.

For grinding spices you can use a couple of different tools. You can use a mortar and pestle or a coffee grinder. (If you are using a coffee grinder, buy one to use just for the spices, since it will take on the smell of the spices.)

The best place to store the spices is in a cupboard or a drawer away from direct sunlight. If you can, use glass or clear plastic jars—this way you can see how much spice you have left. Also, never use a wet spoon to remove spices from a jar. This will keep them fresher longer.

If you live in a very hot area, you can store your spices in the refrigerator to keep them fresher longer. Just make sure that you are using airtight jars.

Tools

This book is about slow cooker recipes, so the most important tool used for the recipes will be a slow cooker, of course. But apart from that, you may need the following utensils:

- **Deep pan**: A dutch oven or a deep sauté pan can be used. To make the cooking process easier, use nonstick pans. In India, a traditional cooking vessel like this is called a *karahi* and is similar to a wok.
- **Tempering pan** (Tadke ka bartan): These are small 1- or 2-cup capacity pans used mainly for the tempering (tadka) process. It has a small handle to make it easier to hold while cooking.
- **Food processor**: This is a real time saver in the kitchen; perfect for mincing, chopping, and grating.
- **Blender**: Wonderful for making chutneys, drinks, and soups.
- **Sieve**: A sieve is perfect for draining whey and straining.
- **Spice grinder/coffee mill/mortar and pestle**: Use any one of these to grind dry spices.

These are the only specialty tools you will need to buy (in case you do not already have them) for the recipes in this cookbook.

Masaledani

Every Indian kitchen has a *masaledani,* which is a typical spice box with five to six basic spices. These basic spices can go a very long way when it comes to Indian cooking. A small introduction of these spices can help you understand the cuisine better and make it less intimidating.

Turmeric *(Haldi)*

Turmeric is one spice that Indians can't cook without, no matter what part of the country they're from. Turmeric can be used fresh, dry, or in ground form. It belongs to the ginger family, so fresh turmeric looks very similar to gingerroot. It has a mild taste and is slightly peppery or bitter. Like any other food, fresh turmeric has a much stronger flavor, but it's the milder ground form that is more commonly used all around India.

More than flavor, turmeric is used to add color to food. In fact, some people call it "Indian saffron," and back in the old days it was used as a cheaper alternative to saffron. Be it a simple stir-fry, a *dal* (lentil soup), a spicy curry, or an Indian pickle, turmeric is used everywhere. In addition to being called on for its brilliant yellow color and mild flavor, turmeric is also used as a preservative. For example, to make pickles, my grandma would coat raw mangoes or vegetables with a mixture of salt and turmeric and leave them out in the sunlight to dry. Those pickles would last for years! Turmeric is also used to color cheese, yogurt, spice mixes, salad dressings, and even butter and margarine.

Outside of the kitchen, this spice is known for its therapeutic properties. Did you know that turmeric is a fabulous anti-inflammatory agent and an antiseptic? As a child, whenever I came home with a cut or bruise, my mom would rub a paste of turmeric and water on the afflicted area and it worked like magic. If I had a fever, she would give me *haldi doodh* (a little turmeric mixed with warm milk). In India, when a girl is about to get married, she gets a body massage with a paste of turmeric, as it is believed to improve the skin tone and is considered a great anti-aging agent.

It is thanks to all these medicinal, culinary, and cosmetic qualities that turmeric has earned a sacred place in Indian culture and history, especially in a Hindu home.

Chili Powder (*Lal Mirch*)

It is believed that chili was first introduced to India by the great Portuguese explorer Vasco da Gama. The spice was a welcome addition to the cuisine, and India's climate helped cultivate many varieties of chili across the country. *Lal mirch*, or Indian chili powder, is very similar to cayenne pepper, which you can find easily in the United States and Europe. Unlike Mexican or American chili powder varieties where salt or spices are added to the pepper, Indian chili powder is pure ground red pepper. Dried red chilies are powdered after being sun-dried until they are nice and crisp. The red chili peppers range from orange to dark red and have a pungent odor with a very strong bite.

There are two main types of chili powders widely used in India—the usual red chili powder described above, which is fiery hot, and the milder type, which is called *Kashmiri lal mirch*. Kashmiri lal mirch is named after Kashmir, where it comes from. It has a much milder heat and, like turmeric, is used primarily to add color to the dish. The tandoori chicken and beautiful red curry that your local Indian restaurant serves get their vibrant hue from Kashmiri lal mirch. Chili powder can be used in practically any dish. An Indian cook cannot live without lal mirch; they like their meals on the spicy side!

Cumin *(Jeera)*

Cumin is another basic spice that can be found in every Indian household. It has a strong, distinctive aroma and can be used whole or ground. There are two types of cumin: white and black. Black cumin, also known as royal cumin, has a slightly sweeter taste to it. It is also a bit more rare than white cumin.

Both types of cumin have a warm and earthy flavor, which works really well with lentil soups or hearty stews. Roasting adds to the aroma of the cumin seeds, making them perfect to flavor cheese or breads. Roasted, ground cumin seeds also make a wonderful garnish for *raita* (a cooling, yogurt-based dip) and yogurt. Cumin also aids digestion, and the most common way it's enjoyed in India is in a beverage called *jal jeera*—an Indian form of lemonade (in Hindi, *jal* means water and *jeera* means cumin).

Asafetida (*Heeng*)

When you smell asafetida for the first time, it might be tough to imagine using this ingredient in cooking—in its raw state, it has a pungent, sulfurous smell. The odor is native to the entire plant, including the stems, from which this spice is derived. Not very common in the Western world, it is a staple in Indian cooking (commonly used in tempering lentils or mixed with ground rice), and it gives a lovely flavor to dishes when cooked in oil.

Asafetida has great medicinal qualities, too. It is thought to aid in digestion and is also believed to help with breathing problems and lung diseases like asthma and bronchitis. Back in the days when people were more superstitious, it was said that the strong smell of asafetida could help drive evil spirits away from children. It was also said to help get rid of alcoholism and anxiety.

Asafetida is very commonly used in lentil dishes. Add a pinch (or even less) in hot oil and it will perfume the whole dish and aid digestion. Just remember, it's potent—a pinch goes a long way.

Mustard Seeds (*Sarson*)

Mustard is a familiar spice to most people. Mainly known for its pungent flavor, it's one of those spices that are used in all regions of India in some form or another. From sarson ka saag (cooked mustard greens) in Punjab in the North to aava pindi (powdered mustard seeds preserved in oil) in the South, mustard plays a part in Indian food culture and traditions.

Unlike in the Western Hemisphere where yellow mustard rules, black mustard is used more frequently and found more easily in India. Mustard seeds make a good ingredient in salad dressings, curries, and vegetables. This spice also plays an important role in preserving pickles. Oil extracted from its seeds (mustard oil) in India is as common as olive oil in Italy. Before vegetable oils and other refined cooking oil hit the market, mustard oil was used for almost all preparations in Indian kitchens and homes, from cooking to body massage, because it's inexpensive and very good for health. However, if you're not used to it, it might take time for your palate to get accustomed to its strong taste.

ESSENTIAL

When I was a child, my grandma would put a teaspoon of salt with a few drops of mustard oil in my palm and tell me to massage my gums with it. She said it would make the gums strong and whiten the teeth. From toothache, colds, and stomach disorders to bronchitis and rheumatism, mustard is said to heal everything. Drink mustard tea before bed and kiss your fever or cold goodbye!

Coriander Seeds (*Dhaniya*)

Last but definitely not least: coriander seeds! Their sweet, earthy smell perfumes your kitchen and house. Coriander, better known in the United States as cilantro, is a very common herb in India. It's used to make marinades, chutney, and pesto; cooked in curries; and used as garnish. The fruit from this herb bears small seeds, which once dry, have a sweet, citrusy flavor and a nutty, spicy smell. In Hindi, coriander seeds are known as *dhaniya*.

Dhaniya is a must in an Indian kitchen. You can buy whole seeds from the market and roast them either in the oven or on medium-low heat in a pan. When you roast them on low heat, they slowly start giving out a beautiful smell and get slightly darker—it's the perfect way to use coriander seeds for full flavor. Then, coarsely crush the seeds and make a marinade or rub on a piece of meat with some salt and citrus before grilling. Or make a powder to use in curries. Or mix them with a couple of other spices and stuff your veggies with them before baking. Coriander seeds can make anything and everything taste like Indian food should taste!

Other Pantry Essentials

- Salt
- Bay leaves
- Cinnamon
- Cloves

- Black peppercorns
- Green and black cardamom
- Carom seeds (also called *ajowan* or *ajwain*)
- Mango powder
- Tamarind pulp
- Dried fenugreek leaves
- *Gur* or jaggery

Apart from these there are several spice mixes that can always be found in an Indian kitchen. Chapter 2 will introduce you to some of them.

Adapting Recipes for Your Slow Cooker

Many recipes that were originally designed for an oven or stovetop can easily be adapted for just about any slow cooker. The main principles of slow cooking are that you cook ingredients in liquid, covered, for a long period of time; but as long as you keep this in mind, you shouldn't be afraid to experiment with other recipes that were not originally intended for a slow cooker.

ESSENTIAL

Dried beans may be prepared in a slow cooker, but you must first soak them overnight and wash thoroughly before using them in recipes in order to remove the toxins found in some beans. This adds a fair amount of time to each recipe, so canned beans are often recommended instead.

Some cooking methods are easier to adapt for a slow cooker than others though. For example, don't attempt to deep-fry food in a slow cooker on the low setting because the oil will not be hot enough to cook your food in a desirable way. Methods that call for cooking in a liquid, such as braising and stewing, adapt well to a slow cooker.

Don't Be Afraid to Take Shortcuts or Improvise

Throughout this book there are recipe steps and sidebar suggestions that explain how you can take shortcuts without compromising a recipe. Straying from the recipe may seem like a daunting task at first, but once you understand the logic behind such shortcuts, you'll begin to look at them as alternative measures rather than total improvisations. Before you know it, you'll be adding a little bit of this and a little bit of that, which is what Indian cuisine is all about. Every household has a different recipe for a dish and every cook has a different take.

QUESTION

Can I use the slow cooker to cook seafood?
Seafood can be cooked in the slow cooker, but use caution because seafood can easily overcook. Most seafood should be added during the last 15–30 minutes of cooking. The only exception is an oily fish like salmon, which can be cooked up to 2 hours on low with no ill effect. In fact, the fish will be amazingly tender and moist due to the lack of evaporation.

Meat

Meat does not brown in the slow cooker. If you want browning for flavor or aesthetic reasons, you need to brown the meat before adding it to the slow cooker. Quickly searing meat in a dry skillet or sautéing it can accomplish this. For stews that need a thicker broth, toss the meat in flour prior to sautéing to help with both browning and thickening. Slow cooking is perfect for recipes that call for cheaper, leaner cuts of meat that need a long cooking time to become tender. Browning on the stovetop before throwing it all into a slow cooker will also help reach the temperature of 180–200°F faster, which can inhibit any microbial growth in the meat.

If the original recipe calls for a high-fat cut of meat, substitute a leaner cut. High-fat meats are not well suited to the slow cooker because they become greasy and tough. For example, instead of using bone-in pork shoulder, use pork tenderloin.

You do not need to marinate food or meat when using a slow cooker. Marinating is a process of mixing spices with food and letting it sit for some time, allowing the food to blend nicely with the spice flavors. But since slow cookers cook food slowly, the flavors penetrate into the food and, hence, prior marinating is not needed.

Boneless cuts of chicken, turkey, or duck cook relatively quickly in the slow cooker; do not cook them for longer than 4 hours on low or 2 hours on high. Boneless poultry works best in the slow cooker when it is paired with wet ingredients such as sauces, tomatoes, or soft fruit. This insures that the lean meat will not dry out during the cooking time.

Dairy Dos and Don'ts

Dairy products, like sour cream, cream cheese, or milk, do not hold up well over long cooking times. To avoid curdling, add them during the last half hour of cooking. If you are making a hot dip, do not heat it for more than an hour unless otherwise instructed. If milk is a major ingredient, for example, in a creamy sauce or soup, substitute an equal amount of evaporated milk.

Evaporated milk can be used directly from the can, and since it has been heat processed, it can withstand long cooking times. Due to the relatively short, low-heat cooking time of the last half hour, low-fat sour cream, cream cheese, or milk can be used with great success in the slow cooker despite having a tendency to separate while cooked using traditional methods.

CHAPTER 2

Basic Sauces and Spice Mixes

Mint-Cilantro Chutney
(Pudine Dhaniye Ke Chutney)
27

Hot Cilantro Chutney
27

Amchoor (Mango Powder)
28

Chaat Spice Mix (Chaat Masala)
28

Chai Masala
29

Chili-Garlic Paste
29

Garam Masala Powder
(Warm Spice Mix)
30

Ginger-Garlic Paste
(Adrak Lasan Ka Paste)
30

Goda Masala Powder
31

Panch Foran Spices
31

Homemade Paneer
(Indian Cottage Cheese)
32

Pav Bhaji Masala
33

Rasam Powder
33

Roasted Saffron (Kesar)
34

Tandoori Spice Mix
(Tandoori Masala)
34

Sambhar Masala
35

Green Chili and Coconut
Chutney (Hari Mirch Aur
Nariel Ke Chutney)
35

Mint-Cilantro Chutney (Pudine Dhaniye Ke Chutney)

Use this as a dipping sauce, salad dressing, or as a topping for grilled meats or seafood.

INGREDIENTS | YIELDS ½ CUP

1 packed cup cilantro

½ packed cup mint

2 serrano green chilies, roughly chopped

2 fresh garlic cloves

Salt, to taste

2 tablespoons fresh lemon juice

1. Blend all the ingredients in a food processor to a smooth paste. To aid in the blending process, you can add 1 tablespoon of water if needed. Chill for about 30 minutes. Serve as a dipping sauce. This chutney will keep, refrigerated, for 4 days.

Chutney Finger Foods

A tablespoon of Mint-Cilantro Chutney served on thinly sliced and lightly buttered baguette is the perfect snack on a hot summer day.

Hot Cilantro Chutney

This is a very popular North Indian chutney used as a dip and also as a base for several recipes, a few of which are mentioned in this book.

INGREDIENTS | YIELDS ½ CUP

1½ packed cups cilantro

4–6 Thai green chilies, roughly chopped

2 fresh garlic cloves

1½" piece of gingerroot

½ tablespoon cumin seeds

1 tablespoon skinless roasted peanuts (optional)

Salt, to taste

2 tablespoons fresh lemon juice

1. Blend all the ingredients in a food processor to a smooth paste. To aid in the blending process, you can add 1 tablespoon of water if needed. Chill for about 30 minutes. Serve as a dipping sauce. This chutney will keep, refrigerated, for 4 days.

Amchoor (Mango Powder)

Amchoor is nothing but dried raw mango powder. It is tart, light brown in color, and used mainly for pickling and sometimes in stir-fries and curries. It's a great way to add a tang to dishes without actually adding to their moisture. It is also a great meat tenderizer.

INGREDIENTS | YIELDS 1 CUP

2 pounds raw mango

Mango Tip

Clean the mangoes thoroughly with the skins on before peeling. Hot summer days are best for drying mango for amchoor.

1. Cut the head of each mango. Using a peeler, peel the outer skin and discard. Next, work on the flesh, peeling thin strips until you reach the seed.

2. Place the strips in a thin layer on a baking sheet or sieve. Dry either outside under the hot sun, or in a dehydrator, or in your convection oven. Turn the oven to a warm setting (around 140–170°F).

3. Let it sit under the heat for 10–12 hours or until the mango strips are as dry as a dry leaf, with no moisture left.

4. Using a spice grinder, grind the dried strips into a fine powder. Store in airtight containers in a cool, dry place; will last about 10 months.

Chaat Spice Mix (Chaat Masala)

This zesty spice mix is sprinkled over dishes once they have been cooked, adding a very tangy flavor.

INGREDIENTS | YIELDS 3 TABLESPOONS

1 tablespoon cumin seeds
1½ teaspoons dried mint leaves
¼ teaspoon black peppercorns
¼ teaspoon carom seeds
Pinch of asafetida
1 teaspoon ginger powder
1 teaspoon dried mango powder
1 teaspoon black salt

1. Heat a small skillet on medium heat. Dry roast the cumin seeds, mint leaves, black peppercorns, and carom seeds for about 2 minutes, until fragrant.

2. Remove from heat and mix in the asafetida, ginger powder, dried mango powder, and black salt.

3. Grind all the ingredients using a mortar and pestle or a spice grinder.

4. Store in an airtight jar for up to 3 months. Sprinkle over salads or cooked dishes.

Chai Masala

Indian sweet milk tea is normally flavored with some spice or other.
The recipe can be tweaked by adding or taking out a couple ingredients.

INGREDIENTS | YIELDS APPROXIMATELY ½ CUP

2 cinnamon sticks
¼ cup green cardamom pods
12–15 cloves
1 tablespoon peppercorns
1 teaspoon nutmeg
1 tablespoon soonth (dried ginger powder)

1. Dry roast the cinnamon, cardamom, cloves, and peppercorns on medium heat for 5 minutes. Cool down completely.

2. Using your spice grinder, make a fine powder of all the ingredients together. Store in an airtight container in a cool dry place; will last for several months.

Dry Ginger

Soonth, or dry ginger, is believed to have great health benefits. It helps to cure colds, coughs, and fevers. Soonth laddus are given to new moms post delivery for a healthy recovery.

Chili-Garlic Paste

This simple paste can be made ahead and stored for weeks. It's a great way
to enhance the taste of curries, or it can be used as a dip when mixed with warm oil.

INGREDIENTS | YIELDS 1 CUP

¼ cup dried whole red chilies
2 bulbs of garlic (approximately ¾ cup)

1. Soak the chilies in ½ cup water for about 1 hour.

2. If using a food processor, place the soaked chilies and garlic into the food processor and make a coarse paste. If using mortar and pestle, start by crushing the garlic and then about halfway through add the chili. Grind, making the paste to a consistency you like.

3. You can either use this paste right away or add oil and store it in an airtight container; will last for a month in the refrigerator.

Grind It Yourself!

You can use a food processor to grind the paste, but it always tastes better when ground with a mortar and pestle. Add about ¼ cup oil and store in an airtight container.

Garam Masala Powder (Warm Spice Mix)

*You can vary this recipe a bit—experiment with various spices
until you find the combination that works for you.*

INGREDIENTS | YIELDS 2 TABLESPOONS

8 cloves
4 teaspoons cumin seeds
3 green whole cardamom pods
2 black whole cardamom pods
1 (2") cinnamon stick
2 teaspoons coriander seeds
1 teaspoon black peppercorns
1 bay leaf
Pinch of grated nutmeg (optional)

1. Heat a small skillet on medium heat. Add all the spices *except* the nutmeg and dry roast the spices, stirring constantly. After about 5 minutes, the spices will darken and begin to release a unique aroma.

2. Remove the skillet from the heat, then add the nutmeg. Transfer the spice mix to a bowl and allow to cool for about 5 minutes.

3. Using a spice grinder, grind the spices to a fine powder. Store in an airtight jar. The spice mixture will keep for up to 3 months.

Ginger-Garlic Paste (Adrak Lasan Ka Paste)

*To freeze convenient portions of this paste, scoop 1-tablespoon portions
into ice trays, freeze, and transfer to a container or plastic bag.*

INGREDIENTS | YIELDS 1 CUP

2 serrano green chilies (optional)
½ cup fresh gingerroot, peeled
½ cup garlic cloves, peeled
1 tablespoon cold water

1. Remove the stems from the green chilies.

2. Place all the ingredients in a food processor and purée to form a smooth paste. Add no more than 1 tablespoon of water to help form a smooth consistency.

3. Store the paste in an airtight jar in the refrigerator. The paste will keep for up to 2 weeks in the refrigerator.

Gingerroot

Ginger is a rhizome native to India and China. Its name comes from a Sanskrit word, which translates to "a body with horns." In addition to its many healing powers, it is said to be quite the aphrodisiac!

Goda Masala Powder

This is typically a Maharashtrian spice mix, which might look very similar to the garam masala (Warm Spice Mix). Unlike garam masala, spices for goda masala are first roasted in oil and then powdered.

INGREDIENTS | YIELDS APPROXIMATELY 1 CUP

1 teaspoon oil
½ cup coriander seeds
1 tablespoon cumin seeds
4–5 bay leaves
1½ teaspoons cloves
3–4 black cardamom pods
1 cinnamon stick
2 teaspoons white sesame seeds
2 teaspoons black peppercorns

1. Heat oil in a pan over medium heat. Roast all the spices together. Stir continuously or the spices can burn. Roast until the spices turn dark, no more than 4–5 minutes. Turn off the heat. Cool down and then grind them together in your spice grinder. Transfer to an airtight container and store in a cool, dry place for 3–4 months.

Panch Foran Spices

Panch in Hindi means number five and foran is the Hindi name for tempering. Panch foran is a blend of five whole spices. All the spices in the spice blend give a distinct flavor to the dish. Panch foran spices are used in stir-fried vegetables, chutneys, and pickles.

INGREDIENTS | YIELDS 5 TABLESPOONS

1 tablespoon fennel seeds
1 tablespoon fenugreek seeds
1 tablespoon cumin seeds
1 tablespoon nigella (onion seeds)
1 tablespoon black mustard seeds

1. Mix all the spices together and store in an airtight container. You can use this mix to make several chutneys, such as, Sweet and Tangy Mango Relish (Chapter 13), Five-Spice Strawberry Chutney (Chapter 13), or in stir-fried potatoes.

Homemade Paneer (Indian Cottage Cheese)

Try stirring the milk with a plastic spatula while heating it. Stirring will prevent the milk from sticking to the bottom. But in the case that some milk still sticks to the bottom and burns, a plastic spatula will not scratch the bottom and spoil the milk.

INGREDIENTS | YIELDS 1½ CUPS

½ gallon milk

3½ tablespoons lemon juice, plus extra if needed

Ice, as needed

Avoid Rubbery Paneer

Stop the cooking process as soon as the milk curdles. Add ice to the milk. This way paneer does not come out rubbery.

1. Boil the milk in a thick-bottomed pan. Stir it from time to time to keep it from sticking at the bottom.

2. Once the milk is boiling, turn off the heat and add lemon juice, stirring continuously. It will take just a few seconds for the milk to curdle, and that's exactly the time you have to stop the cooking process, so add the ice to the pot.

3. Let it sit for about 1 minute and then strain it through a strainer lined with cheesecloth.

4. Wash the collected cheese with cold tap water (this helps wash away that extra lemony flavor). Take all the sides of the cheesecloth and tie them together. Hang it somewhere to let the extra liquid drip off (place an empty bowl below it for the liquid to collect).

5. Once the liquid (or whey) stops dripping, take out the cheese and make a big ball with it. Wrap it again with the cheesecloth. To press the cheese and give it a shape, place it on a chopping board and put a heavy pan or pot over it.

6. Let it sit for an hour or so. When all the liquid is pressed out of the paneer, cut it into pieces and use for butter paneer masala or matar paneer, or just store in zip-top bags in the refrigerator for future use.

Pav Bhaji Masala

If carefully stored in airtight containers, this spice mix will last for months.
There are also several varieties of pav bhaji masala you can easily find at any Indian grocery store.

INGREDIENTS | YIELDS APPROXIMATELY 1 CUP

½ cup coriander seeds

1½ tablespoons cumin seeds

1½ teaspoons caraway seeds

1 tablespoon cloves

1 cinnamon stick

2 teaspoons black peppercorns

8–10 whole dry red chilies

1 tablespoon red chili powder (can also use Kashmiri lal mirch or paprika)

¼ teaspoon asafetida

1½ tablespoons Amchoor (see recipe in this chapter)

2 teaspoons turmeric

1. Roast the coriander seeds, cumin seeds, caraway seeds, cloves, cinnamon, and black peppercorns in a pan over medium heat until it starts to perfume, about 5 minutes. Set aside and let it cool.

2. Grind all the ingredients together in a spice grinder. Transfer to an airtight container and store in a cool dry place.

Rasam Powder

Just like sambhar powder, rasam powder is another special spice blend that is used very commonly in South Indian cooking, especially in lentil soups and curries.

INGREDIENTS | YIELDS APPROXIMATELY 3 CUPS

¼ cup cumin seeds

½ teaspoon asafetida

¾ cup whole dried red chilies

¼ cup toor dal (yellow lentils)

¼ cup chana dal (split bengal gram)

1½ tablespoons turmeric

1½ cups coriander powder

¼ cup black pepper

1. Roast each of the whole spices and lentils separately over medium heat until aromatic, about 5 minutes. Let them cool before grinding together with all the remaining ingredients in a spice grinder. Store in airtight containers.

Roasted Saffron (Kesar)

*Never fry saffron, as it will lose its taste. Saffron is generally added
at the end of the cooking process for flavor and as a garnish.*

INGREDIENTS | YIELDS 2 TABLESPOONS

2 tablespoons whole milk

¼ teaspoon saffron threads

Caution!

Don't try to substitute another spice for saffron. The aroma and flavor of this sophisticated spice cannot be duplicated.

1. Warm the milk over low heat until it is warm to the touch (but not hot).

2. In a dry skillet, dry roast the saffron threads over low heat until fragrant, less than 1 minute. Remove from heat.

3. Pour the milk into a small bowl and add the saffron threads. Use immediately.

Tandoori Spice Mix (Tandoori Masala)

This recipe is quintessential in North India. You can also try adding red chili to it.

**INGREDIENTS | YIELDS ABOUT
2 TABLESPOONS**

½ teaspoon carom seeds

1 tablespoon Garam Masala Powder (see recipe in this chapter)

½ teaspoon ginger powder

¼ teaspoon black salt

½ teaspoon dried fenugreek leaves

¼ teaspoon dried mango powder

Prepacked Spice Mixes

If you need a spice mix in a hurry, you can buy most prepacked spice mixes (like the garam masala, tandoori masala, and chaat masala) at your local Indian grocery stores instead of making them yourself.

1. Place the carom seeds in a resealable plastic bag and crush with a rolling pin.

2. Combine all the ingredients in a bowl and mix thoroughly. Transfer to an airtight jar and store.

Sambhar Masala

*This aromatic spice mix is quintessential in South Indian cooking,
especially in the thin lentil soup called sambhar.*

**INGREDIENTS | YIELDS APPROXIMATELY
2 CUPS**

½ cup coriander seeds
12–15 dried red chilies
1 tablespoon fenugreek seeds
2½ tablespoons cumin seeds
½ teaspoon asafetida
1 tablespoon urad dal
1 tablespoon chana dal
1 tablespoon split mung bean
1 tablespoon black pepper
2 tablespoons turmeric

1. Heat a pan and roast the coriander seeds, red chilies, fenugreek seeds, cumin seeds, and asafetida. Set aside.

2. Now roast all the lentils (urad dal, chana dal, and split mung bean) until they turn very light golden and you can smell the aroma. Set aside. Let it cool.

3. Now grind all the ingredients together in a spice grinder. Store in airtight containers.

Green Chili and Coconut Chutney
(Hari Mirch Aur Nariel Ke Chutney)

*This chutney tastes best when it is made fresh, but refrigerated
it will keep for 4 days. Serve as a topping for grilled fish.*

INGREDIENTS | YIELDS 1 CUP

1 cup shredded coconut
4 serrano green chilies
1" piece fresh gingerroot, peeled
1 tablespoon fresh lemon juice
1 tablespoon minced cilantro
1 tablespoon plain yogurt (optional)
Water, as needed
1 tablespoon vegetable oil
½ teaspoon mustard seeds
2 dried red chilies, roughly pounded
4 fresh curry leaves

1. In a blender, purée the coconut, green chilies, gingerroot, lemon juice, cilantro, yogurt, and ½ cup of water to a smooth paste. Transfer to a nonreactive container with a lid and set aside.

2. In a small skillet, heat the vegetable oil. Add the mustard seeds, red chilies, and curry leaves. In less than 1 minute the mustard seeds will start to sputter. Remove from heat and pour over the coconut chutney.

3. Mix well. Refrigerate, covered, until needed.

CHAPTER 3

Indian Slow Cooker Foundation Recipes

Brown Basmati Rice
37

Perfect Slow Cooker White Rice
37

Hard-Boiled Eggs
38

Caramelized Onions
38

Curry Paste
39

Ghee
40

Khoya (Solidified Milk)
40

Makhani Masala
41

Slow Cooker Yogurt
42

Pasteurized Eggs
43

Brown Basmati Rice

Traditional white basmati rice might not cook the best in a slow cooker and can get mushy. Brown basmati rice comes out great after being slow-cooked and is healthier, too!

INGREDIENTS | YIELDS APPROXIMATELY 6 CUPS OF COOKED RICE

2 cups brown basmati rice
1 tablespoon ghee
4 cups water
Salt, to taste (optional)

Use More Water

Once all the water has been absorbed and you still think the rice is a little tough for you, try adding another cup of warm water and cook.

1. Thoroughly clean rice by rinsing it in water.

2. Brush ghee on the inside walls of the slow cooker. This will keep cooked rice from sticking to the walls, and perfumes the rice, too.

3. Transfer clean rice and 4 cups of water to the slow cooker. Add salt if desired.

4. Cover with the lid and cook on high for 3–4 hours or on low for 6–8 hours.

Perfect Slow Cooker White Rice

Parboiled or converted rice, which is widely used in India, can be made to perfection in a slow cooker.

INGREDIENTS | YIELDS APPROXIMATELY 4 CUPS

2 cups parboiled rice
2 cups water

1. Combine all the ingredients together in a 5-quart slow cooker and cook on high for 3 hours or until the rice is cooked through.

Hard-Boiled Eggs

For even cooking, try to put the eggs in a single layer in the slow cooker and not pile them on top of each other.

INGREDIENTS | YIELDS 1 DOZEN EGGS

1 dozen raw eggs
3 quarts water

1. Add water to a 5-quart slow cooker. Carefully drop in the eggs so they are all touching the base of the slow cooker. Put the lid on and cook on low for 4 hours.

Caramelized Onions

You can freeze and store these caramelized onions in airtight containers for weeks.

INGREDIENTS | YIELDS 2–2½ CUPS

2 tablespoons butter, or ghee
8 cups thinly sliced yellow onions

1. Grease the inner walls of a 6-quart slow cooker with a small amount of the butter. Add the onions to the slow cooker. Put the remaining butter/ghee on top of the onions.

2. Cover the slow cooker and cook on high for about 12 hours or until they turn brown and caramelize.

Curry Paste

Curry paste is the base of many Indian dishes including a spicy biryani and chicken curry. The secret to a perfect curry paste is slow cooking. You can store this curry paste for 2–3 weeks in a refrigerator and for months in a freezer.

INGREDIENTS | YIELDS 2½ CUPS

2 cups sliced onion

1½" piece fresh gingerroot

5–6 cloves garlic

4–5 green Thai chili peppers

2 (14-ounce) cans of tomatoes, drained

3 tablespoons coriander powder

1 teaspoon turmeric powder

3 tablespoons cooking oil

1 tablespoon ghee

Salt, to taste

3 teaspoons Garam Masala Powder (Chapter 2)

Hold Your Water

Try not to add water while grinding the wet ingredients.

1. Grind onion, gingerroot, garlic, chili peppers, and tomatoes in a blender to make a smooth paste.

2. To the wet paste add the dry spices *except* for Garam Masala. Mix it all together.

3. Add oil and ghee to a 3- or 4-quart slow cooker. Transfer the prepared wet paste. Stir everything together. Place the lid on, turn the heat to high, and cook for 2–3 hours.

4. After 1 hour stir in the salt, turn the heat to low, and cook for 4–5 hours. Stir every couple hours and scrape down the sides of the cooker. In the last 30 minutes, add Garam Masala. Cook for another 30 minutes.

5. Wait for the Curry Paste to cool down. Transfer the prepared Curry Paste to a glass container or an airtight container. Can be stored in the refrigerator for 2–3 weeks.

Ghee

*Derived from its Sanskrit name ghrith, ghee is to Indian cooking what olive oil
is to Italian. Ghee, which is nothing but clarified butter, has been used for centuries in
India as a cooking oil and is traditionally made with cream collected from cow's milk.*

**INGREDIENTS | YIELDS APPROXIMATELY
2 CUPS**

4 cups (8 sticks) butter

Fridge Ghee
If refrigerated, liquid ghee solidifies but is
still soft and creamy.

1. In a 3-quart slow cooker, place the sticks of butter in so they are all touching the bottom of the cooker. Set the slow cooker on low and let it cook for about 8–10 hours.

2. In the end you will get clear golden ghee. Scum will be floating on the top; spoon it off and discard it. Burnt milk solids will stick to the walls of the slow cooker.

3. Let the ghee come to room temperature and then filter it using a strainer. Store in airtight bottles.

Khoya (Solidified Milk)

Khoya, or mawa, is soft solidified milk made my reducing whole or reduced-fat milk at low temperature.

INGREDIENTS | YIELDS ABOUT 1½ CUPS

½ gallon milk

Different Types of Khoya
Depending on the amount of liquid in
khoya, it can be named differently. Chikna
khoya is really reduced milk, but it is
smooth and flowing and has the highest
liquid content. When reduced further, you
get daanedar khoya, which is paste-like.
Reduced further, it's called batti khoya.

1. On a stovetop, heat the milk in a large pot to bring it to a temperature of 180°F.

2. Preheat the slow cooker by heating water on high for about half an hour.

3. Discard the water and transfer the warm milk into the slow cooker and cook on high. Leave the lid open just enough for the steam to escape.

4. Stir occasionally, after every 30–40 minutes. In about 5 hours you should get chikna khoya.

Makhani Masala

Makhani masala is the base for some of the most popular Indian curries, such as butter chicken, butter paneer masala, and dal makhani. If you make this ahead of time and store in your refrigerator, whipping up such complicated Indian curries will be a breeze.

INGREDIENTS | YIELDS 2 CUPS

1 teaspoon cloves

3–4 whole black cardamoms

3–4 dried bay leaves

1½ teaspoons cumin seeds (optional)

2 whole cinnamon sticks

2 (14-ounce) cans diced tomatoes, drained

½ cup melted ghee, or butter

4 tablespoons Ginger-Garlic Paste (Chapter 2)

1½ teaspoons fenugreek seeds

1½ teaspoons Kashmiri lal mirch powder

Salt, to taste

2 tablespoons brown sugar

2 tablespoons kasuri methi (dried fenugreek leaves)

Make It Red!

You can add red food coloring for a vibrant masala, if you like a more reddish dish.

1. Grind the cloves, cardamoms, bay leaves, cumin seeds, and cinnamon sticks together in a spice grinder (ground masala). Purée tomatoes in a food processor or blender.

2. Add the ghee to a 4-quart slow cooker. Add the tomato purée, Ginger-Garlic Paste, fenugreek seeds, and Kashmiri lal mirch powder. Mix. Cover with a lid, turn the heat to high and cook for 2 hours. Scrape the sides and stir the mixture a few times during the cooking process.

3. Add salt and brown sugar to the reduced mixture. Stir again and cook for another hour.

4. Once liquid is well reduced, you will see oil slowly bubbling out and separating from the sides. Add dry ground masala and kasuri methi. *You can add food coloring at this time if you want.* Mix well, scraping the sides. Cook for another 30 minutes.

5. You can use this masala either for curries right away by adding cream and rich cashew paste, or cool and store it in the refrigerator in airtight containers for a few weeks, or freeze it for months.

Slow Cooker Yogurt

Yogurt is the base of so many dishes in Indian cuisine. You can add ½–¾ cups of powder along with the culture to get a thicker and firmer yogurt.

INGREDIENTS | YIELDS APPROXIMATELY 6–7 CUPS

6 cups milk (whole or reduced fat)
½ cup plain yogurt with active culture

1. Pour milk into a 5-quart slow cooker. Put the lid on and turn the heat on low setting; cook for 3 hours.

2. Turn the heat off and let the milk sit in the same slow cooker for 3 hours.

3. Take a cup or two of warm milk from the slow cooker, mix it with the yogurt with active culture in a small bowl. Whisk well, transfer it back to the slow cooker, and whisk entire mixture well.

4. Take a thick towel, fold it to a size bigger than the mouth of the slow cooker; place it on top of the slow cooker to cover the mouth and put the lid back on to create a seal. Cover the whole slow cooker with another towel or blanket so that the heat does not escape. Let it sit for at least 8–9 hours or overnight.

Pasteurized Eggs

Pasteurization is a method where the inner temperature of a food product is brought to a desired temperature and then immediately brought back down. This helps kill the microorganisms in the food.

INGREDIENTS | YIELDS 1 DOZEN EGGS

3 quarts water

1 dozen raw eggs

1. Fill a 4-quart slow cooker with water. Cover the lid and turn it to low for 2 hours. Usually water reaches a temperature of 145–160°F around this time. Check with a thermometer, if you can.

2. Once the water reaches this desired temperature range, slowly drop the eggs in the water. Put the lid back on and cook for 5 minutes.

3. Take the eggs out and transfer them to a bowl of cold water. The eggs should now be pasteurized, but you should still cook your eggs well before eating.

CHAPTER 4

Appetizers

Chicken Bites
45

Dhaniye Waale Aloo
(Potato Bites in Cilantro Sauce)
45

Citrusy Beets
46

Gingered Sweet Potatoes
46

Keema Pav (Indian Sloppy Joes)
47

Lamb Kofta
48

Lasuni Gobhi
49

Masala Nuts
50

Papdi Chat
50

Pav Bhaji
51

Pork Tikkas (Pork Ke Tikke)
52

Reshmi Kabab
53

Roasted Chickpeas
54

Shakarkandi (Spicy Baked
Indian Sweet Potatoes)
54

Slow Cooker Hara Bhara Kabab
55

Slow Cooker Roasted Potatoes
56

Spice Potatoes
56

Spiced Fingerling Potatoes
57

Sweet and Spicy Pineapple
Pumpkin Curry
58

Sweet and Tangy
Slow Cooker Almonds
59

Tangy Sweet Potato Bites
59

Tandoori Chicken Wings
60

Tikki Chaat
61

Chicken Bites

*These sweet and tangy chicken bites will be great for kids since they are not very spicy—
you just need to drop everything in the slow cooker in the morning,
and they will be ready to please when the kids get home.*

INGREDIENTS | SERVES 8–10

3 pounds chicken breast, cut into bite-size pieces

½ cup pineapple, diced

1½ teaspoons curry powder

1½ teaspoons Ginger-Garlic Paste (Chapter 2)

½ tablespoon coriander powder

2 tablespoons cornstarch

1 tablespoon oil

Salt, to taste

1. Mix everything together in a mixing bowl and put into your slow cooker. Set the cooker on low setting and cook for approximately 5–6 hours. If after the chicken is cooked you still feel that there's more liquid than you want, you can cook it off in a separate pan on the stovetop before serving.

Dhaniye Waale Aloo (Potato Bites in Cilantro Sauce)

These fiery hot appetizers are one of the most popular street foods in the north of India.

INGREDIENTS | SERVES 8

4 cups russet potatoes, peeled and cut into 1" cubes

½ cup Caramelized Onions (Chapter 3)

1½ teaspoons olive oil

Salt, to taste

1 teaspoon turmeric (optional)

2 cups water

4 tablespoons Hot Cilantro Chutney (Chapter 2)

1 tablespoon coriander powder

1. In a large bowl, mix together the potatoes, Caramelized Onions, oil, salt, and turmeric (optional).

2. Pour the water into a 5-quart slow cooker. Transfer the potatoes. Cover and cook it on low for about 3 hours or on high for about 1½ hours.

3. Toward the last half-hour add the Hot Cilantro Chutney and coriander powder; replace the lid and let it cook until the potatoes are cooked through. Serve hot with tea.

Tips

Add the cilantro chutney toward the end of the cooking. Slow-cooking fresh herbs for longer times makes them lose their flavor and aroma.

Citrusy Beets

Beets can be served as a warm side dish or a chilled salad over a bed of greens.

INGREDIENTS | SERVES 4

12 baby beets, ends trimmed and halved
1 cup orange juice
Juice of ½ lime
¼ red onion, sliced
½ teaspoon pepper

1. Add all ingredients to a 2-quart or a 4-quart slow cooker and cook on low for 4 hours.

Gingered Sweet Potatoes

For this festive recipe, look for candied ginger that is not coated in sugar; it's called uncrystallized ginger.

INGREDIENTS | SERVES 10

2½ pounds sweet potatoes
1 cup water
1 tablespoon grated fresh ginger
½ tablespoon minced uncrystallized candied ginger
½ tablespoon butter

1. Peel and quarter the sweet potatoes. Add them to a 4-quart slow cooker. Add the water, fresh ginger, and candied ginger. Stir.

2. Cook on high for 3–4 hours or until the potatoes are tender. Add the butter and mash. Serve immediately or turn them down to low to keep warm for up to 3 hours.

Sweet Potatoes or Yams?

Yams are not grown domestically in the United States, so the yams commonly found in supermarkets are actually varieties of sweet potato. True yams can be found in Asian or specialty stores and come in colors ranging from purple to yellow to white.

Keema Pav (Indian Sloppy Joes)

Do not let the long list of ingredients frighten you. This dish is easy to put together if you have a slow cooker. This fiery hot Indian version of Sloppy Joes will take you straight to the core of Indian old school cafés.

INGREDIENTS | SERVES 4–6

2 tablespoons cooking oil

2 teaspoons black mustard seeds

12–15 curry leaves

1 cup chopped onion

2 tablespoons Ginger-Garlic Paste (Chapter 2)

2 pounds ground lamb

1 (14-ounce) can tomato sauce

½ tablespoon garam masala

1 tablespoon coriander powder

1 teaspoon Kashmiri lal mirch

2 teaspoons minced green chili

2 tablespoons brown sugar

1 teaspoon turmeric powder

Salt, to taste

1 (8-ounce) can coconut milk

2 tablespoons lemon juice

6–8 pav (dinner roll)

1. Heat the oil in a skillet. Add the mustard seeds and curry leaves. As they pop and splatter, add the onion and Ginger-Garlic Paste. When the onion becomes translucent, add the ground lamb. Cook it on high until it browns.

2. Transfer the browned meat mixture to a slow cooker. Add the tomato sauce, Garam Masala, coriander, Kashmiri lal mirch, green chili, brown sugar, turmeric, and salt. Cover and cook on low for 3 hours.

3. Add the coconut milk, stir, and cook on high for another 30 minutes.

4. When done add the lemon juice, stir, and serve on pav.

Tips
Browning the meat on the stovetop before cooking it in the slow cooker prevents contamination.

Lamb Kofta

Koftas are the Indian version of meatballs. With vegetarianism being so prevalent in India, vegetarian koftas are hugely popular, too. Here is an easy lamb kofta recipe used as an appetizer.

INGREDIENTS | YIELDS APPROXIMATELY 4 DOZEN MEATBALLS

2 pounds ground lamb

1 cup potatoes, boiled and mashed

1 cup chopped red onion

1 tablespoon minced green chili

1 tablespoon Ginger-Garlic Paste (Chapter 2), plus 1 tablespoon for the sauce

2 tablespoons cilantro, chopped

Salt, to taste

1½ tablespoons cooking oil, or ghee

1½ cups tomato purée

1 teaspoon ground cumin

1 teaspoon turmeric powder

½ tablespoon garam masala

1 tablespoon coriander powder

1 teaspoon Amchoor (Chapter 2)

1 teaspoon salt

½ cup heavy cream

Another Option

You can use ½ cup boiled rice along with potatoes to mix in with the lamb. This helps in binding.

1. Preheat the oven to 300°F. In a large bowl, combine the ground lamb, potatoes, chopped red onion, minced chili, 1 tablespoon Ginger-Garlic Paste, cilantro, and salt to taste. Divide the mixture into equal parts and make balls out of it. This recipe should make around 4 dozen balls. Line them up on lightly oiled baking sheets. Then bake the meatballs for 15 minutes.

2. In the meantime, pour the oil or ghee into a 5-quart slow cooker. Add the tomato purée, all the dry spices, 1 teaspoon salt, and the remaining Ginger-Garlic Paste. Cover with a lid and turn the slow cooker to high setting. After the meatballs have baked for 15 minutes, take them out and transfer to the slow cooker, stirring the tomato sauce before adding meatballs. Cover and cook for 45 minutes.

3. Add heavy cream, stir, cover, and cook for another 30 minutes or until the meatballs are cooked through and there is no pink in the middle.

4. Carefully transfer the meatballs onto a serving platter. Drizzle sauce over them. If the sauce is too thin for you, reduce it by cooking on a stovetop for 15 minutes. Serve hot.

Lasuni Gobhi

Lasun or lehsun *is a Hindi name for garlic. In this mildly spicy dish, gobhi (cauliflower)
is deep-fried and then served with a garlic and tomato sauce.*

INGREDIENTS | SERVES 6

1 tablespoon ghee
1 tablespoon ginger paste
6–8 cloves garlic, grated
½ teaspoon turmeric powder
1 (14-ounce) can tomato purée
½ teaspoon fennel seeds
¼ cup thick hung yogurt
1 teaspoon garam masala
¼ cup rice flour
½ cup besan (chickpea flour)
½ teaspoon salt
1 teaspoon cayenne pepper
Water, as needed
1 large head cauliflower, cut into florets
Oil for deep-frying
2–3 cloves garlic, sliced

Save Some Time

You can always prepare the sauce in advance and refrigerate it to reheat and use later. The sauce stores well in an airtight container in your refrigerator for 2–3 weeks and can be reheated on a stovetop or microwave before served with the dish.

1. Pour the ghee into a 3-quart slow cooker. Add the ginger paste, grated garlic, turmeric, tomato purée, and fennel seeds. Mix well together. Cover and turn the heat to high setting. Let it cook and reduce for 2½ hours on high or for 4 hours on low setting.

2. Once all the excess water is reduced from the sauce, add the yogurt and Garam Masala. Mix well together, scraping the walls. Cook for another 20–25 minutes on high. Your sauce for lasuni gobhi is ready.

3. In a mixing bowl, mix together rice flour, besan, salt, and cayenne pepper. Slowly add about ¼ cup of water, whisking thoroughly, making a dipping batter the consistency of pancake batter.

4. Heat oil in a deep-fryer or wok to 350°F. Dip the cauliflower florets in the batter, coating it well, and then deep-fry until they turn dark golden in color. Place on paper towels to absorb excess oil.

5. In a little oil, fry the sliced garlic until it turns golden and crispy. Place the cauliflower florets on a plate, pour a nice serving of sauce, garnish with some garlic chips, and serve hot.

Masala Nuts

Masala nuts go very well with cocktails or beverages, such as tea and coffee. You can use any kind of nuts for this recipe. Almonds, peanuts, or mixed nuts are all good alternatives.

INGREDIENTS | YIELDS 3 CUPS

3 cups dried nuts

3 teaspoons mild curry powder

1 tablespoon vegetable oil

½ teaspoon salt

1 teaspoon white granulated sugar

1. Mix all of the ingredients together. Transfer into a 4-quart slow cooker.

2. Cook on low for 1 hour. Then uncover and cook until the nuts look dry and toasty.

Papdi Chat

Leftover Chole Masala (Chapter 7) works wonderfully as a substitute to curried yellow peas for this recipe and can turn out to be a delicious quick-fix meal.

INGREDIENTS | SERVES 8

2 cups dried whole yellow peas, soaked overnight

6 cups water

1½ teaspoons salt

1 teaspoon turmeric powder

1 tablespoon Curry Paste (Chapter 3)

1 tablespoon coriander powder

2 dozen store-bought papdi (deep-fried, thin, crispy wheat crackers)

1½ cups boiled potatoes, peeled and diced

2 tablespoons Hot Cilantro Chutney (Chapter 2)

2 tablespoons Tamarind Chutney (Chapter 13)

1 teaspoon curry powder

1 tablespoon Amchoor (Chapter 2)

1 tablespoon roasted cumin powder

½ cup chopped onion

1½ cups thin sev

1. In a 5-quart slow cooker, add yellow peas (water drained), water, salt, turmeric, Curry Paste, and coriander powder. Cover and cook on high for 4 hours, or on low for 8 hours, or until the yellow peas are well cooked. Once cooked, stir the peas well with a wooden spoon.

2. For serving, place the papdi in a single layer. Spoon cooked yellow peas over it. Then spoon boiled potatoes, followed by a drizzle of both the chutneys, a sprinkle of curry powder, Amchoor, cumin powder, and some onion and sev on top.

Pav Bhaji

Pav bhaji, where pav means simple bread rolls and bhaji means a vegetable dish, is a popular street food in the state of Maharashtra. Different vegetables are continuously cooked on low heat while vendors hand out servings after servings of bhaji to a hungry crowd.

INGREDIENTS | SERVES 8

2 tablespoons olive oil

½ pound coarsely chopped cabbage

2 cups peeled and diced potatoes

3–4 green chili peppers, chopped

1 cup chopped carrots

1½ cups thawed green peas

1½ cups chopped tomatoes

Salt, to taste

1½ tablespoons Pav Bhaji Masala (Chapter 2)

1 tablespoon Ginger-Garlic Paste (Chapter 2)

2 tablespoons lime juice

1½ tablespoons butter, plus extra for bread

16–18 dinner rolls (pav)

Chopped onions, for garnish

Chopped cilantro, for garnish

Lemon wedges (optional)

1. In a 6-quart slow cooker add oil, greasing the walls. Throw in all the vegetables, tomatoes, and salt. Turn the slow cooker to low setting, cover, and cook for 4 hours or until the vegetables are almost cooked.

2. Add Pav Bhaji Masala, Ginger-Garlic Paste, and lime juice. Stir well and cook on high for another 30 minutes or until the vegetables are well cooked.

3. Add butter and mix together well with the bhaji, mashing everything well into a homogenous thick gravy.

4. Before serving, place remaining butter in a hot skillet. Cut pav into two, sliced sideways, and add it, cut side down, to the butter in pan. Allow cut side to brown and remove from pan.

5. Garnish bhaji with chopped onions and cilantro. You can serve with some lemon wedges, browned pav, and butter on the side.

Tips

You can add any vegetable to bhaji. If the vegetables lose a lot of liquid, add ½ cup of water.

Pork Tikkas (Pork Ke Tikke)

Yogurt is used as a tenderizer in meat dishes such as this one and provides a perfect base for marinades. It is "hung" to drain out the whey and give it a creamier consistency.

INGREDIENTS | SERVES 4

1 cup Slow Cooker Yogurt (Chapter 3)

1 small onion, peeled and minced

1 tablespoon Ginger-Garlic Paste (Chapter 2)

1 teaspoon garam masala

¼ teaspoon red chili powder

¼ teaspoon turmeric powder

Salt, to taste

1 pound lean boneless pork, cubed

1 tablespoon oil

1. In a bowl (or resealable plastic bag) mix together all the ingredients *except* the oil. Cover and refrigerate for at least 1 hour or, maximum, overnight.

2. Remove pork and mix oil onto the pork. Thread the pork onto skewers. (If you are using wooden skewers, soak them in water for 30 minutes so that they don't scorch or burn.) Discard any remaining marinade.

3. Place the skewered pork into the slow cooker, each touching the bottom surface. Cover and cook on high for 4 hours (turning occasionally) or until the meat is cooked to your liking. Serve hot.

Reshmi Kabab

Resham in Hindi means "silk," so reshmi kabab refers to any bite-size grilled or baked kabab that is soft and silky when you bite on it. To make that happen, rich heavy cream or sour cream is used along with cashews as a marinade.

INGREDIENTS | SERVES 6–8

½ cup fresh mint

2–3 green chili peppers

1 tablespoon Ginger-Garlic Paste (Chapter 2)

¼ cup cashew paste

3 pounds chicken breasts, cut into ½" pieces

Salt, to taste

2 pinches nutmeg

1½ tablespoons ghee

½ cup sour cream

½ tablespoon lime juice

Tips

You can use 1½ teaspoons mint paste if fresh mint is not available.

1. Grind the mint leaves, chili peppers, Ginger-Garlic Paste, and cashew paste together. Place mixture into a large bowl and add the chicken, salt, nutmeg, and ghee. Toss it all together. Poke toothpicks through each chicken piece. Transfer the chicken into a 5-quart slow cooker. Turn the heat to high, cover, and cook for 2 hours.

2. In a small bowl, mix together the sour cream and lime juice. Pour it over the chicken. Toss and cook for another 30–45 minutes or until the chicken is cooked through.

3. Take the chicken out of the slow cooker. Place it on a baking sheet; put it under the broiler for 5 minutes on each side.

4. Reduce the extra liquid left in the slow cooker. Pour it over the chicken and serve hot with chutney or raita.

Roasted Chickpeas

Dry snacks, or as we call them namkeen or chakna, are hugely popular all across India. Every state and region has their variety of namkeen, which they serve with beverages and drinks.

INGREDIENTS | YIELDS 3 CUPS

2 (14-ounce) cans garbanzo beans
1 tablespoon lime juice
1½ teaspoons curry powder
1 teaspoon cumin powder

Canned Beans

Canned beans are already salty, so you do not need to add extra salt. But if you rinse them, then add a teaspoon of salt.

1. Drain garbanzo beans. In a large mixing bowl, combine all the ingredients and mix well.

2. Transfer mixture to a 5-quart slow cooker. Cover, but prop the lid open on the side for the steam to escape. Turn the heat to high and cook for 5–6 hours, or on low for 10 hours, or until the beans are dry and crunchy.

Shakarkandi (Spicy Baked Indian Sweet Potatoes)

This is a great option when hungry and looking for a healthy snack alternative. Instead of digging into a bag of chips, pull out some prebaked shakarkandi from the refrigerator and enjoy!

INGREDIENTS | SERVES 8–10

10 shakarkandi (Indian sweet potatoes)
½ teaspoon Chaat Masala (Chapter 2)
2 teaspoons lime juice

1. Wrap each sweet potato in aluminum foil. Place them in the slow cooker so that each one touches the bottom. Cook on low for 8 hours or until cooked through.

2. Let the sweet potatoes cool a little before opening the foil. Peel and cut into big chunks. Sprinkle with Chaat Masala and some lime juice. Toss it together and serve.

Slow Cooker Hara Bhara Kabab

Hara is a Hindi name for the color green, so you can imagine these kababs are green in color. They get their green color from spinach and green peas, which are added to the batter.

INGREDIENTS | SERVES 8

¾ cup skinless urad dal, soaked overnight
1 cup spinach
½ cup peas
1 teaspoon green chili pepper
1 teaspoon ginger, grated
1½ cups boiled and mashed potatoes
2 tablespoons cilantro, chopped
½ teaspoon cumin powder
1½ teaspoons coriander powder
¼ cup chickpea flour
¼ cup bread crumbs
Salt, to taste
3 tablespoons oil

1. In a food processor, blend together urad dal, spinach, peas, chili pepper, and ginger making a thick paste. (Do not add extra water.)

2. Scrape the blended paste into a large bowl and add the rest of the ingredients *except* for the oil. Combine the mixture and divide it into 16–18 equal parts. Make a patty from each part.

3. Pour 2 tablespoons of oil in an oval slow cooker. Place the patties so that each one touches the bottom of the slow cooker. (It's okay if they overlap or touch each other.) Brush remaining oil on top of each patty. Cover and cook approximately 3–4 hours on high or until they are brown on the outside. You can flip the patties halfway through the cooking time, if you desire. Serve with your choice of chutney or raita.

Slow Cooker Roasted Potatoes

This is a simple roasted potato recipe that goes great with Indian deep-fried breads (poori) or pan-fried breads (parathas).

INGREDIENTS | SERVES 8

7–8 medium-size potatoes
1 teaspoon ghee
1½ tablespoons olive oil
½ cup sliced onions
1 teaspoon turmeric powder
1 teaspoon black mustard seeds
2 tablespoons curry leaves

Choose Your Potato

You can use any kind of potato. Yellow or red potatoes work best though and can be used with the skin on.

1. Cut the potatoes lengthwise into big chunks. Wash with water.

2. Pour the ghee and oil into a 4-quart slow cooker.

3. In a large bowl, mix the potatoes with the rest of the ingredients. Transfer to the slow cooker.

4. Turn the slow cooker on and cook on high for 3 hours or until the potatoes are cooked through. Once done, the potatoes should be lightly browned. Serve with your choice of bread.

Spice Potatoes

Really kick it up by adding an extra teaspoon of cayenne to these potatoes!

INGREDIENTS | SERVES 4

6 cups red potatoes, cubed
1 teaspoon chili powder
½ teaspoon sugar
½ teaspoon paprika
⅛ teaspoon cayenne pepper
⅛ teaspoon garlic powder
¼ teaspoon cumin
½ teaspoon salt
⅛ teaspoon black pepper
½ cup water

1. Add all ingredients into a 4-quart slow cooker, cover, and cook on medium heat for 4 hours.

Spiced Fingerling Potatoes

Fingerling potatoes are small, long potatoes that look a little like fingers.

INGREDIENTS | SERVES 6

2 tablespoons extra-virgin olive oil
1½ pounds fingerling potatoes
1 teaspoon salt
¼ teaspoon black pepper
½ teaspoon cumin seeds
1 teaspoon whole coriander seeds
1 tablespoon fresh lemon juice

Time Saver

To save on time when cooking potatoes, always cut them into the smallest pieces the recipe will allow and cook at the highest temperature. For this recipe, you can quarter the potatoes and cook on high heat for about 2 hours.

1. Add the olive oil, potatoes, salt, and pepper to a 4-quart slow cooker, cover, and cook on low heat for 3–4 hours.

2. Remove the cover and mix in the rest of the ingredients. Put the lid back on, turn off the heat, and let it sit covered for 15 minutes before serving.

Sweet and Spicy Pineapple Pumpkin Curry

*Keep an eye on the pumpkin; it should be cooked just beyond
the stage of raw. It should be chunky and not mushy.*

INGREDIENTS | SERVES 6–8

2½ cups pumpkin, peeled and cut into 1" chunks

1½ cups pineapple, peeled, cored, and cut into 1" chunks

1 tablespoon ginger, thinly sliced

1 teaspoon turmeric

1½ teaspoons salt

1 tablespoon sugar

2 tablespoons coconut oil

1 teaspoon black mustard seeds

1 teaspoon cumin seeds

3–4 green chilies, deseeded and cut lengthwise

18–20 curry leaves

1 cup coconut, dry and shredded

1. In a large bowl, mix together the pumpkin, pineapple, ginger, turmeric, salt, and sugar. Transfer to a 5-quart slow cooker. Cover and cook for 1½ hours on high setting, or about 3 hours on low setting, or until the pumpkin is cooked.

2. In a tempering pan, heat the oil. Add the mustard seeds, cumin seeds, chilies, and curry leaves quickly one after the other; cook just until they sputter, approximately 30 seconds. This is your *tadka*.

3. Add the coconut to the cooked pumpkin. Pour tadka over it. Stir together and serve. The dish should be dry, and you should be able to eat it using a toothpick.

Sweet and Tangy Slow Cooker Almonds

You can substitute almonds with any other nut like pistachios, peanuts, or cashews.
They pair well with beer and any other cold beverage.

INGREDIENTS | YIELDS 3 CUPS

¼ cup salted butter

3 cups almonds

½ cup brown sugar

1 tablespoon Amchoor (Chapter 2)

1. Add the butter to a 4-quart slow cooker and turn the heat to high. After about 15–20 minutes, add the almonds and brown sugar. Mix everything together so that the almonds are well coated in the sugar and butter. Cover and cook for 15 minutes. Then reduce the heat to low and cook for another hour, stirring occasionally.

2. Uncover, add the Amchoor, and toss everything together. Let sit for 15–20 minutes before transferring the almonds into a bowl.

Tangy Sweet Potato Bites

If you're in a hurry, just bake the sweet potatoes for 15–20 minutes
at 425°F and toss them with the rest of the ingredients.

INGREDIENTS | SERVES 6–8

6–8 sweet potatoes

1½ tablespoons olive oil

½ teaspoon salt

1½ teaspoons lime juice

1 teaspoon Chaat Masala (Chapter 2)

1. Peel and cut sweet potatoes into 1" chunks. Mix with oil and salt. Place in a 4–5 quart slow cooker. Cover and cook for 3 hours on high setting, or 6 hours on low setting, or until sweet potatoes are cooked through.

2. Transfer the cooked sweet potatoes to a mixing bowl. Drizzle with lime juice, sprinkle with Chaat Masala, mix together, and serve.

Tandoori Chicken Wings

Tandoori chicken is one of the most popular Indian appetizers, but you will not believe how easy it is to fix, and even easier to make in a slow cooker.

INGREDIENTS | SERVES 6

4 pounds chicken wings

Salt, to taste

1 teaspoon ground pepper

1½ tablespoons Ginger-Garlic Paste (Chapter 2)

1 tablespoon Tandoori Masala (Chapter 2)

¼ cup thick hung yogurt

2 tablespoons lemon juice

1 tablespoon brown sugar

1. Wash the chicken, place in bowl, and add salt and pepper. Mix. Place on a baking sheet and broil for 5–7 minutes on each side or until browned.

2. Take the chicken out of the broiler, add the Ginger-Garlic Paste and Tandoori Masala. Transfer it into a 6-quart slow cooker and cook on high for 2 hours, or on low for 4–5 hours, or until the chicken is cooked through.

3. In a small bowl, mix together the yogurt, lemon juice, and brown sugar. Around a half hour before the cooking time is over, pour in the yogurt mixture. Spread the coating all over the chicken wings. Cook for another 30 minutes.

4. Remove the chicken from the slow cooker. Pour the remaining liquid into a saucepan and reduce it over medium heat. Use it to coat the chicken before serving it hot.

Tikki Chaat

Tikki chaat is another popular Indian street food. Originally from the north of India, it has become a popular Indian appetizer all around the country. Tikki refers to small potato patties served with chickpea curry and spicy chutneys.

INGREDIENTS | SERVES 8

5–6 cups Chole Masala (Chapter 7)

3 cups boiled potatoes, peeled and mashed

½ cup bread crumbs

2 teaspoons ginger paste

1 teaspoon curry powder

1 teaspoon fennel seeds

Salt, to taste

Oil for pan frying

3–4 tablespoons chickpea curry

Green Chutney Raita (Chapter 13)

2 tablespoons Tamarind Chutney (Chapter 13), or to taste

½ cup yogurt, whisked and smooth

½ cup chopped onion

1. Using your slow cooker, cook the Chole Masala as explained in Chapter 7.

2. In a large mixing bowl, combine together the mashed potatoes, bread crumbs, ginger paste, curry powder, fennel seeds, and salt.

3. Divide the mixture into 8 equal parts. Using both your hands, make circular patties. Heat oil in a skillet and pan-fry the patties, browning both sides. Patties should be crispy golden brown in color.

4. Before serving, place one patty on each plate. Pour 3–4 tablespoons of chickpea curry over it followed by both the chutneys, a dollop of yogurt, and onion. Serve hot.

CHAPTER 5

Soups and Stews

Beef Stew
63

Black Bean Soup
64

Bottle Gourd Stew
(Lauki Ka Stew)
65

Butternut Squash Soup
with Cilantro Chutney
66

Cauliflower Soup
67

Chhurpi Soup
68

Curried Cauliflower Soup
69

Dudhi Ni Tarkari (Squash Soup)
69

Kerala Mutton Stew
70

Khurdi (White Stock Soup)
71

Lamb Soup
72

Mulligatawny Soup
73

Murghi ka Shorba
(Chicken Soup)
74

Palak ka Soup (Spinach Soup)
75

Roasted Red Bell Pepper Soup
76

Spicy Chicken Stew
77

Split Pea Soup with Fried Paneer
78

Sweet and Sour
Bottle Gourd Soup
79

Tamatar ka Soup
80

Tomato Basil Soup
81

Tomato Coconut Soup
82

Beef Stew

Browning the outside of meat, specially red meat, before cooking in the slow cooker prevents it from any bacterial growth while cooking for a prolonged time at low temperature.

INGREDIENTS | SERVES 6

3 tablespoons cooking oil

2 pounds beef stew meat

12–15 fingerling potatoes, skins on

1½ cups sliced onions

1 teaspoon cayenne pepper

1½ teaspoons Garam Masala Powder (Chapter 2)

2–3 bay leaves

1 teaspoon turmeric

½ teaspoon fennel seeds

1 tablespoon Ginger-Garlic Paste (Chapter 2)

½ cup Curry Paste (Chapter 3)

Salt, to taste

½ cup diced canned pineapple, with juice

1 (8-ounce) can tomato sauce

1½ tablespoons ghee

½ cup chopped cilantro

1. Heat the oil in a skillet. Add the meat and cook it for 8–10 minutes, browning it on all sides. Drain excess fat and discard.

2. Layer the bottom of the slow cooker with potatoes and onion. Top it with the beef.

3. In a medium bowl, mix all the spices, the Ginger-Garlic Paste, the Curry Paste, salt, pineapple, and tomato sauce, and pour it over the meat. Add the ghee. Cover and cook on low for 8–10 hours.

4. Garnish with cilantro and serve with your favorite roti or rice dish.

Black Bean Soup

You may substitute the black beans with any other kind of bean like pinto,
red kidney beans, or even black-eyed peas.

INGREDIENTS | SERVES 6

2 tablespoons olive oil

½ green bell pepper, diced

½ red bell pepper, diced

½ red onion, sliced

2 cloves garlic, minced

2 (15-ounce) cans black beans, drained and rinsed

2 teaspoons cumin, minced

1 teaspoon red chili powder

1 teaspoon salt

4 cups vegetable broth or water

¼ cup cilantro, chopped

1. In a sauté pan, heat the olive oil over medium heat; then sauté the bell peppers, onion, and garlic for 2–3 minutes.

2. Add the sautéed vegetables, black beans, cumin, red chili powder, salt, and vegetable broth to a 4-quart slow cooker, cover, and cook on low for 6 hours.

3. Let the soup cool slightly; then pour half of it into a blender, process until smooth, and then pour it back into the pot. Add the chopped cilantro and stir.

Bottle Gourd Stew (Lauki Ka Stew)

Bottle gourd, or lauki, is a variety of squash very popular in India. Would you believe that this highly nutritious vegetable is used not only for cooking in India; it is also made into floatation devices (to assist in learning to swim) and into musical instruments.

INGREDIENTS | SERVES 6–8

1 tablespoon peppercorn

2–3 bay leaves

1 stick cinnamon

3–4 whole black cardamom pods

2 tablespoons cooking oil

2 pounds bottle gourd, peeled, cored, and cut into ½" chunks

2½ cups potatoes, peeled, and cut into ½" chunks

Salt, to taste

½ cup water

1 cup yogurt

3 green chilies, cut lengthwise

1. Coarsely crush the peppercorns, bay leaves, cinnamon, and cardamom with a mortar and pestle.

2. Heat the oil in a tempering pan. Add the crushed spices and cook for about 30 seconds. Set aside.

3. In a 4–5 quart slow cooker, add the bottle gourd and potatoes. Pour in the oil with spices. Add salt and ½ cup water, cover, and cook on high for 2 hours, or on low for 4 hours, or until the vegetables are cooked through.

4. Whisk the yogurt making it smooth. Pour it into the stew along with green chilies. Add more water if you like your stew thinner. Stir, cover, and cook for another 20 minutes or longer if the vegetables are still not cooked well.

5. Serve with some rice on the side.

Butternut Squash Soup with Cilantro Chutney

Layer the vegetables in a bed starting with carrots at the bottom, followed by celery, squash, apples, and then onions. This will help all the vegetables cook in the same amount of time.

INGREDIENTS | SERVES 8

1 tablespoon butter

1½ cups carrots, peeled and cut into chunks

4 celery stalks

2½ pounds butternut squash, peeled and cut into 1" chunks

1 medium-size apple, peeled and cut into chunks

½ cup Caramelized Onions (Chapter 3)

1 teaspoon thyme

1 teaspoon pepper

3 cups chicken or vegetable stock

Salt, to taste

1 tablespoon olive oil

2 tablespoons Hot Cilantro Chutney (Chapter 2)

1. Grease the inside of a 6-quart slow cooker with butter. Add all the ingredients *except* the oil and chutney into the slow cooker. Mix well.

2. Drizzle the olive oil and any remaining butter on top. Cover and cook for 4–5 hours on high or 9 hours on low.

3. Once the vegetables are cooked through, take them out of the slow cooker and purée using a hand blender. Drizzle some Hot Cilantro Chutney on top and serve hot with fried poppadum (crisp Indian bread).

Keep It Even

Try to cut all the vegetables the same size. Different sizes lead to uneven cooking.

Cauliflower Soup

Be sure to cut the cauliflower and potatoes the same size so they cook evenly.
Add another vegetable of your liking to make the soup colorful.

INGREDIENTS | SERVES 6–8

3 tablespoons butter

2 tablespoons chopped garlic

3–4 bay leaves

1½ cups chopped onions

1 pound potatoes, peeled and chopped

3 pounds cauliflower, chopped

Salt, to taste

4 cups chicken stock

1 cup heavy cream

2 teaspoons crushed red pepper

1. Add the butter, garlic, bay leaves, and onion into a large-size slow cooker. Turn the slow cooker on high. Cover and cook for 20 minutes.

2. Once the onion and spices start to sizzle, add the potatoes, cauliflower, salt, and chicken stock. Cover and cook for 3 hours on high or 6–7 hours on low.

3. Uncover; add the heavy cream and red pepper. Cover and cook for another 20–30 minutes or until all the vegetables are cooked and almost mushy.

4. Once the vegetables are cooked, transfer everything into a large pot. Remove the bay leaves. Blend the mixture into a smooth, creamy liquid using your hand blender or a regular smoothie maker. Serve with some croutons on top.

Chhurpi Soup

Chhurpi is a kind of cheese that is very popular in the northern hills region of India. Buttermilk is cooked, and its solid mass is then strained through cheesecloth and hung to drain the excess liquid. There's soft and harder chhurpi.

INGREDIENTS | SERVES 8

2–3 whole tomatoes
1 tablespoon cooking oil
½ teaspoon fennel seeds
½ teaspoon cumin seeds
¼ teaspoon carom seeds
1 tablespoon finely chopped ginger
1 cup onion
½ teaspoon cayenne pepper
1 tablespoon powdered jaggery
1 cup water
Salt, to taste
½ cup grated chhurpi
1½ cups cooked rice

1. Boil water in a saucepan. Turn off the heat and add the whole tomatoes and cover for 1 minute. Take the tomatoes out and peel the outer skin. Cut into quarters and transfer into a 3–4 quart slow cooker.

2. Heat the oil in a sauté pan; add the fennel, cumin, and carom seeds. Once they pop, add the ginger and cook till they turn light golden. Add the onion. Sauté for 3–4 minutes.

3. Transfer mixture into the slow cooker. Add the rest of the ingredients *except* for the chhurpi and rice. Cover and cook on low for 4 hours.

4. Add the chhurpi. Stir, cover, and cook on high setting for 30 minutes. Add the rice. Turn the heat off. Let it stay covered for 5–8 minutes. Serve hot.

Curried Cauliflower Soup

Orange cauliflower is an excellent variety to use in this recipe.
It has 25 percent more vitamin A than white cauliflower and lends an attractive color to the soup.

INGREDIENTS | SERVES 4

1 pound cauliflower florets

2½ cups water

1 onion, minced

2 cloves garlic, minced

3 teaspoons curry powder

¼ teaspoon cumin

1. Place all the ingredients into a 4-quart slow cooker. Stir. Cook on low for 8 hours.

2. Use an immersion blender or blend the soup or in batches in a standard blender until smooth.

Dudhi Ni Tarkari (Squash Soup)

To find a good and fresh bottle gourd, look for one with a light green skin, a green stem, and no dark spots on its body.

INGREDIENTS | SERVES 6

4–5 cups bottle gourd, peeled, cored, and cut into 1" cubes

5 cups chicken or vegetable stock

Salt, to taste

1 teaspoon red chili powder

½ teaspoon green chili paste

1½ tablespoons Ginger-Garlic Paste (Chapter 2)

1½ tablespoons cooking oil

1½ teaspoons cumin seeds

½ teaspoon turmeric

2 tablespoons lemon juice

1. In a slow cooker, add the bottle gourd, stock, salt, chili powder, chili paste, and Ginger-Garlic Paste. Cover and cook on high setting for 2 hours.

2. Heat the oil in a tempering pan and add the cumin seeds. As they begin to pop, add the turmeric and immediately transfer the contents to the slow cooker. Put the cover back on and cook for another 45 minutes to an hour or until the bottle gourd is fork tender.

3. Stir in the lemon juice. Garnish with coriander leaves or a dollop of butter and serve hot.

Kerala Mutton Stew

This stew, or ishtoo, *is popular in typical Syrian Christian homes in Kerala. The use of coconut milk gives a sweet, creamy, and yet light feel to it.*

INGREDIENTS | SERVES 6

2 tablespoons cooking oil
1½ pounds mutton
1 (14-ounce) can coconut milk
¾ cup Caramelized Onions (Chapter 3)
1 tablespoon ginger, thinly sliced
3–4 green chilies, thinly sliced
1 cup yellow potatoes, cubed
1 cup baby carrots
¾ cup frozen corn, thawed
Salt, to taste
1 tablespoon coconut oil
¼ teaspoon cloves
1 stick cinnamon
½ teaspoon turmeric
15–18 curry leaves
1 teaspoon cayenne pepper

1. On the stovetop, heat the cooking oil in a skillet over medium heat. Add the mutton and brown it. Set aside.

2. Open the can of coconut milk. Skim out all the cream on top and put in a separate bowl, leaving just the diluted water in the bottom. Set aside.

3. In the slow cooker, add the Caramelized Onions, ginger, green chilies, meat, and vegetables. Add the salt and reserved coconut water. Cover and cook for 4 hours on high setting or on low for about 8–9 hours.

4. In a tempering pan, heat the cocounut oil. Add the cloves, cinnamon stick, turmeric, and curry leaves. As they splutter, turn off the heat. Set aside.

5. Uncover the slow cooker. Add the skimmed coconut cream, cayenne pepper, and tempered oil and spices. Stir well. Cover and cook for another hour on high or until the meat is well cooked. Serve hot with steamed rice or *appam* (fermented rice pancake).

Khurdi (White Stock Soup)

This is a traditional meat soup made from mutton stock and comes from the Bohra community. Soup, an important part of the Bohra cuisine, is normally served with rice. In this cuisine, meat is generally boiled in water with some spices instead of grilling or searing it.

INGREDIENTS | SERVES 6–8

2 tablespoons oil, plus extra to brown the meat

1 pound goat meat

6 cups water

2 tablespoons Ginger-Garlic Paste (Chapter 2)

3–4 green chilies, minced

1½ cups sliced red onion

Salt, to taste

1 teaspoon cumin seeds

2 cinnamon sticks

1 teaspoon cloves

2 teaspoons black peppercorns

3 tablespoons all-purpose flour

2 cups milk

1 tablespoon lime juice

1. Heat oil in a skillet over medium heat. Add the meat and brown it for 7–10 minutes before transferring into a slow cooker.

2. Add the meat, water, Ginger-Garlic Paste, green chilies, onion, and salt to the slow cooker. Cover and cook on high for 4 hours or until the meat is tender.

3. Heat 2 tablespoons of oil in a skillet. Add the whole spices. Once they splutter, add the flour. Roast on low heat for 2–3 minutes, stirring constantly as the mixture can burn easily. Add the milk and bring it to boil while constantly whisking.

4. Add the gravy to the slow cooker. Cover and cook for another 30 minutes. Once it is done, stir in the lime juice and serve.

Meat Alternative

Traditionally goat is used for this recipe, but any kind of red meat can be used. You can also add some vegetables.

Lamb Soup

Lamb is not very easily available in India so this dish is traditionaly cooked with goat meat.

INGREDIENTS | SERVES 5–6

3 tablespoons cooking oil

1 teaspoon turmeric

1 tablespoon Tandoori Masala (Chapter 2)

1 teaspoon Garam Masala Powder (Chapter 2)

2 tablespoons coriander powder

2 tablespoons Ginger-Garlic Paste (Chapter 2)

2 pounds boneless lamb stew meat

1 cup Caramelized Onions (Chapter 3)

1 cup baby carrots

1 cup baby potatoes, skin on

1 tablespoon minced green chili

2 (28-ounce) cans diced tomatoes, drained

1 (14-ounce) can chicken broth

Salt, to taste

1½ tablespoons corn starch

4–5 tablespoons water

½ cup chopped cilantro

1. Heat the oil in a skillet. Add all the dry spices. Cook for 3–4 seconds and then add the Ginger-Garlic Paste. Cook for 30 seconds.

2. Add the lamb to the skillet. Cook the lamb on medium heat for 10 minutes, browning it on all sides. Drain excess fat.

3. Add the vegetables to the bottom of the slow cooker. Transfer the browned meat from the skillet to the slow cooker. Add the drained canned tomatoes, broth, and salt. Cover and cook on high for 4 hours or on low for 7–8 hours.

4. In a small bowl, mix the corn starch with the water, just enough to dissolve it (about 4–5 tablespoons). Add it to the cooked lamb. Cover and cook on high for another 20 minutes or until the lamb is cooked enough to fall apart. Serve hot; garnish with cilantro.

Mulligatawny Soup

Mulligatawny in Tamil literally means "pepper water." This is a perfect example of Indian slow cooking using simple ingredients but with a complex flavor.

INGREDIENTS | SERVES 6–8

1 tablespoon oil

1½ teaspoons garlic paste

1 cup diced onion

3 cups chicken breast, boneless, skinless, and diced

1 cup diced carrots

1 tablespoon curry powder

12–15 curry leaves

1 teaspoon minced green chili

6 cups chicken stock

2 cups flour, dissolved in 1 cup water

Salt, to taste

1 (8-ounce) can coconut milk

1½ cups cooked white rice

1 cup tart apple, chopped

1. Heat the oil in a large pan over medium heat. Add the garlic paste and onion. Cook until the onion gets translucent. Add chicken and cook for 3–4 minutes.

2. Transfer the contents to a slow cooker. Add the carrots, curry powder, curry leaves, chili, chicken stock, flour and water mixture, and salt. Cover and cook on low for 3–4 hours or until the chicken is cooked.

3. Add the coconut milk, rice, and apple. Cover and cook for another 15 minutes. Serve hot.

Murghi ka Shorba (Chicken Soup)

You can use any part of the chicken breasts, thighs, or even drumsticks if you can manage to get the bone out. Cut the chicken into 1" chunks.

INGREDIENTS | SERVES 8–10

1 tablespoon ghee, or butter

1½ teaspoons cumin seeds

1 teaspoon turmeric powder

2 pounds boneless chicken

1 (8-ounce) can diced tomatoes, drained

5 cups chicken stock

1½ teaspoons garam masala

1 teaspoon cayenne pepper

Salt, to taste

1 cup thick hung yogurt (optional)

1. Add the ghee to a large slow cooker. Add the cumin seeds and turmeric. Turn the slow cooker to high setting. Cover. As soon as the ghee melts, add the rest of the ingredients *except* for the yogurt. Cover again and cook for 4 hours on high, or for 7–8 hours on low, or until the chicken is well cooked. Stir occasionally.

2. Serve hot with a dollop of yogurt.

Tips

Do not forget to brown the chicken on the stovetop for 5 minutes before dropping in the slow cooker.

Palak ka Soup (Spinach Soup)

It's no secret that spinach is one of the healthiest vegetables. Adding just a few ounces in your diet can provide you with a great supply of iron, vitamins, calcium, and carotenoids.

INGREDIENTS | SERVES 4–6

1 tablespoon ghee
1 teaspoon fennel seeds
2–3 cloves
1 medium-size onion, chopped
8 cups spinach
1 cup potatoes, peeled and chopped
1 cup carrots
1 tablespoon grated garlic
1 teaspoon garam masala
Salt, to taste
1 cup water

1. In a large sauté pan, heat the ghee. Add the fennel seeds, cloves, and onion one after the other. Sauté until the onion turns translucent. Add the rest of the ingredients *except* the water. Sauté for about 5 minutes or until the spinach shrinks.

2. Add the mixture to the slow cooker. Add the water. Cover and cook on high for 2½ hours or until the vegetables are cooked well.

3. Transfer the slow cooker contents into a blender or a large pot and blend, making a smooth-consistency soup. Serve hot with a little cream on top, if desired.

Roasted Red Bell Pepper Soup

Roasting a bell pepper gives it a nice charred taste. If you do not have a broiler or oven, you can roast peppers on the stovetop by setting a cooling rack over the burner and roasting the peppers on it.

INGREDIENTS | SERVES 4–6

5 pounds red bell peppers
3 tablespoons butter
3–4 bay leaves
3–4 green cardamom pods
2 teaspoons ginger powder
1½ tablespoons cayenne pepper
1 bulb (8–10 cloves) garlic
2 cups chopped onion
Salt, to taste
4 cups chicken stock
Ground black pepper, to taste

1. Wash the bell peppers. Halve them and lay them on oiled baking sheets, cut-side down. Roast them under a broiler for 15–20 minutes or until the outer skins of the bell peppers are charred.

2. Transfer the roasted bell peppers to a large pot and cover the top with plastic wrap to trap the steam. (This will help later with the pealing of the peppers.) Set aside.

3. Add the butter and spices to a large slow cooker. Cover and turn the heat on high for 20 minutes. After 20 minutes, add the garlic and onion. Stir, cover, and cook for another 30 minutes.

4. In the meantime, clean the peppers. Take off the skin, deseed them, and transfer them to the slow cooker. Add the salt and chicken stock. Cover and cook for 2½ hours on low setting or until everything is mushy enough to be blended easily with a blender.

5. Transfer the cooked contents to a large pot. Blend everything into a smooth purée using a hand blender or a regular blender (take out the whole spices if you want). Sprinkle with some ground pepper and serve.

Spicy Chicken Stew

The peppercorns give this stew a slightly sweet taste along with the heat.
The amount of heat can be controlled with the amount of black pepper in this dish.

INGREDIENTS | SERVES 6

3 tablespoons cooking oil

3 teaspoons coarsely crushed black peppercorns

2 cinnamon sticks

4–5 green whole cardamom pods

6–7 cloves

1½ pounds boneless, skinless chicken pieces

1 tablespoon coriander powder

1½ teaspoons Garam Masala Powder (Chapter 2)

1 teaspoon turmeric

Salt, to taste

1 cup thinly sliced onion

1 (14-ounce) can diced tomatoes, drained

1 (14-ounce) can chicken broth, or water

1½ tablespoons Ginger-Garlic Paste (Chapter 2)

3 cups baby spinach

1. Heat the oil in a pan. Add the spices. As they sizzle, add the chicken. Stir-fry for 3–4 minutes. Drain the extra liquid. Transfer the chicken to the slow cooker.

2. Add all the ingredients to the slow cooker *except* for the spinach. Stir. Cover and cook on high for 4–5 hours or on low for 8–9 hours.

3. Add the spinach. Stir everything together well. Turn off the heat. Cover and let it sit for 5–10 minutes. Serve hot with your favorite bread or Saffron Rice (Chapter 11). If the stew has more liquid than you prefer, transfer it to a pan (before adding the spinach) and cook on the stovetop on high for 5 minutes before serving.

Cooking Chicken Thighs

Slow-cooked chicken thighs stay juicier than breast pieces. Adding a teaspoon of papaya powder or a couple tablespoons of pineapple juice also helps.

Split Pea Soup with Fried Paneer

*Try adding some acid to the dish like a squirt of lemon juice,
some tamarind pulp or amchoor powder to give the dish a different face.*

INGREDIENTS | SERVES 6

2 cups split peas (soaked overnight), or 2 (14-ounce) cans

4 cups water

Salt, to taste

1 teaspoon turmeric

1½ tablespoons cooking oil

1 cup paneer cubes

1 tablespoon ghee

1 teaspoon mustard seeds

1 tablespoon coriander powder

1 teaspoon cayenne pepper

½ cup fried brown onion

1. Drain the water in which the split peas were soaked (or if using canned split peas, drain the water from the can).

2. Add the peas to a 4–5 quart slow cooker along with 4 cups of water. Add salt to taste and turmeric. Cover and cook on high for 1 hour and then on low for 3–4 hours or until they are cooked through.

3. Heat the cooking oil in a skillet. Pan-fry paneer cubes on medium-high heat until they turn golden brown on all sides. Place the paneer on a paper towel to absorb the extra oil. Set aside.

4. Heat the ghee in a tempering pan. Turn the heat off, add mustard seeds, coriander powder, and cayenne pepper. Cook for 30 seconds. Transfer this mixture (*tadka*) to the slow cooker. Stir well.

5. Serve the soup, while hot, into serving bowls. Add fried brown onions and 4–5 cubes of paneer per bowl and serve.

Sweet and Sour Bottle Gourd Soup

The sweetness of sugar and the tanginess of tamarind sauce gives so-called bland bottle gourd an interesting flavor. And heat from the chilies adds to the taste.

INGREDIENTS | SERVES 8

4–5 cups bottle gourd, peeled and cut into 1" cubes

1 teaspoon turmeric

Salt, to taste

2 cups water

1½ tablespoons oil

1 pinch asafetida

1 teaspoon mustard seeds

3–4 whole red chilies

12–15 curry leaves

2 tablespoons brown sugar

2 teaspoons Amchoor (Chapter 2)

1. Transfer the bottle gourd, turmeric, salt, and 2 cups water into the slow cooker. Cover and cook for 2 hours on high setting.

2. Heat the oil in a tempering pan. Add the asafetida, mustard seeds, red chilies, and curry leaves. Once they pop, transfer to the slow cooker.

3. Add the remaining ingredients. Cover and cook for another 45 minutes to 1 hour on high setting or until the bottle gourd is cooked through. Serve hot.

Oh, My Gourd!

Clean the bottle gourd with the skin on before cutting. Cleaning with water after cutting leads to a longer cooking time.

Tamatar ka Soup

Tamatar ka soup, or tomato soup, is probably one of the oldest and most popular soups in urban India. You can find it at almost every dinner party and function, probably because it's vegetarian and tomatoes grow almost all year long in India, in one variety or another.

INGREDIENTS | SERVES 8

12–15 large ripe tomatoes

1½ tablespoons butter

1 teaspoon black mustard seeds

1 teaspoon cumin seeds

½ teaspoon turmeric powder

2–3 bay leaves

1 tablespoon ginger paste

1 tablespoon dark brown sugar

Salt, to taste

1 cup water

¼ cup cream

Tomato Tip

Fresh tomatoes taste better for this recipe, but you can also use canned tomatoes.

1. In a large pot, bring enough water to cover the tomatoes to a boil. Drop in the tomatoes and cover with a lid. After 1 minute, take the tomatoes out. Let them cool and then peel off the outer skin. Cut into quarters. Transfer them to the slow cooker.

2. Heat a tempering pan. Add the butter and then the mustard and cumin seeds. As soon as the mustard and cumin seeds start to pop, transfer this mixture into the slow cooker.

3. Add the rest of the ingredients into the slow cooker *except* for the cream. Cover and cook on low for approximately 5 hours or until the tomatoes are cooked and turn mushy.

4. After the tomatoes are cooked, add the cream. Cover and cook for another 30 minutes.

5. Transfer the contents to a large pot or blender and blend it into a smooth soup. Serve hot.

Tomato Basil Soup

Fresh basil adds a different flavor to dishes than dried basil, and the fresh variety is more complementary to this soup. This soup is great for colds or sore throats.

INGREDIENTS | SERVES 5

2 tablespoons ghee
½ onion, diced
2 cloves garlic, minced
1 (28-ounce) can whole peeled tomatoes
½ cup vegetable broth, or water
1 bay leaf
1 teaspoon salt
1 teaspoon pepper
½ cup unsweetened soymilk
¼ cup sliced fresh basil (holy Tulsi, if you can find it)

1. In a sauté pan over medium heat, melt the ghee. Then sauté the onion and garlic for 3–4 minutes.

2. Add the onion and garlic, tomatoes, vegetable broth, bay leaf, salt, and pepper to a 4-quart slow cooker. Cover and cook over low heat 4 hours. During the last 20 minutes add the soymilk. Put the lid back on and continue cooking. Turn the heat off. Add basil leaves. Stir well and serve hot.

Tomato Coconut Soup

Try garnishing this soup with some spicy roasted peanuts
or chickpeas, instead of toasted coconut flakes.

INGREDIENTS | SERVES 8–10

2 tablespoons butter

1 cup chopped onion

½ cup chopped carrots

½ cup chopped celery

1 (28-ounce) can diced tomatoes

3–4 bay leaves

1 teaspoon black pepper

Salt, to taste

1 (8-ounce) can coconut milk

⅓ cup toasted coconut flakes

1. Melt the butter in a sauté pan. Sauté the onion. Add the carrots and celery. Sauté for 5 minutes.

2. Transfer the sautéed ingredients to the slow cooker. Add the canned tomatoes and the rest of the ingredients *except* for the coconut milk and coconut flakes. Cover and cook for 2½ hours on high or until tomatoes turn mushy.

3. Add the coconut milk to the slow cooker. Stir well. Cover and cook for another 45 minutes.

4. Transfer the contents to a blender, or hand blend in a large pot. Serve hot, topped with toasted coconut flakes.

CHAPTER 6

Lentils and More

Bengal Gram Dal and Bottle
Gourd Soup (Chana Dal Lauki)
84

Black-Eyed Peas Curry
(Tarewale Lobhiya)
85

Creamy Red Lentils
(Masoor Ki Dal)
86

Curried Chana Dal
87

Dal Makhanai (Slow-Cooked
Beans with Spices and Cream)
88

Drumstick Sambhar
(Murungaikkai Sambhar)
89

Gujarati Yellow Mung Beans
(Peele Moong Ki Dal)
90

Lentil Chili
91

Maharastrian Pigeon Pea Curry
(Ambat Varan)
92

Mung Ki Dal Palak (Split Mung
Beans Cooked with Spinach)
93

Punjabi Kadhi Pakoda
94

Puneri Dal
95

Rajma Masala
96

Rasam
97

Restaurant-Style Dal Fry
98

Sambhar
99

Simple Chickpea Sandal
100

Simple Mung Bean Curry
(Tadka Dal)
101

Split Black Lentil Soup (Urad Dal)
102

Split Pea and Cheese Curry
(Paneeri Chana Dal)
103

Tadka Tomato Dal
104

The Five-Lentil Delight
(Paanch Dalo Ka Sangam)
105

Tomato Rasam
106

Vegetable Kadhi
107

Yogurt Green Curry
(Hariyali Kadhi)
108

Bengal Gram Dal and Bottle Gourd Soup
(Chana Dal Lauki)

Bengal gram dal (or chana dal as Indians call it) is one of the most fibrous legumes and a great source of protein. When mixed with bottle gourd and some basic Indian spices, it is not only good but is very good for you.

INGREDIENTS | SERVES 6–8

2 cups dry Bengal gram dal

4 cups water

Salt, to taste

1 teaspoon turmeric powder

4 cups bottle gourd (peeled, deseeded, and cut into bite-size chunks)

1 cup diced Roma tomatoes

1 tablespoon gingerroot, coarsely chopped

1 teaspoon chopped green chili

1 teaspoon ghee

1 pinch asafetida

1 teaspoon cumin seeds

1 tablespoon coriander powder

1 tablespoon chopped cilantro

1. Wash the dal and transfer it to a 5–6 quart slow cooker. Add 4 cups water, salt, and turmeric powder. Cook on high for 1 hour.

2. Transfer the diced bottle gourd, tomatoes, gingerroot, and green chili into the slow cooker. Cook on low for 5 hours, or until everything is cooked through. With a spatula, stir everything together well.

3. Heat the ghee in a pan for tempering. Add the asafetida and cumin seeds. Once the cumin seeds pop, add the coriander powder. Turn heat off immediately. Stir this tadka with a spoon and then add it to the soup along with the cilantro. Mix well and serve with rice or warm bread.

Tomato Options

You can use any kind of tomatoes for this dish. For a tangy soup, try using green tomatoes.

Black-Eyed Peas Curry (Tarewale Lobhiya)

This dish is unusual and quite delicious. Serve with your favorite bread.

INGREDIENTS | SERVES 4

2 tablespoons vegetable oil

½ teaspoon turmeric powder

1 teaspoon red chili powder

1 (10-ounce) can diced tomatoes, drained

2 teaspoons coriander powder

Salt, to taste

1 teaspoon tamarind pulp, concentrate

2 (14-ounce) cans black-eyed peas (*lobhiya*), rinsed

1½ cups water

1 tablespoon minced cilantro

1. Mix all the ingredients together in the slow cooker *except* the cilantro. Stir well. Cover and cook on high for 2 hours, or on low for 4 hours, or until the peas are tender and blended well in the gravy.

2. Garnish with cilantro and serve hot with your choice of fresh flatbread or rice dish, and a raita on the side.

Edible Spoons?

Indians use their bread, torn into small pieces, as spoons to scoop up yummy lentils and gravies. Try it and see the difference it makes.

Creamy Red Lentils (Masoor Ki Dal)

This dish tastes as beautiful as it appears. Serve with Hot Cilantro Chutney (Chapter 2) or garlic chutney, and your choice of fresh flatbread or Perfect Slow Cooker Basmati Rice (Chapter 11).

INGREDIENTS | SERVES 4

1½ cups red split lentils (*masoor dal*), well rinsed

4 cups water, plus ½ cup more as needed

½ teaspoon turmeric powder

1 teaspoon salt, or to taste

4 tablespoons vegetable oil

½ teaspoon cumin seeds

2 garlic cloves, minced

½ teaspoon red chili powder

A Change of "Season-*ings*"

Changing the final seasoning, or *tadka*, can completely change the taste of a dish. Take this dish or the Simple Mung Bean Curry (see recipe in this chapter), for instance. Change the final seasoning from cumin seeds to black mustard seeds and add a few fresh curry leaves, and taste the difference.

1. In a slow cooker, combine lentils, 4 cups of water, turmeric powder, salt, and 2 tablespoons of the vegetable oil. Cover and cook on high for 2–2½ hours, or on low setting for 4–5 hours, or until the lentils are soft. If the water begins to dry out, add up to ½ cup more. (The consistency should be like a creamy soup).

2. Using a spoon, mash the cooked lentils to a creamy consistency. Set aside.

3. In a medium-size pan, heat the remaining vegetable oil. Add the cumin seeds. When they begin to sizzle, add the garlic and red chili powder. Sauté for about 20 seconds.

4. Remove from heat and pour over the lentils. Mix well and serve hot.

Curried Chana Dal

Chana dal is produced by removing the outer skin of black chickpeas,
which are smaller than normal chickpeas or garbanzo beans.

INGREDIENTS | SERVES 6–8

2 cups chana dal/split Bengal gram

1 cup sliced tomatoes

1 cup curry paste

½ teaspoon turmeric

5 cups water

Salt, to taste

1 tablespoon ghee

1 teaspoon cumin seeds

1 teaspoon cayenne pepper

1. Wash the chana dal with water before transferring it to the slow cooker. Add the tomatoes, Curry Paste, turmeric, water, and salt. Stir to combine. Cover and cook for 3 hours on high setting, or on low for about 5–6 hours, or until the chana dal is completely cooked.

2. Heat the ghee in a tempering pan. Add the cumin seeds and cayenne pepper and heat them until they sputter. Transfer to the cooked lentils immediately and mix well. Serve hot.

Dal Makhanai
(Slow-Cooked Beans with Spices and Cream)

*Dal makhanai is a perfect example of a slow-cooked Indian recipe.
The spices can be either slow-cooked for hours with the beans or added halfway through
the cooking to retain their aroma during the course of the long cooking process.*

INGREDIENTS | SERVES 6–7

¾ cup red kidney beans

2 cups urad dal

6 cups water

1 teaspoon turmeric powder

Salt, to taste

8–10 peppercorns

4–5 cloves

2 tablespoons olive oil or ghee

1–2 bay leaves

1 cup chopped onion

1" piece ginger, chopped

3–4 cloves chopped garlic

1 tablespoon tomato paste, or 1 cup chopped tomato

1½ teaspoons cayenne pepper

2 tablespoons coriander powder

2 teaspoons curry powder

½ cup heavy cream

2–3 tablespoons shaken buttermilk

Curry Paste

½ cup curry paste can also be used in place of all the spices, onion, and Ginger-Garlic Paste (Chapter 2). Although fresh paste will taste better in this recipe.

1. Soak the red kidney beans in water overnight or for at least for 6–8 hours.

2. Wash the lentils (urad dal) thoroughly and put into the slow cooker. Add 6 cups of water. Add turmeric, salt, peppercorns, and cloves. Turn heat on and cook on high setting for 4 hours, or on low for 6–7 hours, or until they are well cooked.

3. In a thick-bottomed pan, heat oil over medium-high heat. Throw in bay leaves and then chopped onion. Sauté onions until translucent.

4. Make a paste by combining the ginger and garlic and then add it to the onions. Fry it until everything looks golden in color, approximately 10 minutes. Then add the tomato paste (or chopped tomato), cayenne pepper, and coriander powder. Fry until the tomato is almost dissolved and then add the curry powder. After 1 minute add the heavy cream to the mixture.

5. Add the buttermilk to the slow-cooked beans. Stir well so that lentils are completely mixed into each other and then add the onion masala (bay leaves and onion) that has been prepared.

6. Garnish it with coriander leaves and a dollop of butter, if desired. Serve hot with tandoori roti or plain basmati rice.

Drumstick Sambhar (Murungaikkai Sambhar)

*I am sure the word "drumsticks" will take you to your favorite drum player,
but here it refers to a long, slender, triangular seed pods that are very popular
in India and are used to make curries, soups, and stir-fries.*

INGREDIENTS | SERVES 6

2 tablespoons cooking oil

1 pinch asafetida

½ teaspoon cumin seeds

½ teaspoon mustard seeds

3–4 whole dry red chilies

¾ cup chopped white onion

8–10 curry leaves

1½ cups toor dal (yellow lentil)

2 cups drumstick (peeled and cut finger length)

1½ cups chopped tomato

1½ tablespoons tamarind pulp

2 tablespoons Sambhar Masala (Chapter 2)

½ cup coconut milk

1 teaspoon turmeric

4 cups water (extra, if needed)

1. Heat the oil in a pan. Add the asafetida, cumin, and mustard seeds. As they splutter, add the red chilies. After 3–5 seconds add the onion and curry leaves. Sauté for 2–3 minutes. Set aside cooked mixture.

2. Add the lentils and the remaining ingredients to the slow cooker. Transfer the sautéed ingredients from the pan to the slow cooker. Cover and cook for 2½–3 hours on high or 5–6 hours on low setting. Serve hot.

Gujarati Yellow Mung Beans (Peele Moong Ki Dal)

This simple dal is a staple in the western Indian state of Gujarati. Serve garnished with minced cilantro.

INGREDIENTS | SERVES 4

2 cups yellow split mung beans (yellow *moong dal*), rinsed

6 cups water, as needed

½ teaspoon turmeric powder

2 tablespoons vegetable oil

4 packed teaspoons jaggery or brown sugar

Salt, to taste

1 teaspoon vegetable oil

½ teaspoon black mustard seeds

5–6 fresh curry leaves

Pinch of asafetida

2 dried red chilies, roughly pounded

1. In a slow cooker add the mung beans, 6 cups of water, turmeric, and 2 tablespoons vegetable oil. Cover and cook on high for 2–3 hours or on low for 4–6 hours. If the dal begins to dry up, add up to 1 cup of hot water.

2. Once cooked, use a hand mixer or the back of a wooden spoon to mash the dal to a coarse purée. Add the jaggery and salt; mix well. Set aside.

3. Just before serving, heat 1 teaspoon vegetable oil in a small pan. Add the mustard seeds. When they begin to sputter (about 30 seconds), in quick succession add the curry leaves, asafetida, and red chilies. Sauté for another 30 seconds.

4. Remove from heat and pour over the dal. Mix well and serve hot.

Lentil Chili

Before using dried lentils, rinse them well and pick through to remove any debris or undesirable pieces.

INGREDIENTS | SERVES 6

1 cup lentils, uncooked

1 onion, diced

3 cloves garlic, minced

4 cups vegetable broth or water

¼ cup tomato paste

1 cup chopped carrots

1 cup celery, chopped

1 (15-ounce) can diced tomatoes, drained

2 tablespoons chili powder

½ tablespoon paprika

½ teaspoon turmeric

1 teaspoon cumin

1 teaspoon salt

¼ teaspoon black pepper

1. Add all the ingredients to a 4-quart slow cooker, cover, and cook on low heat for 8 hours.

Maharastrian Pigeon Pea Curry (Ambat Varan)

A tangy dish from the western Indian state of Maharastra, this is traditionally served with steamed rice sprinkled with 1 tablespoon of warmed ghee.

INGREDIENTS | SERVES 4

4 cups water, as needed
½ teaspoon turmeric powder
4 tablespoons vegetable oil
1 cup split pigeon peas (*toor dal*), rinsed
1 teaspoon minced garlic
Pinch of asafetida
½ teaspoon cumin seeds
½ teaspoon mustard seeds
1 teaspoon tamarind pulp concentrate
1 teaspoon sugar
Salt, to taste

Reducing the Cooking Time for Dals

Soak dal in hot water instead of cold water. Also, add salt, lemon juice, or tamarind only at the end of the cooking process for dal. If you add it earlier, the dal will take a lot longer to cook. Additionally, while boiling, add a little bit of oil and turmeric powder to dal to considerably shorten the cooking process.

1. In a slow cooker, combine 4 cups of water, the turmeric, and 2 tablespoons of the vegetable oil. Add the toor dal and stir. Cover and cook on high for 2–3 hours, or on low for 4–5 hours, or until dal is cooked through.

2. In a small skillet, heat the remaining vegetable oil. Add the garlic and sauté for 30 seconds. In quick succession, add the asafetida, cumin, and mustard seeds. When the mustard seeds begin to sputter, remove from heat and pour over the toor dal.

3. Transfer the toor dal to a pan on the stovetop and add the tamarind; mix well. Add the sugar and salt, and mix well. Add ½ cup of water and bring to a quick boil. Remove from heat and serve hot.

Mung Ki Dal Palak
(Split Mung Beans Cooked with Spinach)

Here is a simple one-pot meal. It is very high in protein and vitamins.
Throw in some grilled naans and you have a whole meal.

INGREDIENTS | SERVES 6

2 cups split mung beans
½ pound spinach, coarsely chopped
6 cups water
1 tablespoon chopped green chili
1 tablespoon chopped fresh gingerroot
Salt, to taste
1 tablespoon ghee
Pinch of asafetida
2 teaspoons cumin seeds

1. Rinse mung beans and spinach in water. Place in the slow cooker.

2. Add the water, green chili, gingerroot, and salt to the mung beans and spinach. Cover the lid and cook for 6 hours on low heat.

3. Check to see if the beans are cooked. If not, then cook longer. Add water, if needed.

4. Heat the ghee in a tempering pan over high heat. Add the asafetida and cumin seeds to the hot ghee for no more than 1 minute. They should pop.

5. Add the spice mixture to the beans. Mix everything together and serve hot.

Punjabi Kadhi Pakoda

*Punjab, the land of five rivers, is famous for its fertile land, colorful life,
and rich food loaded with makkhan, or butter. One of the most popular Punjabi dishes
is Punjabi kadhi pakoda: chickpea flour fritters simmered in yogurt sauce.*

INGREDIENTS | SERVES 4–6

For Besan (Chickpea Flour) Fritters:

2 cups besan (chickpea flour)

½ teaspoon ajwain seeds

Pinch baking soda

Salt, to taste

1–1½ cups water

Oil for deep frying

For Kadhi:

4 cups water

1 cup besan

3 cups yogurt

1½ tablespoons cooking oil

Pinch asafetida

½ teaspoon cumin seeds

½ teaspoon black mustard seeds

½ teaspoon fenugreek seeds

2 whole dried red chilies

1 tablespoon chopped ginger

1 tablespoon chopped garlic

1 tablespoon curry leaves

1 teaspoon turmeric powder

Salt, to taste

Tips

To add an extra crunch, you can add fried
onions on top of your kadhi. In fact, you
can add them to any kind of kadhi.

1. In a large bowl, mix the chickpea flour, ajwain seeds, and baking soda. Add the salt. (Chickpea fritters should be very lightly salted because they will absorb juices and flavor from the kadhi later.)

2. Add water while thoroughly whisking so that there are no lumps in the batter. Batter should be light, smooth, and thicker than a pancake batter. Heat the oil in a deep fryer and slowly spoon batter into the oil. Fry until the fritters are golden brown. Place the fritters on paper towels to drain the excess oil. Set the fritters aside.

3. In a large mixing bowl, whisk together half of the water (2 cups) and besan (chickpea flour) until it's smooth. Set aside. Add the other half of the water to the yogurt and whisk it into a thin liquid. Set aside.

4. Heat the oil in a wok or a big wide pan over medium heat. Add the asafetida, cumin seeds, mustard seeds, fenugreek seeds, and red chili. When the spices start to pop, add the chopped ginger, garlic, and curry leaves. Cook until the mixture is golden brown, approximately 3–5 minutes. Add water and besan mixture. Add the turmeric. Mix everything together well and transfer the contents into the slow cooker. Cover and cook on high for 1 hour or until the mixture is thickened like a loose paste. Whisk a couple times during cooking using your hand whisk.

5. Once the mixture in the slow cooker is thickened, add the thinned-out yogurt to it. Cover and cook on high for another 1 hour or until the mixture begins to thicken to a consistency of your liking.

6. About 20–25 minutes after adding the yogurt, drop the fritters into the slow cooker. Add salt to your taste. Cover and cook until the kadhi has the desired consistency.

Puneri Dal

The use of goda masala, a vibrant spice blend, and tangy tamarind gives this soup its distinct flavor.

INGREDIENTS | SERVES 4–6

2 cups split pigeon peas (toor dal)

2 tablespoons tamarind (soaked in ½ cup water for 30 minutes)

6 cups water, as needed

½ teaspoon turmeric powder

Salt, to taste

2 tablespoons jaggery, or dark brown sugar

2 tablespoons ghee

½ teaspoon black mustard seeds

½ teaspoon cumin seeds

12–15 curry leaves

1 tablespoon Goda Masala Powder (Chapter 2)

1 teaspoon cayenne pepper

¼ cup unsweetened grated coconut

Cilantro, for garnish

Puneri Dal

This soup originates from the kitchens of the Puneri Brahmins, a sect of Hindus from the state of Maharashtra.

1. Rinse the toor dal with water. Drain the water and set aside. Mash the tamarind in the soaking water and filter out the pulp. Set aside.

2. In a slow cooker, combine the rinsed toor dal, 6 cups water, turmeric, salt to taste, and jaggery. Cover and cook on high for 2½–3 hours or on low setting for 4–5 hours. If the water begins to dry out, add up to ½ cup more. (The consistency should be thinner than a creamy soup.)

3. Toward the last 30 minutes of cooking add the tamarind pulp.

4. Heat the ghee in a skillet over medium heat. Add the mustard seeds, cumin seeds, and curry leaves one after the other. As they sputter, add the Goda Masala and cayenne pepper. Cook for another 5–7 seconds and then add the grated coconut. Turn the heat off.

5. Transfer the spice mixture into the cooked lentil soup. Stir well and serve hot, garnished with cilantro.

Rajma Masala

No North Indian would believe you if you said that red kidney beans are not native to India. The bean is an integral part of the North Indian cuisine, especially food from the states of Punjab, Haryana, Delhi, Kashmir, and Himachal Pradesh.

INGREDIENTS | SERVES 6

1 cup dry red kidney beans, or 2 (8-ounce) cans red kidney beans

2–3 cloves

Salt, to taste

¾ cup Curry Paste (Chapter 3)

¼ cup chopped cilantro

Soaking Water

Drain the water in which the beans are soaked. Wash the beans with water and only then use it for cooking. Using the same soaking water makes the dish heavy on the stomach.

1. Wash the dry beans with water. Then soak the beans in water three times the quantity of beans (in this case, 3 cups of water). Let them soak in water for 6–8 hours or overnight. Drain all the water. Add fresh water, this time four times the quantity of beans (in this case, 4 cups).

2. Add the cloves, salt, and Curry Paste to the slow cooker and cook on high for 3–4 hours, or on low for 6–7 hours, or until the beans are cooked well. If using canned beans, cook on high for 2 hours or on low for about 4 hours.

3. Garnish with chopped cilantro and serve with white steamed rice.

Rasam

In Hindi, rasa *means juice; but in Tamil* rasam *simply means a thin lentil soup cooked with tamarind/tomato juice and several spices. Sometimes vegetables are added, too. It's a common Indian soup staple in the South Indian cuisine.*

INGREDIENTS | SERVES 6–8

1 lime-size ball of tamarind
1 cup toor dal (yellow lentil)
½ teaspoon turmeric powder
2 tablespoons rasam powder
Salt, to taste
4–5 cups water
1 tablespoon cooking oil
Pinch asafetida
½ teaspoon cumin seeds
1 teaspoon black mustard seeds
½ teaspoon cayenne pepper
12–18 curry leaves
2 tablespoons chopped cilantro leaves

1. Soak the tamarind in ½ cup water for 2 hours. Collect all the pulp, filtering out the waste.

2. Add the lentils, turmeric, tamarind pulp, rasam powder, salt, and water to the slow cooker. Cover and cook on high for 3 hours or on low for 5 hours.

3. In a tempering pan, heat the oil. Add the asafetida. After 5 seconds, add the cumin seeds, mustard seeds, cayenne pepper, and curry leaves one after the other. Transfer the pan mixture (tadka) to the slow cooker. Mix well, garnish with cilantro, and serve with rice.

Thinning It Out

This soup is very thin and flow-y, so extra water can be added if lentils end up absorbing too much liquid or if vegetables are added.

Restaurant-Style Dal Fry

When you ask for dal in most North Indian restaurants, you will be served fried yellow lentils.
But you can use this same recipe to make a dal fry for any other kind of lentil.

INGREDIENTS | SERVES 4–6

1½ cups yellow lentils, washed (toor dal)

4 cups water, and more if needed

½ teaspoon turmeric powder

Salt, to taste

4–5 tablespoons oil or ghee

1 teaspoon cumin seeds

1 teaspoon garlic (minced)

3–4 dried whole red chilies

¼ cup chopped red onion

½ cup diced tomato

3 tablespoons chopped cilantro

1. In a slow cooker, combine the lentils, 4 cups of water, turmeric powder, salt, and 1 tablespoon of the oil. Cover and cook on high for 2–2½ hours, or on low for 4–5 hours, or until the lentils are soft. If the water begins to dry out, add up to ½ cup more. (The consistency should be like a creamy soup.)

2. Using a spoon, mash the cooked lentils to a creamy consistency. Set aside.

3. In a medium pan, heat the remaining vegetable oil. Add the cumin seeds. When they begin to sizzle, add the garlic and red chilies. Sauté for about 20 seconds. Add the red onion and sauté until it turns light brown. Add the tomato and cook uncovered on low 5 minutes or until the tomato melts.

4. Add the tomato mixture to the cooked dal. Garnish with cilantro and serve hot over Perfect Slow Cooker Basmati Rice (Chapter 11).

Sambhar

Sambhar (or sambar, or kuzhambu) is a traditional vegetable stew, a staple in the southern states of India. In the dish, vegetables are cooked for a long time with some lentils, spices, and tamarind, typical in the southern cuisine.

INGREDIENTS | SERVES 6–8

1½ cups pigeon peas

5 cups water

Salt, to tatse

2 cups eggplant, cut into ½" cubes

1 cup carrots, peeled and cut into ½" cubes

1 cup chopped cauliflower heads

2 tablespoons cooking oil

Pinch asafetida

½ teaspoon cumin seeds

½ teaspoon mustard seeds

½ cup frozen shallots

1 teaspoon chopped green chili

10–12 curry leaves

1 teaspoon turmeric

2 tablespoons Sambhar Masala (Chapter 2)

½ cup coconut milk

1 tablespoon jaggery, or brown sugar

1 lemon-size ball of tamarind, soaked in water and pulp extracted

1. Wash the pigeon peas in running water. Transfer to the slow cooker; add the water and soak them overnight or for 6–8 hours.

2. Add salt to the soaked pigeon peas. Cover and cook on low for 5 hours or on high for 2 hours. Add the eggplant, carrots, and cauliflower. Cook for another 1½ hours on high.

3. Heat the oil over medium heat in a sauté pan. Add the asafetida, cumin, and mustard seeds. As they splutter, add shallots, green chili, and curry leaves. Sauté for 5 minutes.

4. Add the turmeric, Sambhar Masala, coconut milk, jaggery, and tamarind pulp. Bring the mixture to a quick boil. Transfer the contents to the slow cooker. Cook for another ½ hour.

5. Serve hot over rice or with steamed rice cakes (or *idly*).

Simple Chickpea Sandal

*Dal ki poori, or flatbreads stuffed with mashed chickpea sandal,
is also a popular dish in the North of India.*

INGREDIENTS | SERVES 5–6

1½ cups chickpeas, soaked overnight in water

3 cups water, plus extra as needed

Salt, to taste

1 teaspoon baking soda

3–4 tablespoons oil

3–4 whole dried red chilies

1 teaspoon black mustard seeds

12–15 curry leaves

½ cup unsweetened grated coconut

1. Drain out the soaking water from the chickpeas. Rinse with running water. Set aside.

2. In a slow cooker, combine together the 3 cups of water, salt to taste, and baking soda. Add the rinsed chickpeas. Cover and cook on high for 3–4 hours, or on low for 6–7 hours, or until the chickpeas are cooked. Add extra water if the chickpeas are not yet cooked.

3. When the chickpeas are completely cooked, all the water should be absorbed. If not, then drain all the extra water.

4. Heat the oil in a large pan over medium heat. Add all the dried spices. As they sputter, add the grated coconut. Stir-fry for 3–5 minutes. As soon as the mixture starts turning brown, add the chickpeas. Stir everything together and serve either as a snack or with rice and lentils.

Simple Mung Bean Curry (Tadka Dal)

Tadka in Indian cooking means "seasoning." This yellow dal is a North Indian favorite.
Serve atop steamed Indian basmati rice.

INGREDIENTS | SERVES 6

2 cups yellow split mung beans (yellow *moong dal*), well rinsed

6 cups water, more if needed

½ teaspoon turmeric powder

4–5 tablespoons vegetable oil, divided

1 teaspoon cumin seeds

1 small red onion, minced

1 teaspoon grated ginger

1 serrano green chili, seeded and minced

1 small tomato, minced (optional)

Salt, to taste

1 tablespoon minced cilantro (optional)

Removing Gas

Some lentils contain gas-forming compounds. In order to reduce these, rinse them well. Never cook them in the soaking water—always use fresh water.

1. In a slow cooker, combine the mung beans, 6 cups of water, turmeric, and 1 tablespoon vegetable oil. Cover and cook on high for 2½–3 hours, or on low for 4–5 hours, or until the mung beans are very soft. If the water starts to dry up, you can add another ½–1 cup water. Turn off the heat and set aside.

2. In a medium-size skillet, heat the remaining vegetable oil. Add the cumin seeds; when they begin to sizzle, add the red onion. Sauté for 7–8 minutes or until the onions are well browned.

3. Add the ginger, green chili, and tomato. Cook for another 8 minutes or until the tomato is soft.

4. Add the salt and cilantro and mix well. Add the onion mixture to the mung beans and mix well. Reheat gently and serve hot.

Split Black Lentil Soup (Urad Dal)

*Urad dal or black lentils are popularly consumed in the
northern states of India specially Punjab and Haryana.*

INGREDIENTS | SERVES 4–6

1½ cups black split lentil (urad dal)

1 tablespoon minced gingerroot

½ teaspoon turmeric powder

1 teaspoon minced green chili

½ teaspoon asafetida

Salt, to taste

4 cups water, plus more as needed

2–3 tablespoons ghee

1 teaspoon cumin seeds

1 teaspoon minced garlic

½ cup chopped red onion

¼ cup chopped cilantro

1. Rinse the lentils thoroughly with water. Drain the water and set lentils aside.

2. Transfer the washed lentils, gingerroot, turmeric, chili, and half the asafetida to the slow cooker, along with salt to taste. Add 4 cups of water. Cover and cook on high for 2½–3 hours, or on low for 4–5 hours, or until the lentils are cooked through. If the dal begins to dry up, add up to 1 cup of hot water.

3. Heat the ghee in a pan. Add the rest of the asafetida, followed by cumin seeds. As they sputter, add the garlic. Cook for 1 minute and as it browns add the onion. Let the onion turn light golden in color. Transfer the hot mixture to the cooked lentils. Stir well.

4. Garnish with cilantro. Serve hot with Perfect Slow Cooker Basmati Rice (Chapter 11) or your choice of flatbread.

Split Pea and Cheese Curry (Paneeri Chana Dal)

A cozy combination of creamy chana dal *and soft* paneer *(Indian cheese),
serve this with warm simple Indian bread or roti. Garnish with minced cilantro.*

INGREDIENTS | SERVES 4

½ teaspoon turmeric powder

1 teaspoon red chili powder

3 tablespoons vegetable oil, divided

4 cups water

1 cup chana dal (or yellow split peas),
well rinsed

1 cup fried paneer

Salt, to taste

1 teaspoon minced garlic

1 small red onion, minced

Cilantro, for garnish

1. In a slow cooker, combine the turmeric powder, red chili powder, 1 tablespoon of the vegetable oil, and 3½ cups of water. Add the chana dal. Cover and cook on high for 2–3 hours, or on low for 4–6 hours, or until the split peas are cooked, stirring occasionally.

2. Toward the last 30 minutes, add the fried paneer to the slow cooker and let it cook with the dal.

3. Once the split peas are cooked, turn the slow cooker off. Add the salt; mix well with a wooden spoon. Set aside.

4. In a medium-size pan, heat the remaining vegetable oil. Add the garlic and sauté for 30 seconds.

5. Add the onion and sauté for 7 minutes or until the onions are browned. Remove from heat and add to the dal. Mix well. Serve hot, garnish with cilantro.

Tadka Tomato Dal

Tadka, as discussed in Chapter 1, "Basics of Indian Cooking," is a simple tempering where some whole spices are tempered in oil or ghee and then added to soups, rice dishes, and even raita and chutney.

INGREDIENTS | SERVES 4–6

2 cups toor dal (yellow lentil)

3 cups sliced tomatoes

Salt, to taste

1½ teaspoons turmeric

4 cups of water

2 tablespoons ghee

¼ teaspoon asafetida

1 tablespoon black mustard seeds

1 teaspoon cumin seeds

3 cloves garlic, minced

2 tablespoons chopped curry leaves

4–5 cherry tomatoes, sliced into halves

1 teaspoon cayenne pepper

1. Wash the lentils thoroughly till the water runs clear when added to it.

2. In a slow cooker, add the lentils, tomatoes, salt, and turmeric, along with 4 cups of water. Cover and cook on high for 2–3 hours or on low for 4–5 hours. If the dal (lentils) begins to dry up, add up to 1 cup of hot water.

3. For the tadka, heat the ghee in a tempering pan. Add the asafetida. When it starts sizzling, add the mustard and cumin seeds. When the seeds start to pop, add the garlic. Let it brown and then add curry leaves. Cook for 10–15 seconds.

4. Add the sliced cherry tomatoes. Cook the mixture for about 4–5 minutes and just before the tomatoes start to melt, add the cayenne pepper. Turn the heat off immediately and add the tadka to the hot lentils. Mix well. Serve with rice.

The Five-Lentil Delight (Paanch Dalo Ka Sangam)

Also called Panchratan, *or "The Five Jewels," this creamy dahl (*dal*)
is a gourmet's delight. Serve with simple naan or roti.*

INGREDIENTS | SERVES 4–6

½ cup yellow split peas (*chana dal*), rinsed

½ cup red split lentils (*masoor dal*), rinsed

½ cup split black gram, or black lentil (*safeed urad dal*), rinsed

½ cup pigeon peas (*toor dal*), rinsed

½ cup green split mung beans (green *moong dal*), rinsed

Water, as needed

1 teaspoon turmeric powder

2 teaspoons salt

5 tablespoons vegetable oil, divided

1 teaspoon cumin seeds

1 teaspoon Ginger-Garlic Paste (Chapter 2)

1 medium-size red onion, minced

1 teaspoon red chili powder

½ teaspoon cumin powder

½ teaspoon Garam Masala Powder (Chapter 2)

1. In a slow cooker, combine all the dals, 6 cups of water, the turmeric powder, salt, and 2 tablespoons of the vegetable oil. Cover and cook on high for 2½–3 hours, or on low for 5–6 hours, or until the dals are cooked. If the water begins to dry out, add more. (The consistency should be like a creamy soup.) Remove from heat and set aside.

2. In a medium-size skillet, heat the remaining vegetable oil. Add the cumin seeds; when they begin to sizzle, add the Ginger-Garlic Paste. Sauté for 30 seconds and then add the onion. Sauté for 7–8 minutes or until the onions are well browned.

3. Add the red chili, cumin powder, and Garam Masala Powder spice mix to the skillet; mix well.

4. Add the prepared mixture in the skillet to the dal and mix well. Serve hot.

Tomato Rasam

You can get creative and try adding some sweet or citrus fruits like cherry or blood orange to experiment with flavors. You will be surprised how much you can do with just a simple lentil soup.

INGREDIENTS | SERVES 6–8

1 lime-size ball of tamarind

1½ tablespoons jaggery powder

1 cup toor dal (yellow lentil)

2 cups diced tomatoes

2 cups frozen mixed vegetables (beans, carrots)

½ teaspoon turmeric powder

2 tablespoons rasam powder

Salt, to taste

4–5 cups water

1 tablespoon cooking oil

Pinch asafetida

½ teaspoon cumin seeds

1 teaspoon black mustard seeds

½ teaspoon cayenne pepper

12–18 curry leaves

2 tablespoons chopped cilantro leaves

1. Soak the tamarind in ½ cup water for a couple hours. Collect all the pulp, filtering out the waste. Add the pulp and the jaggery to a small saucepan and bring it to boil. Set aside.

2. In a slow cooker, add the lentils, tomato, vegetables, turmeric, tamarind and jaggery sauce, rasam powder, salt, and water. Cover and cook on high setting for about 3 hours or on low for 5 hours.

3. In a tempering pan, heat the oil. Add the asafetida and after 5 seconds add the cumin seeds, mustard seeds, cayenne pepper, and curry leaves one after the other. Transfer this mixture to the lentils. Mix well; garnish with cilantro and serve with rice.

Vegetable Kadhi

Practically any kind of vegetable can be used for this recipe. Eggplants, broccoli, and potatoes are a few examples other than the ones used in this recipe.

INGREDIENTS | SERVES 4–6

4 cups water

1 cup besan (chickpea flour)

3 cups yogurt

¼ tablespoon cooking oil

Pinch asafetida

½ teaspoon cumin seeds

½ teaspoon black mustard seeds

½ teaspoon fenugreek seeds

2 whole dried red chilies

1 tablespoon chopped ginger

1 tablespoon chopped garlic

1 tablespoon curry leaves

2 cups mix of string beans, carrots, and peas (or any vegetable of your choice)

1 teaspoon turmeric powder

Salt, to taste

1. In a large mixing bowl, whisk together 2 cups water and besan until it's smooth. Set aside.

2. Add the other 2 cups of the water to the yogurt and whisk it into a thin liquid. Set aside.

3. Heat the oil in a wok or a big wide pan. Add the asafetida, cumin seeds, mustard seeds, fenugreek seeds, and red chilies. When the spices start to pop, add the chopped ginger, garlic, and curry leaves. Cook until the mixture is golden brown. Add the vegetables. Sauté for 5 more minutes.

4. Add the water and besan mixture to the pan. Add the turmeric and salt to taste. Mix everything together well and transfer the contents to the slow cooker. Cover and cook on high for 1 hour or until the mixture is thickened like a loose paste. Whisk a couple times during cooking using your hand whisk.

5. Once the mixture in the slow cooker is thickened, add the thinned-out yogurt to it. Cover and cook on high for 1 hour or until the mixture begins to thicken to a consistency of your liking.

6. Serve hot with Perfect Slow Cooker Basmati Rice (Chapter 11) or a flatbread, such as a soft and warm naan.

Yogurt Green Curry (Hariyali Kadhi)

A variation on the classic spicy yogurt kurry (Punjabi kadhi), serve this nutritious curry with Perfect Slow Cooker Basmati Rice (Chapter 11).

INGREDIENTS | SERVES 4

1 (10-ounce) package chopped frozen spinach, thawed

½–¾ cup chickpea flour

Water, as needed

2 tablespoons vegetable oil

Pinch of asafetida

2 dried red chilies, broken

1 teaspoon minced garlic

1½ cups plain yogurt

Salt, to taste

Stinking Spice

Asafetida is a stinky resin that is used for flavoring and as a digestive aid. Don't let the smell discourage you; it dissipates during the cooking process.

1. Place the spinach in a deep pan and add enough water to cover. Boil until the leaves are cooked through, about 10 minutes. Remove from heat, drain thoroughly, and cool to room temperature. In a food processor, purée the spinach to a thick paste. Transfer to a deep bowl.

2. Whisk together the chickpea flour and 1 cup water in a mixing bowl, making sure there are no lumps. Next, whisk this mixture into the spinach paste. Set aside.

3. In a deep pan, heat the vegetable oil. Add the asafetida, red chilies, and garlic; sauté for 30 seconds.

4. Add the spinach-chickpea mixture into the seasoned oil. Mix well.

5. Transfer the contents to a slow cooker. Cover and cook on high for 1 hour or until the mixture is thickened like a loose paste. Whisk a couple times during cooking using your hand whisk.

6. In the meantime, whisk together the yogurt and salt. Add 3 cups of water (or more or less according to your taste).

7. Once the mixture in the slow cooker is thickened, add the thinned-out yogurt to it. Cover and cook on high for another 1 hour or until the mixture begins to thicken to a consistency of your liking. Adjust salt. Serve hot.

CHAPTER 7

Vegetarian

Acorn Squash
with Fenugreek Seeds
and Garlic
110

Aloo Matar Masala
110

Aloo Methi
(Potatoes Cooked in
Fenugreek Leaves)
111

Aloo Saag ki Sabji
(Potato and Spinach
Cooked with Red Chili)
112

Avial (Mixed Vegetables
in Coconut Sauce)
113

Baigan Bharta
114

Baigan Nu Bharta
(Roasted Eggplant
in Yogurt)
115

Bandhagobhi ki Sabji
(Cabbage with
Potatoes and Peas)
116

Bell Pepper and
Vegetables Cooked with
Fennel Seeds
117

Chili Pepper Curry
(Mirchi Ka Salan)
118

Chole Masala
119

Curried Black-
Eyed Peas
119

Curried Soy Chunks
120

Tempeh in
Coconut Cream
121

Dry-Spiced
Carrot and Peas
(Gajar Mattar ki Subzi)
121

Dum Aloo
122

Eggplant Cooked with
Panch Foran Spices
123

Gobhi Aloo (Potato
and Cauliflower)
124

Indian Curry Tempeh
124

Jeera Aloo (Cumin-
Scented Potatoes)
125

Kathal Do Pyaza
126

Malai Kofta
127

Matar Paneer
128

Palak Paneer
129

Paneer Makhani
130

Potato Curry
(Assami Ril Do)
131

Rajma Masala
132

"Roasted" Beets
132

Royal Mushrooms with
Cashew Nut Sauce
(Nawabi Guchhi)
133

Slow-Cooked Mustard
Greens (Sarson ka Saag)
134

Spiced "Baked"
Eggplant
135

Stuffed Eggplants
136

Tamatar Aloo
(Curried Potato with
Tomato Sauce)
137

Til waali Bandhagobhi
(Cabbage with
Peas, Carrots, and
Sesame Seeds)
138

Acorn Squash with Fenugreek Seeds and Garlic

Traditional in India, this dish is prepared with a variety of pumpkin, which tastes the closest to the acorn squashes easily available in Western markets.

INGREDIENTS | SERVES 6

1 tablespoon oil (mustard, olive, or vegetable oil)

1 teaspoon fenugreek seeds

1 tablespoon freshly minced garlic

2 dried whole red chilies

1 medium-size acorn squash, skinned, seeded, and cut into 1" cubes

1 teaspoon turmeric powder

1½ teaspoons amchoor powder (Chapter 2), or 1 tablespoon lime or lemon juice

½ tablespoon brown sugar

1 tablespoon coriander powder

Salt, to taste

1. Heat the oil in a wok or thick-bottom pan. Add the fenugreek seeds. As they start to sizzle, add the garlic and whole chilies (broken into pieces).

2. When the garlic starts to brown, add the acorn squash. Add turmeric. Toss everything together. Add the remaining ingredients.

3. Transfer the contents to a slow cooker. Cover and cook on low for 4–5 hours, stirring occasionally and scraping the sides and bottom. Cook until the squash is cooked through but not mushy.

4. Serve hot with hot puffed roti (Indian flatbread) and a cup of hot yellow lentil soup.

Aloo Matar Masala

Poori (Chapter 15) or Paratha (Chapter 15) are popular accompaniments of Aloo Matar Masala other than rice.

INGREDIENTS | SERVES 5–6

2½ cups potatoes (peeled and cut into cubes)

1 cup frozen green peas

1 cup diced tomatoes

¾ cup curry paste

1½ tablespoons ghee

Salt, to taste

Water, as needed

¼ cups chopped cilantro

1. Mix all the ingredients together *except* the cilantro in a slow cooker. Add up to 2 cups of water. Cover and cook on high for 2 hours, or on low for 4 hours (stirring a couple times), or until the vegetables are cooked well.

2. Garnish with cilantro and serve hot with Perfect Slow Cooker Basmati Rice (Chapter 11).

Aloo Methi (Potatoes Cooked in Fenugreek Leaves)

Methi or fenugreek is a very popular herb in India and is used in several forms from fresh leaves to dried or even seeds and is very commonly used for tempering and with stir-fries.

INGREDIENTS | SERVES 4–5

3–4 tablespoons oil, plus 1 tablespoon ghee

1 teaspoon cumin seeds

1 tablespoon minced garlic

2–3 dry whole red chilies

½ teaspoon turmeric powder

1½ cups potatoes (peeled and cut into cubes)

3 cups fenugreek leaves (clean, discard the tougher stems and chop the rest of the stems with the leaves)

Salt, to taste

1. Heat the oil in a large pan over medium heat. Add the cumin seeds. As they sputter, add the garlic and red chilies. Cook for 1 minute. As they brown, add the turmeric powder followed by the potatoes. Cook for another 5 minutes and then transfer the contents to the slow cooker.

2. Add the fenugreek leaves and salt. Mix well. Cover and cook on high for 1½ hours, or on low for 3–4 hours, or until the potatoes are cooked through (stirring occasionally, scraping the bottom or sides).

3. Toward the last 30 minutes of cooking, check to see if the potatoes are cooked. If they are, then cook on high, uncovered, stirring frequently to cook off the excess liquid, if any. You can even perform this step over a stovetop to quicken the process.

Aloo Saag ki Sabji
(Potato and Spinach Cooked with Red Chili)

Practically every green and leafy vegetable easily available in India can and is cooked with potatoes. Cook until the leaves lose most of their moisture and then serve with a bread and dal on the side.

INGREDIENTS | SERVES 4

3–4 tablespoons oil, preferably mustard oil

1 teaspoon fenugreek seeds

3–4 dried red chilies

1 tablespoon minced garlic

½ teaspoon turmeric powder

2 cups potatoes, peeled and cut into 1" cubes

6 cups chopped fresh spinach

Salt, to taste

Methi Dana or Fenugreek Seeds

Apart from adding flavor to food, fenugreek seeds are believed to have great medicinal values, ranging from alleviating arthritis pain to promoting good lactation to warming the kidneys to dispersing colds, and more.

1. Heat the oil in a pan; add the fenugreek seeds followed by the dried chilies. As they sputter, add the garlic. Cook for 10 seconds or until the garlic turns brown.

2. Add the turmeric powder, and after a couple seconds add the potatoes. Stir-fry for 5 minutes or until the potatoes begin to brown on the sides.

3. Transfer the contents to the slow cooker. Add the washed and chopped spinach. Add salt. Stir it together well. Cover and cook on high (stirring occasionally) for 2–2½ hours or until the potatoes are cooked through and the spinach has lost all its moisture.

4. Serve hot with a lentil soup and fresh warm bread on the side.

Avial (Mixed Vegetables in Coconut Sauce)

*Use your choice of seasonal vegetables to make this dish. Serve with
Perfect Slow Cooker Basmati Rice (Chapter 11) and your choice of any hot pickle.*

INGREDIENTS | SERVES 4

1 cup unsweetened desiccated coconut

1 tablespoon cumin seeds, toasted

2 serrano green chilies, seeded

Water, as needed

½ pound carrots, peeled

2 small potatoes, peeled

1 green banana or plantain, peeled (optional)

½ pound frozen cut green beans, thawed

½ cup plain yogurt, whipped

½ teaspoon turmeric powder

Salt, to taste

1 tablespoon vegetable oil

1 teaspoon black mustard seeds

8 curry leaves

Vegetable Drumsticks

The next time you are at your Indian grocer, ask for a can of vegetable drumsticks and use it in this dish. Add this along with the other vegetables in Step 2. These delightful vegetables add something special to your dishes. Eat only the jelly-like portion inside, discarding the outside skin.

1. In a food processor, grind the coconut, cumin seeds, and green chilies along with a few tablespoons of water to make a thick paste. Set aside.

2. Cut the carrots and potatoes into ¼" sticks. Peel and chop the banana.

3. In a slow cooker, combine the carrots, potatoes, banana, green beans, and 1½ cups of water. Cover and cook on high for 1½ hours, or on low for 3 hours, or until the vegetables are soft. Drain off any remaining water.

4. Add the yogurt, the reserved coconut paste, turmeric, and salt to the vegetables. Simmer until the vegetables are completely cooked through, another 45 minutes on high or 1½ hours or low. When cooked through, turn off the heat and set aside.

5. In a small skillet, heat the vegetable oil over medium heat. Add the mustard seeds and curry leaves. When the seeds begin to crackle, remove from heat and pour over the cooked vegetables. Serve hot.

Baigan Bharta

Bharta, or bhurta, in Hindi refers to any lightly spiced, mashed mix of vegetables. There are several recipes for bharta that are popular in India, with baigan (Hindi for eggplant) being the most popular.

INGREDIENTS | SERVES 6–8

1 medium-size whole eggplant

2 Thai green chilies

3 cloves garlic, peeled

2 medium-size tomatoes

1 cup boiled potatoes, peeled and mashed

3–4 tablespoons oil

½ teaspoon black mustard seeds

½ teaspoon cumin seeds

½ teaspoon turmeric

1½ tablespoons coriander powder

½ cup chopped onion

1 cup frozen green peas, thawed

Salt, to taste

1 teaspoon Garam Masala Powder (Chapter 2)

¼ cup chopped cilantro

1. Wash the eggplant and tomatoes with water. Wipe off dry. Make 5–6 small slits on the eggplant. (Not very deep). Carefully push the whole green chilies and garlic cloves, one each, into the slits. Use aluminum foil sheets to wrap the eggplant and tomatoes individually.

2. Place the packets into the slow cooker, making sure each one touches the surface. Cover and cook on low for 10–12 hours or until they are cooked and soft inside. The tomatoes will take less time to cook, so add them to the slow cooker toward the last 2 hours of cooking or take them out when they are cooked.

3. Take the cooked eggplant and tomatoes out of the foil and let them cool down before peeling the outer skin. Take the skin off the vegetables and then mash them together with the boiled potatoes. Set aside.

4. Heat the oil in a pan over medium heat. Add the mustard and cumin seeds. As they sputter, add the turmeric and coriander powder. Cook for 2–4 seconds and then add the onion. Cook until the onions turn translucent. Then add the thawed green peas and salt. Cover and cook for 4–5 minutes.

5. Add the Garam Masala Powder and the mashed vegetables. Cook on medium-high heat for 7–10 minutes, stirring occasionally. Garnish with cilantro and serve hot with warm puffed flatbreads and Tadka Tomato Dal (Chapter 6).

Baigan Nu Bharta (Roasted Eggplant in Yogurt)

This recipe comes from a dear friend who claims to be a hater of eggplants. Roasting an eggplant and then mixing it with a few simple spices and tangy yogurt just adds an extra kick to it.

INGREDIENTS | SERVES 4–5

1 medium eggplant

2 tablespoons oil, or ghee

1 teaspoon roasted cumin seeds, coarsely crushed

¾ cup chopped green onions

½ teaspoon red chili flakes

Salt, to taste

1½ cups Slow Cooker Yogurt (Chapter 3)

1. Rub the outside of the eggplant with 1 teaspoon ghee or oil. Either roast it over an open flame, or in a convection oven wrapped in aluminum foil until cooked and then under the broiler for the last 10 minutes to char the skin. (You could also cook the eggplant in a slow cooker like Baigan Bharta (see recipe in this chapter) or Shakarkandi (Chapter 4).)

2. Once cooked through, place the eggplant in a glass bowl and cover it with plastic wrap. (This will quicken the peeling process.) Let it sit for 10 minutes and then uncover and peel the skin off. Mash the eggplant and set it aside.

3. Heat rest of the ghee in a pan, add the cumin seeds. As they sputter, add the chopped green onion. Sauté for 1 minute and as they soften, add the eggplant. Add the chili flakes and salt. Stir everything together.

4. In a serving bowl, whisk the yogurt smooth and add the sautéed vegetables. Mix together and serve chilled.

Bandhagobhi ki Sabji (Cabbage with Potatoes and Peas)

This recipe can be varied in several ways by just substituting different vegetables.

INGREDIENTS | SERVES 4

3–4 tablespoons oil, or ghee

1–2 pinches asafetida

1 teaspoon cumin seeds

1 tablespoon Ginger-Garlic Paste (Chapter 2)

¼ cup chopped red onion

¾ teaspoon turmeric powder

1 tablespoon coriander powder

1 teaspoon Garam Masala Powder (Chapter 2)

Water, as needed

4–5 cups chopped cabbage (about ½ medium cabbage)

1½–2 cups potatoes (peeled and cut into ½–1" cubes)

¾ cup frozen peas, thawed

Salt, to taste

1. Heat the oil in a pan or wok. Add the asafetida followed by cumin seeds. As they sputter, add the Ginger-Garlic Paste. Cook for 10–15 seconds and then add chopped onion. Cook until they turn brown.

2. Add the turmeric, coriander, and Garam Masala. Add 3–4 tablespoons of water and simmer on low for 1 minute until all the water evaporates.

3. Add the remaining ingredients and mix everything together well. Transfer the contents to the slow cooker. Cover and cook on high for 2½ hours, or on low for 4–5 hours (stirring occasionally), or until all the vegetables are cooked well. If necessary, cook uncovered toward the end to help evaporate excess water.

4. Garnish with cilantro if desired and serve hot with a side of lentil soup, Perfect Slow Cooker Basmati Rice (Chapter 11), and/or warm flatbread of your choice.

Bell Pepper and Vegetables Cooked with Fennel Seeds

When in a hurry, this can be your go-to recipe. Use any kind of root vegetable to replace the ones used in this recipe.

INGREDIENTS | SERVES 5–6

4 tablespoons oil

1 teaspoon cumin seeds

1 tablespoon Ginger-Garlic Paste (Chapter 2)

½ cup chopped onion

½ teaspoon turmeric powder

1 cup chopped potatoes

1 cup frozen mix of green peas and carrots

½ cup yellow sweet frozen corn

Salt, to taste

2 cups chopped green bell pepper

1 tablespoon coriander powder

1. Heat the oil in a pan over medium heat. Add the cumin seeds, followed by the Ginger-Garlic Paste and onion. Sauté for 2–4 minutes or until the onions turn translucent.

2. Add the turmeric powder and stir. Add the potatoes, peas and carrots, and corn. Add the salt; toss everything together and transfer to the slow cooker. Cover and cook on high for 1 hour or on low for 2–2½ hours.

3. Add the bell pepper and cook covered for 1 hour on high, or on low for 2 hours, or until the bell pepper is fork tender.

4. Add the coriander powder. Stir well and cook uncovered for another 15–20 minutes. Serve hot on the side with warm Paratha (Chapter 15).

Chili Pepper Curry (Mirchi Ka Salan)

This dish is not for the weak of stomach or heart. Serve with Perfect Slow Cooker White Rice (Chapter 3) and a large pitcher of cold water!

INGREDIENTS | SERVES 4

8 large green chilies, anaheim or cubanelle

1 teaspoon tamarind pulp

1 cup warm water, divided

1 teaspoon cumin seeds

2 teaspoons coriander seeds

¼ teaspoon fenugreek seeds

1 teaspoon white poppy seeds

2 tablespoons sesame seeds

2½ tablespoons unsweetened desiccated coconut

4 tablespoons vegetable oil

¾ cup Caramelized Onions (Chapter 3)

1 tablespoon Ginger-Garlic Paste (Chapter 2)

¼ teaspoon red chili powder

¼ teaspoon turmeric powder

Salt, to taste

1. Remove the stems from the green chilies. Cut a slit down the side of each chili to remove the seeds, but don't separate the halves; discard the stems and seeds and set aside the peppers.

2. Add the tamarind pulp to 2 tablespoons of warm water and set aside to soak.

3. In a small skillet, roast the cumin, coriander, fenugreek, poppy, and sesame seeds. As the spices start to darken and release their aroma (less than 1 minute), add the coconut and roast for another 15 seconds. Remove from heat and let cool. Grind to a powder using a pestle and mortar or spice grinder.

4. In a large skillet, heat the oil over medium heat. Add the green chilies. As soon as the chilies develop brown spots, use a slotted spoon to remove them from the skillet and set aside. Place the chilies in the bottom of a 3–4 quart slow cooker.

5. In a large bowl, mix the Caramelized Onions, Ginger-Garlic Paste, and rest of the ingredients *except* for tamarind pulp. Mix the ingredients with water making a thin paste. Drizzle it on top of the chilies in the slow cooker. Cover and let it simmer on high for 1½ hours or on low for 3–3½ hours.

6. Strain the tamarind and discard the residue. Add the strained tamarind pulp to the slow cooker and mix well. Cook for another 10 minutes. Serve hot.

Chole Masala

Chole is the Hindi name for chickpeas and masala and is also commonly known as a mix of spices or a spice blend. This might be one of the easiest recipes to put together if you do a little homework beforehand.

INGREDIENTS | SERVES 6

1 (10-ounce) can diced tomatoes

2 (14-ounce) cans chickpeas

¾ cup Curry Paste (Chapter 3)

1 teaspoon Garam Masala Powder (Chapter 2)

Salt, to taste

Water, as needed

3–4 tablespoons chopped cilantro

Canned or Dried

Instead of canned chickpeas you can also start with dried chickpeas. Soak them overnight and adjust the cooking time accordingly.

1. Drain the excess water from the canned tomatoes and chickpeas. Wash the chickpeas under running water to wash out extra sodium. Transfer the contents to the slow cooker.

2. Add the rest of the ingredients *except* the cilantro to the slow cooker, along with the chickpeas and tomatoes. Add 14 ounces of water. Cover and cook on high for 2–3 hours, or on low for 5–6 hours, or until the chickpeas are cooked well. Add up to 1 cup of water if the chickpeas dry out in the cooking process. Stir occasionally during cooking.

3. Garnish with cilantro and serve with Perfect Slow Cooker Basmati Rice (Chapter 11) and a raita of your choice.

Curried Black-Eyed Peas

Lobhiya or chawali is the Hindi name for black-eyed peas, which are very rich in protein. It's one of the most popular beans used in India mostly because they are easy to grow and hence inexpensive.

INGREDIENTS | SERVES 6

2 (14-ounce) cans black-eyed peas

¾ cups Curry Paste (Chapter 3)

Salt, to taste

3 cups water, plus more as needed

¼ cup chopped cilantro

1. Drain the soaking liquid from the canned beans. Wash the black-eyed peas with water 2–3 times. Transfer them into the slow cooker along with the Curry Paste and salt. Add 3 cups of water. Cover and cook on high for 2 hours, or on low for 4–5 hours, or until the beans are cooked through. Add extra water if the water dries up during cooking. Garnish with cilantro and serve hot with rice or naan.

Curried Soy Chunks

Nutrela is a hugely popular brand of dried soy chunks and other soy products in India.

INGREDIENTS | SERVES 5–6

1½ cup dried soy chunks

4 tablespoons oil

1½ cups potatoes, peeled and chopped into 1" chunks

1 cup curry paste

Salt, to taste

2 cups water, or as needed

3–4 tablespoons chopped cilantro

1. Soak the soy chunks in hot salted water until they absorb water and get soft. Squeeze out all the water by pressing the soy chunks between your hands. Set aside.

2. Heat 2 tablespoons of oil in a pan over medium heat. Add the soy chunks and pan-fry them for about 7–10 minutes or until the sides of the soy chunks are browned.

3. Transfer the soy chunks into the slow cooker. Add the potatoes, Curry Paste, remainder of oil, and salt. Mix together. Add up to 2 cups of water. Stir well. Cover and cook on high for 2–3 hours, or on low for 4–5 hours, or until the potatoes are cooked through.

4. Garnish with cilantro and serve hot with warm puffed Roti (Chapter 15) or over Perfect Slow Cooker Basmati Rice (Chapter 11).

Tempeh in Coconut Cream

Try serving tempeh over rice or on cool, crisp lettuce leaves.

INGREDIENTS | SERVES 4

2 cloves garlic, minced

1 teaspoon minced fresh ginger

¾ cup soy sauce

1 tablespoon vegetable oil

1 tablespoon sriracha sauce

1 (13-ounce) can coconut milk

1 cup water

1 (13-ounce) package tempeh, cut into bite-size squares

¼ cup fresh basil, chopped

1. Add all ingredients *except* for the basil to a 4-quart slow cooker. Cover and cook on low heat for 4 hours.

2. When the tempeh is done cooking, stir in the basil and serve.

Sriracha

Sriracha is a very hot chili sauce, popular in many Thai dishes. The most commonly sold brand is made by Huy Fong Foods and is available at grocery and specialty stores around the country.

Dry-Spiced Carrot and Peas (Gajar Mattar Ki Subzi)

The carrots and peas sautéed in cumin provide a healthy dish with a mild flavor.

INGREDIENTS | SERVES 4

2 tablespoons vegetable oil

1 teaspoon cumin seeds

3 cups frozen mix of carrots and peas, thawed

½ teaspoon red chili powder

¼ teaspoon turmeric powder

1 teaspoon coriander powder

Salt, to taste

Water, as needed

1. In a medium-size skillet, heat the vegetable oil over high heat. Add the cumin seeds. When the seeds begin to sizzle, turn off the heat and set aside.

2. Transfer the carrots and peas mix to a small slow cooker. Add the dry spices and salt along with the cumin oil. Stir and cover and cook on high for 2 hours (if the dry spices begin to stick, add a few tablespoons of water). Stir occasionally. Serve hot.

Spices as Medicine

Indian cuisine rests on the shoulders of ancient medicine. Each spice or herb that is used is deemed to have value in the world of medicine. For example, turmeric is an antiseptic, and cumin and carom seeds aid in digestion.

Dum Aloo

Dum aloo is a perfect example of a slow-cooking technique used in Indian cooking for generations. In ancient times, the lid to the cooking dish was sealed using a simple flour dough and would be cooked on low heat for hours.

INGREDIENTS | SERVES 6

2 tablespoons coriander powder

1 teaspoon turmeric powder

1 teaspoon cumin

5–6 peppercorns

1 teaspoon cinnamon powder

2 black cardamom pods

2–3 cloves

1 bay leaf

½ pound small potatoes, fingerling or small red potatoes work

2–3 tablespoons olive oil, plus extra for pan- or deep-frying

½ cup onion paste

1" piece of ginger, peeled

3–4 cloves garlic

2 Thai green chilies (or 1 teaspoon cayenne pepper or whole red chili)

Salt, to taste

½ cup water

2 tablespoons milk

½ cup yogurt

Cilantro, for garnish

Dum Pukht

Slow oven, or *dum pukht*, is a cooking technique used in India and is more than 200 years old. Slow oven is cooking food, mostly sealed in a container over low flame, and letting it cook slowly in its own juices over a long period of time.

1. Using a spice grinder, grind coriander, turmeric, cumin, peppercorn, cinnamon powder, black cardamom, cloves, and bay leaf making it a fine powder. Set aside.

2. Clean the potatoes with their skin on and poke a few holes into them using a toothpick or a fork. This will help the spices enter deep into the potatoes. Then either pan- or deep-fry them in oil. Set aside.

3. Make a paste of onion, garlic, ginger, cloves, and Thai green chilies.

4. Heat a thick-bottom pan. Add oil and then the paste you created in Step 3. Fry it until it all turns golden brown. Add salt while frying the mixture (masala) and fry until the paste starts leaving oil on the periphery. Add the prepared spice powder from Step 1 and mix well. (To quicken this process you can completely omit this step and use prepared Curry Paste (Chapter 3).)

5. Transfer the masala to a slow cooker. Add the potatoes. Add ½ cup water. Adjust salt if needed. Cover and cook on high for 30 minutes. Then reduce the heat to low and add the milk. Cook for 1 hour.

6. Add a smooth-whisked yogurt to the slow cooker and cook for another 30–45 minutes or until the potatoes are cooked well. Garnish with cilantro and serve hot with Perfect Slow Cooker Basmati Rice (Chapter 11) or your choice of rice dish.

Eggplant Cooked with Panch Foran Spices

Panch *in Hindi means number five and* foran/phoran *stands for the spices used for tempering. So* panch foran *literally refers to the five spices used for tempering.*

INGREDIENTS | SERVES 5–6

4 tablespoons oil

1½ teaspoons Panch Foran Spices (Chapter 2)

2–3 whole dried red chilies

1½ teaspoons minced garlic

½ teaspoon turmeric powder

4–5 Chinese eggplants, chopped to 1" chunks

2 medium potatoes, peeled and chopped to 1" chunks

Salt, to taste

1 tablespoon coriander powder

3–4 tablespoons chopped cilantro

Panch Foran Spices

Panch foran spices are commonly used in the western state of Bengal in India but have now gained popularity across the country, too. It is also used in other cuisines.

1. Heat the oil in a pan over medium heat. Add the Panch Foran Spices. As they sputter, add the whole red chilies followed by the garlic. Cook for 30 seconds or until the garlic starts turning brown. Add the turmeric. Cook for 5 seconds.

2. Toss the vegetables into the pan, along with the salt, and mix everything well. Transfer the contents to the slow cooker. Cover and cook on high for 2½–3 hours, or on low for 5 hours (stirring occasionally), or until the vegetables are cooked through.

3. Add the coriander powder and mix everything well. Uncover and cook further, if there's more liquid than you like. You can also transfer the contents into a pan and cook off the extra liquid over a stovetop. This will also help to brown the vegetables. Garnish with cilantro and serve hot as a side vegetable.

Gobhi Aloo (Potato and Cauliflower)

Try adding some Curry Paste (Chapter 3) to make a spicy gobhi aloo.

INGREDIENTS | SERVES 8

1½ tablespoons olive oil

1½ teaspoons black mustard seeds

1 cup chopped yellow onion

1 teaspoon turmeric

1 tablespoon coriander powder

Salt, to taste

1 medium-size cauliflower, cut into 2" pieces

2 cups potato, peeled and cut lengthwise

1 cup chopped tomatoes

1 teaspoon curry powder

1. Heat the oil in a pan over medium heat. Add the mustard seeds, and once they pop add the onion. Cook until the onion is soft and translucent.

2. Add the turmeric, coriander powder, and salt.

3. Add the rest of the ingredients. Mix it all well and transfer it to a 5-quart slow cooker. Cook on low for 5 hours. If the cauliflower leaves more liquid than you'd like, transfer the mixture to a pan and cook on the stovetop for 2–3 minutes. Serve hot with rice or bread.

Indian Curry Tempeh

Any type of curry powder you have on hand will work in this recipe, but Madras curry powder is best.

INGREDIENTS | SERVES 4

1 (13-ounce) package tempeh, cut into bite-size squares

3 cloves garlic, minced

1 teaspoon ginger, minced

1 onion, sliced

2 carrots, peeled and julienned

1 cup cauliflower, chopped

⅓ cup tomato paste

1 (15-ounce) can coconut milk

1 cup water

¼ cup curry powder

1 (15-ounce) can chickpeas, drained

1 teaspoon salt

¼ teaspoon black pepper

1. Add all the ingredients to a 4-quart slow cooker, cover, and cook on low heat for 4 hours.

Jeera Aloo (Cumin-Scented Potatoes)

Jeera is a Hindi name for cumin, a spice widely used in Indian cuisine irrespective of the region the dish belongs to.

INGREDIENTS | SERVES 5–6

4 medium-size potatoes

Water, as needed

2 tablespoons oil or ghee

1 teaspoon cumin seeds

½ teaspoon turmeric

2 green Thai chilies, minced

Salt, to taste

Vrata or Fasting

In several religions, including Hinduism, *Vrata* is a religious practice performed to achieve the divine blessings of god. Eating simple, minimally spiced food is one such practice, and a whole cuisine called *Vrata ka bhojan* has been developed around it.

1. Place the potatoes in a slow cooker. Cover them with water ½" above the top of the potatoes. Cover and cook on high for 2–3 hours, or on low for 5–6 hours, or until the potatoes are boiled.

2. Take the boiled potatoes out of the slow cooker. Let them cool for 10 minutes and then peel and discard the outer skin. Dice the potatoes and set aside.

3. Heat the oil or ghee in a pan. Add the cumin seeds. As they sputter, add the turmeric and minced chilies. Cook for 5 seconds and then add the potatoes, followed by salt. Toss everything together well and serve hot with deep-fried Indian flatbreads or *poori*.

Kathal Do Pyaza

Kathal, or jackfruit, is a starchy and fibrous fruit, which in Indian cuisine is commonly used to replace meat. Rubbing oil on the knife while peeling the outer skin or cutting the fruit helps when working with this sticky fruit.

INGREDIENTS | SERVES 5–6

1 pound jackfruit, peeled and cut into 2–2½" pieces

¼ cup ghee or oil (preferably mustard oil)

4–5 dried red chilies

3–4 bay leaves

4–5 black cardamom pods

1½ teaspoons cloves

1 cinnamon stick

1 tablespoon whole coriander seeds

5 cups thinly sliced onions

Salt, to taste

1 teaspoon turmeric powder (optional)

Kathal (Jackfruit)

Jackfruit is a fruit that belongs to the mulberry (Moraceae) family and grows well in the tropical lowlands.

1. With a well-oiled knife, peel off the outer skin and cut the jackfruit into pieces. Boil a pot of salted water. Drop the jackfruit pieces into the boiled water for 30 minutes. Drain the water; set the fruit aside.

2. Heat the oil in a tempering pan over medium heat. Add all the dried spices *except* the tumeric. Fry them for 1 minute and then transfer the mixture to the slow cooker. Add the onion. Cover and cook on high for 45 minutes, or on low for 1½ hours, or until the onion softens and sweats (stirring occasionally).

3. Add the jackfruit and salt, to taste. Add the turmeric, if using. Mix well. Cover and cook on high for 2½–3 hours, or on low for 5–6 hours, or until the jackfruit is fork tender. Stir occasionally, scraping the bottom and sides.

4. By the end of this cooking time, all the onions should have reduced and caramelized. The dish will have a slight amount of liquid curry, and the oil should cause the contents to separate on the sides. Serve hot with Simple Naan (Chapter 15), Paratha (Chapter 15), or your choice of Indian bread.

Malai Kofta

The malai kofta served at your Indian restaurant is more likely to be made of potato dumplings, where mashed potatoes are mixed with the remaining ingredients for kofta and then deep-fried. This recipe is a healthier version of that.

INGREDIENTS | SERVES 5–6

2 teaspoons fennel seeds

2 teaspoons coriander seeds

1 teaspoon red pepper flakes

Salt, to taste

1 cup corn flour (to bind kofta together), or as needed

Oil, for deep-frying

1 cup Curry Paste (Chapter 3)

1 (12-ounce) can tomato sauce

¼ cup olive oil

Salt, to taste

6–8 cashews

3 tablespoons milk

¼ cup low-fat cottage cheese

¼ cup cilantro

1. Coarsely crush the fennel seeds and coriander seeds and mix them with the red pepper flakes and salt. Add the corn flour, enough for everything to bind together well.

2. Make lime-size balls and deep-fry them in 350°F oil. Fry them until the dumplings turn nice and brown, about 2–4 minutes. Pull them out and place them on a paper towel to absorb all the extra oil.

3. To prepare the sauce, mix together the Curry Paste, tomato sauce, oil, and salt in the slow cooker. Cover and cook on high for 1½ hours, or on low for 3 hours, or until the sauce is bubbling and does not have any excess liquid.

4. In the meantime, soak the cashews in the milk for about 1 hour and 45 minutes and then make a paste out of them in a blender. Set aside.

5. Add the cottage cheese and prepared cashew paste into the sauce. Mix everything together. If cooking on low, now turn the heat to high and cook further for another 1 hour. Add up to 2½ cups of water.

6. When the sauce starts bubbling on the sides, add koftas. When the sauce has reduced to the consistency of your liking, turn off the heat. Garnish with cilantro and serve hot with hot and soft Simple Naan (Chapter 15).

Matar Paneer

Fresh peas will take longer to cook than frozen and thawed peas, so adjust the cooking time accordingly.

INGREDIENTS | SERVES 6

2½ tablespoons oil

1½ cups tomato sauce

1 cup Curry Paste (Chapter 3)

½ pound sweet green peas, frozen or fresh

⅓ cup cream, or half-and-half

1 teaspoon green chili paste (optional)

1 teaspoon freshly ground pepper

1½ teaspoons garam masala

Salt, to taste

2 cups cubed paneer

2 tablespoons oil for paneeer (optional)

Sour cream and chopped cilantro for garnish (optional)

1. Add the oil to the slow cooker followed by the tomato sauce. Mix, cover, and cook for 1 hour on high setting to reduce the sauce.

2. Add the Curry Paste and green peas. Cover and cook on low for 2 hours if the peas are frozen, or for 4–5 hours if the peas are fresh, or until they are cooked well.

3. One hour before the end of cooking time, add the cream and the rest of the spices to the slow cooker. Stir well. Cover and continue cooking.

4. About 30 minutes before the end of cooking time, heat water in a saucepan (enough to cover all the paneer). Drop the paneer in the hot water for 5–10 minutes to extract excess fat and soften the paneer. Drain the water; set the paneer aside.

5. This step is optional: Heat some oil in a pan and pan-fry the paneer. Place the paneer on a paper towel to drain the extra oil and set it aside.

6. Add the paneer to the slow cooker. Cook for another 30 minutes. If the sauce is thicker than your liking, add about ½–1 cup of water.

7. Add a dollop of sour cream and garnish with cilantro and serve hot with Perfecty Slow Cooker Basmati Rice (Chapter 11) or Brown Basmati Rice (Chapter 3).

Palak Paneer

If you are using Homemade Paneer (Chapter 2), then soaking the room temperature paneer in hot water might not be necessary since it is softer and lighter than the store-bought paneer.

INGREDIENTS | SERVES 6

1 pound fresh green spinach

1 teaspoon fennel seeds

3–4 cloves

3 tablespoons olive oil or cooking oil

1 cup tomato sauce

½ cup curry paste

¼ cup heavy cream, or 2 tablespoons sour cream

1 tablespoon Ginger-Garlic Paste (Chapter 2)

2–3 Thai green chilies

1½ teaspoons Garam Masala Powder (Chapter 2)

Salt, to taste

1 (8-ounce) packet of paneer, cut into cubes

Fennel and Cloves in Spinach

Cooking/boiling the fennel seeds and cloves with the spinach helps to take away the *spinachy* taste of it. But if you like it, just omit that step.

1. Boil the spinach in a big pot, adding the fennel seeds and cloves to it. Let it cool and then blend it in a blender. Save the water in which you boiled your spinach.

2. Add the oil to the slow cooker followed by the tomato sauce. Mix, cover, and cook for 1 hour on high setting to reduce the tomato sauce.

3. Add the Curry Paste and reserved spinach purée. Cover and cook on low for 2 hours. Add up to 2 cups of saved water from boiling the spinach to achieve the consistency of the curry that you like.

4. One hour before the end of cooking time, add the cream and the rest of the spices to the slow cooker. Stir well. Cover and continue cooking.

5. About 30 minutes before the end of the cooking time, heat water in a saucepan (enough to cover all the paneer). Drop the paneer in the hot water for 5–10 minutes to extract excess fat and soften the paneer.

6. This step is optional: Heat some oil in a skillet and pan-fry the paneer. Place the paneer on a paper towel to drain the extra oil; set aside.

7. Add the paneer to the slow cooker. Cook for another 30 minutes. Serve hot with warm flatbread/naan or Perfect Slow Cooker Basmati Rice (Chapter 11).

Paneer Makhani

*If you have Makhani Masala (Chapter 3) already prepared,
then fixing Paneer Makhani or Butter Chicken (Chapter 8) will be much easier.*

INGREDIENTS | SERVES 5–6

Water, as needed

2 cups Homemade Paneer (Chapter 2), cubed

3 tablespoons ghee

1 cup onion, cut into big chunks

1 cup Makhani Masala (Chapter 3)

1 teaspoon chili flakes

Salt, to taste

2 tablespoons sugar

½ cup heavy cream

3–4 tablespoons cashew paste

1. Heat water in a saucepan (enough to cover all the paneer). Drop the paneer in the hot water for 5–10 minutes to extract excess fat and soften the paneer. Drain the water; set the paneer aside.

2. Heat the ghee in a pan on the stovetop. Sauté the onion until it is translucent. Add the Makhani Masala followed by the chili flakes. Stir well. Add the salt and sugar. Cook for another minute.

3. Add the heavy cream and cashew paste. Cook for 1 minute and then add up to 1½ cups of water. As the contents start bubbling, add the paneer. Turn the heat to low and simmer the paneer cubes in the sauce, uncovered, for 5–8 minutes or until the sauce reduces to your liking.

4. Serve hot with any hot Indian flatbread or Perfect Slow Cooker Basmati Rice (Chapter 11).

Potato Curry (Assami Ril Do)

Serve this mouthwatering curry with hot puffed bread.

INGREDIENTS | SERVES 4

10 small baby potatoes, peeled

3 tablespoons vegetable oil

2 teaspoons Ginger-Garlic Paste (Chapter 2)

1 dried red chili, roughly pounded

¼ teaspoon turmeric

1 small tomato, finely chopped

½ cup plain yogurt, whipped

½ cup water

Salt, to taste

Avoid Staining Your Tupperware

Turmeric will turn things yellow—your Tupperware or other plastic containers, for instance. To avoid staining any Tupperware in which you store turmeric-flavored dishes, spray the Tupperware with nonstick spray before using it.

1. Place the potatoes in a slow cooker with enough water to cover them. Boil the potatoes on high for about 2½ hours or until fork tender. Drain. Lightly prick the potatoes with a fork. Set aside.

2. In a large skillet, heat the oil on high. Add the Ginger-Garlic Paste and sauté for about 10 seconds. Add the dried red chili and turmeric; mix well. Add the tomato and sauté for another 2–3 minutes.

3. Add the yogurt and cook for about 5 minutes. Add the potatoes. Sauté for 1 minute. Add the water and lower the heat. Cover and cook for about 20 minutes. Add salt to taste. Serve hot.

Rajma Masala

Another popular North Indian comfort food. It's commonly paired with a simple steamed rice and a sweet dish.

INGREDIENTS | SERVES 5–6

1 cup dry red kidney beans, or 2 (8-ounce) cans red kidney beans

2–3 cloves

Salt, to taste

¾ cup Curry Paste (Chapter 3)

1. Wash the dry beans with water, then soak them in water three times the quantity of beans. (In this case use 3 cups of water.) Let them soak in water for 6–8 hours or overnight, depending on how fast your beans absorb water and get soft.

2. Drain the soaking water and transfer all the ingredients into the slow cooker. Add 3 cups of water if using dried beans or 2 cups if using canned beans. Cover and cook on low for 5–6 hours or until the red kidney beans, or rajma, is cooked through. Serve with Perfect Slow Cooker Basmati Rice (Chapter 11).

"Roasted" Beets

Slice and eat as a side dish or use in any recipe that calls for cooked beets.

INGREDIENTS | SERVES 8

2 pounds whole beets, stems and leaves removed

2 tablespoons lemon juice

¼ cup balsamic vinegar

1. Place the beets in the bottom of a 4-quart slow cooker. Pour the lemon juice and vinegar over the top. Cook for 2 hours on low or until they are easily pierced with a fork.

2. Remove the beets from the slow cooker. Allow to cool slightly. Wrap a beet in a paper towel and rub it to remove the skin. Repeat for the remaining beets.

Easy Pickled Beets

Pickled beets are easy to make on the stovetop too. First, slice 1 pound roasted beets. Place in a small saucepan and add ½ cup sugar, ½ cup white distilled vinegar, ¼ teaspoon cinnamon, and ½ small onion, sliced. Bring to a boil. Cool and store in an airtight container overnight before serving.

Royal Mushrooms with Cashew Nut Sauce (Nawabi Guchhi)

The Nawabs, the Muslim royals of ancient India, introduced nuts into Indian cuisine.

INGREDIENTS | SERVES 4

2 tablespoons unsalted cashew nuts

Water, as needed

4 tablespoons vegetable oil

2 green cardamom pods

1 black cardamom pod

2 cloves

1 (1") cinnamon stick

1 bay leaf

1 teaspoon minced garlic

½ teaspoon red chili powder

1 teaspoon coriander powder

1 small red onion, minced

½ cup plain yogurt, whipped

½ cup whole milk

Salt, to taste

1 pound white button mushrooms, cleaned

Hot Water

Heating water in the slow cooker before the ingredients are added will help keep the slow cooker warm when you add hot contents. Adding hot contents to a cold slow cooker can damage the slow cooker.

1. Soak the cashews in 1 cup of water for about 20 minutes. Drain and grind to a paste in a food processor. Set aside.

2. Fill a 3–4 quart slow cooker halfway with water. Put on the lid and turn the heat to high. Turn the slow cooker on for a couple hours before you start cooking.

3. In a medium skillet, heat the vegetable oil over medium heat. Quickly add the green cardamom, black cardamom, cloves, cinnamon stick, bay leaf, and minced garlic; sauté for about 30 seconds.

4. Add the red chili powder, coriander powder, and minced onion; sauté for 2 minutes. If the spice mixture sticks to the pan, add a few tablespoons of water. Continue to sauté until the onions are golden brown, about 7 minutes. Add the cashew nut paste and stir for 1 more minute.

5. Add the yogurt, milk, salt, and mushrooms; mix well.

6. Discard the hot water in the slow cooker and transfer the yogurt sauce to the cooker. Cover and let it simmer on high heat until the oil starts to separate from the spice mixture, about 1 hour. Serve hot.

Slow-Cooked Mustard Greens (Sarson ka Saag)

This is a delicious dish from the Indian state of Punjab. Serve along with Indian corn flatbread.

INGREDIENTS | SERVES 4

1 pound frozen mustard leaves, thawed

¼ pound frozen spinach leaves, thawed

1 small turnip, peeled and diced

Salt, to taste

3 cups water (or more, as needed)

2 tablespoons ghee

1 teaspoon Ginger-Garlic Paste (Chapter 2)

2 tablespoons cornmeal

Butter, cut into cubes, for garnish

Cornmeal *Does* Come from Corn

Cornmeal comes from maize, or corn, as the name suggests. This coarse yellow flour is used to provide texture to dishes. Don't mistake it for cornstarch, which is white and powdery and generally used as a thickening agent.

1. Transfer the greens (mustard and spinach) along with the turnip to a slow cooker. Add salt and 1 cup water. Cover and cook on high for 2 hours or on low for 4 hours. Use a food processor or hand blender to purée the vegetable mixture into a thick paste. Transfer it back to the slow cooker.

2. In a large pan, heat the ghee. Add the Ginger-Garlic Paste and sauté for 30 seconds. Add to the vegetables in the slow cooker.

3. Mix the cornmeal with a ¼ cup of water. To ensure that the cornmeal does not form lumps, use the back of your cooking spoon to blend it in. Stir it into the vegetables. Cover and let it simmer on high for 30–40 minutes. Stir a couple times during the cooking process. Add more water if the vegetables start to become dry. Serve hot, garnished with a few butter cubes.

Spiced "Baked" Eggplant

Serve this as a main dish over rice or as a side dish as-is.

INGREDIENTS | SERVES 4

1 pound eggplant, cubed

⅓ cup sliced onion

½ teaspoon red pepper flakes

½ teaspoon garam masala

1½ teaspoons coriander powder

¼ cup lemon juice

1. Place all the ingredients in a 1½–2-quart slow cooker. Cook on low for 3 hours or until the eggplant is tender.

Cold Snap

Take care not to put a cold ceramic slow cooker insert directly into the slow cooker. The sudden shift in temperature can cause it to crack. If you want to prepare your ingredients the night before use, refrigerate them in reusable containers, not in the insert.

Stuffed Eggplants

This recipe can work with any thin eggplant, such as, Japanese, Chinese, Filipino, or other small varieties.

INGREDIENTS | SERVES 6

6 Chinese eggplants

2 tablespoons Ginger-Garlic Paste (Chapter 2)

⅓ cup coriander powder

½ teaspoon cayenne pepper

1 teaspoon Amchoor (Chapter 2)

1 teaspoon Garam Masala Powder (Chapter 2)

3–4 tablespoons oil (preferably mustard oil), plus extra for greasing the slow cooker

1 teaspoon salt, or more if needed

3–4 tablespoons water

Make It a Curry!

Another variation to this recipe is to use small Indian eggplants and stuff them with a mild curry paste.

1. Wipe the eggplants clean. Make a long slit through its stomach on one side but do not cut through to the other side. Set aside.

2. Mix all the spices with the oil and salt in a bowl. Add water to moisten the spice blend, making it easier to stuff into the eggplants. Divide the spice blend into 6 equal parts. Stuff into the eggplants.

3. Grease the inner walls of the slow cooker. Place the stuffed eggplants into the slow cooker (each touching the bottom) making a single layer. Cover and cook on high for up to 3 hours, or on low for 5–6 hours, or until the eggplants are cooked through, turning the eggplants every 30–45 minutes.

4. Once cooked, carefully take the eggplants out of the slow cooker. Place them on a serving dish and pour the liquid over them. Serve hot or warm with Perfect Slow Cooker Basmati Rice (Chapter 11) and lentil soup.

Tamatar Aloo (Curried Potato with Tomato Sauce)

*Tamatar aloo is another dish very commonly used as a Vrata ka Bhojan
(Jeera Aloo, in this chapter). But with a few extra spices it can be turned into a spicy delight.*

INGREDIENTS | SERVES 6

3 tablespoons oil, or ghee

2–3 dried whole red chilies

1 teaspoon cumin seeds

1 teaspoon Ginger-Garlic Paste (Chapter 2; omit if using for *Vrata*)

1 teaspoon Garam Masala Powder (Chapter 2; optional)

½ teaspoon turmeric

3 medium-size tomatoes, diced

Salt, to taste

3 medium potatoes, peeled and cut into cubes

2–3 cups water

1. Heat the oil in a pan over medium heat. Add the dried red chilies and cumin seeds. As the spices pop, add the Ginger-Garlic Paste. Sauté for about 30 seconds and then add the Garam Masala, turmeric, and diced tomatoes.

2. Let the tomatoes cook for 2–3 minutes and then add salt and the potatoes. Toss everything together and transfer the contents to the slow cooker.

3. Add 2–3 cups of water. Stir, cover, and cook on high for 2½–3 hours, or on low for 5–6 hours, or until the potatoes are cooked well. Serve hot with your choice of warm bread or a rice dish.

Curry Up!

Instead of adding the five spices, you can add ½ cup of curry paste to make it a spicier dish.

Til waali Bandhagobhi
(Cabbage with Peas, Carrots, and Sesame Seeds)

Til, Hindi for sesame, is a seed extracted from the flowers of the sesame plant. Both white and dark sesame are used in India mainly for sweet treats like gajak or pitha but can also be used in stir-fries.

INGREDIENTS | SERVES 4–6

3–4 tablespoons oil

1–2 green Thai green chilies

1 teaspoon black mustard seeds

½ teaspoon turmeric powder

4 cups chopped cabbage

1½ cups blend of frozen peas and carrots

Salt, to taste

¼ cup sesame seeds

Sesame Seeds

Sesame seeds have strong roots in Hindu mythology where they are believed to bring immortality. Sesame oil is revered next to ghee.

1. Heat the oil in a pan or wok. Add the chilies and mustard seeds. As they sizzle and sputter, add the turmeric followed by all the vegetables and salt. Toss everything together.

2. Transfer the contents to a slow cooker. Cover and cook on high for 2 hours or on low for 4 hours, stirring occasionally.

3. Toward the last 15 minutes, add the sesame seeds to the cooked vegetables and cook uncovered for 15 minutes. Serve hot as a side dish.

CHAPTER 8

Poultry

Almond-Flavored Chicken
(Badaami Murgh)
140

Butter Chicken
141

Chicken Braised in Beer
142

Chicken Curry with
Red Potatoes
142

Chicken in a Creamy Sauce
(Murgh Korma)
143

Chicken Makhani
144

Chicken Tikka Masala
145

Chili Coconut Chicken
(Mangalorian Murgh Gassi)
146

Coriander Chicken
(Dhaniye Wala Murgh)
147

Fenugreek-Flavored Chicken
(Murgh Methiwala)
148

Ginger-Flavored Chicken Curry
(Murgh Adraki)
149

Goan Chicken Curry
(Goan Murgh Xcautti)
150

Kati Roll
151

Lehsun Wala Chicken
(Garlic Chicken)
152

Green Chutney Wings
153

Mango Duck Breast
153

Murgh Achari
(Chicken with Pickling Spices)
154

Murgh Musallam
155

Slow Cooker Tandoori Chicken
156

Slow-Roasted Chicken with
Potatoes, Parsnips, and Onions
157

Spiced Chicken in Green Curry
(Murgh Hariyali)
158

"Teekha" Peanut Chicken
159

Whole Roast Chicken
160

Almond-Flavored Chicken (Badaami Murgh)

Serve this rich chicken dish with Simple Naan or Roti (Chapter 15).

INGREDIENTS | SERVES 4–5

¼ cup blanched almonds

Water, as needed

4 tablespoons vegetable oil

1 bay leaf

2 cloves

5 peppercorns

1 green chili, seeded and minced

1 tablespoon Ginger-Garlic Paste (Chapter 2)

8 pieces skinless, bone-in chicken thighs

½ teaspoon red chili powder

¼ teaspoon turmeric powder

1 teaspoon coriander powder

½ teaspoon Garam Masala Powder (Chapter 2)

Salt, to taste

¼ cup plain yogurt, whipped

¼ cup heavy cream

1. In a blender or food processor, blend the almonds with a few tablespoons of water to make a thick, smooth paste. Set aside.

2. In a large pan, heat the vegetable oil over medium heat. Add the bay leaf, cloves, peppercorns, green chili, and Ginger-Garlic Paste. Sauté for about 10 seconds. Add the chicken and sauté for 2–3 minutes.

3. Add the red chili, turmeric, coriander, the Garam Masala, and salt; transfer into the slow cooker. Cover and cook on high for 2–3 hours, or on low for 5–6 hours, or until the chicken is cooked through.

4. Toward the last 45 minutes, add the yogurt and up to ½ cup of water, if needed. Cover and continue cooking. Stir occasionally, adding a few tablespoons of water if the dish seems too dry.

5. Toward the last 15 minutes, add the almond paste and the cream. Serve hot.

Butter Chicken

Butter chicken is probably one of the most popular Indian dishes. Rumor has it that this Punjabi dish originated from a famous old restaurant in Delhi. Besides chicken, this buttery dish has two main ingredients: tomato sauce as a base and makhan, or butter, which makes its sauce rich and silky.

INGREDIENTS | SERVES 4–6

2 tablespoons lemon juice

1 teaspoon Garam Masala Powder (Chapter 2)

1 tablespoon Ginger-Garlic Paste (Chapter 2)

1 teaspoon Tandoori Masala (Chapter 2)

Salt, to taste

2 pounds boneless, skinless chicken

1 cup Makhani Masala (Chapter 3)

2 tablespoons ghee

1 tablespoon brown sugar

½ cup heavy cream

1 tablespoon kasuri methi

Tips

Marinate the chicken for at least half an hour before baking it in the oven. Add the heavy cream toward the very end, when the chicken is almost cooked.

1. Preheat oven to 350°F. In a large mixing bowl, mix together the lemon juice, Garam Masala, Ginger-Garlic Paste, Tandoori Masala, and 1 teaspoon salt. Add the chicken. Mix. Transfer to a baking dish and bake for 10 minutes.

2. Transfer the baked chicken to the slow cooker (discarding extra liquid). Add Makhani Masala and the rest of the ingredients *except* for the heavy cream and kasuri methi. Adjust salt if needed. Mix well. Cover and cook on high for 2 hours or on low for 4 hours.

3. Add the heavy cream and kasuri methi. Stir well. Cover and cook on high for another 20 minutes or until the chicken is well cooked. Serve with warm Simple Naan (Chapter 15), Paratha (Chapter 15), or just simple steamed rice.

Chicken Braised in Beer

Serve this as-is or in any recipe that calls for cooked chicken, such as, Kati Roll (see recipe in this chapter).

INGREDIENTS | SERVES 6

3 boneless, skinless chicken breasts

1 onion, quartered

6 ounces beer

1½ cups water

1 tablespoon Ginger-Garlic Paste (Chapter 2)

1 teaspoon Tandoori Masala (Chapter 2)

1. Place all ingredients in a 4-quart slow cooker. Cook on low for 6 hours.

2. Remove the chicken breasts and discard the cooking liquid.

Chicken Curry with Red Potatoes

Traditional curries are cooked for long periods of time on the stovetop, making them a logical fit for the slow cooker. The spices meld together and the chicken is meltingly tender.

INGREDIENTS | SERVES 8

1 tablespoon Madras curry powder

1 teaspoon allspice

½ teaspoon ground cloves

½ teaspoon ground nutmeg

1 teaspoon ground ginger

2 pounds boneless, skinless chicken thighs, cubed

1 teaspoon canola oil plus 1 tablespoon

1 onion, chopped

2 cloves garlic, chopped

2 jalapeños, chopped

½ pound red skin potatoes, cubed

⅓ cup light coconut milk

1. In a medium bowl, whisk together the curry powder, allspice, cloves, nutmeg, and ginger. Add the chicken and toss to coat each piece evenly.

2. Heat 1 tablespoon oil in a nonstick skillet. Place the chicken in the skillet and quickly sauté until the chicken starts to brown. Add to a 4-quart slow cooker along with the remaining spice mixture.

3. Heat 1 teaspoon oil in a nonstick skillet and sauté the onions, garlic, and jalapeños until fragrant. Add to the slow cooker.

4. Add the potatoes and coconut milk to the slow cooker. Stir. Cook 7–8 hours on low.

Tips

Garam Masala Powder (Chapter 2) is a good substitute for Madras curry powder.

Chicken in a Creamy Sauce (Murgh Korma)

The secret to preparing the perfect sauce is to let it simmer slowly until it thickens completely.

INGREDIENTS | SERVES 4–5

3 tablespoons unsalted cashew nuts, soaked in water for 10 minutes

2 tablespoons white poppy seeds, soaked in water for 20 minutes

2 tablespoons almonds, blanched

Water, as needed

3 tablespoons ghee

1 teaspoon cumin powder

2 (1") cinnamon sticks

2 black cardamom pods, bruised

1 large bay leaf

4 cloves

2 green cardamoms pods, bruised

¾ cup Curry Paste (Chapter 3)

Salt, to taste

1½ pounds boneless diced chicken

1 cup plain yogurt, whipped

1 teaspoon Garam Masala Powder (Chapter 2)

Roasted cumin seeds, for garnish

1. Process or blend together the cashew nuts, poppy seeds, almonds, and just enough water to make a smooth, thick paste. Set aside.

2. In a deep pan, heat the ghee over medium heat. Add the cumin, cinnamon sticks, black cardamom, bay leaf, cloves, and green cardamom; sauté until fragrant, about 1½ minutes. Add the Curry Paste and salt. Cook for 1 minute as the ghee separates from the Curry Paste (this indicates that the onion paste is cooked).

3. Add the chicken, cook for 3–5 minutes. Transfer the contents to the slow cooker. Cover and cook on high for 2½–3 hours or on low for 5–6 hours. You can add up to ½ cup of water if the gravy is too thick.

4. During the last 45 minutes of cooking, add the yogurt and the nut paste and continue cooking.

5. Once the chicken is cooked, add the Garam Masala. Garnish with roasted cumin seeds and serve hot.

Chicken Makhani

*Just like Paneer Makhani (Chapter 7), if you have a Makhani Masala
(Chapter 3) in place, fixing this dish would a breeze!*

INGREDIENTS | SERVES 4

1 pound boneless, skinless chicken breasts or thighs
2 shallots, minced
2 cloves garlic, minced
½" knob ginger, minced
2 tablespoons lemon juice
2 teaspoons garam masala
1 teaspoon ground cumin
½ teaspoon cayenne
½ teaspoon ground cloves
½ teaspoon fenugreek
¼ teaspoon salt
½ teaspoon freshly ground black pepper
1 tablespoon butter
1 tablespoon tomato paste
¾ cup fat-free Greek yogurt

1. Place the chicken and all the other ingredients *except* the yogurt into a 4-quart slow cooker. Stir. Cook on low for 5 hours.

2. Stir in the yogurt. Serve immediately.

Chicken Makhani

Chicken Makhani is commonly known as butter chicken. Traditionally, the dish has a good combination of sweetness from sugar and spiciness from the fresh ground spices.

Chicken Tikka Masala

This same recipe can be used for a vegetarian version using paneer tikkas or a meat dish using beef, lamb, or pork. Cooking time may vary.

INGREDIENTS | SERVES 4–5

1 teaspoon Kashmiri red pepper powder

1½ teaspoons Ginger-Garlic Paste, plus 1 tablespoon (Chapter 2)

1½ teaspoons coriander powder, plus 1 tablespoon

1 teaspoon Garam Masala Powder, plus 1 teaspoon (Chapter 2)

½ cup yogurt

1½ teaspoons lemon juice

½ teaspoon red food color (optional)

4 boneless, skinless chicken thighs (cut into cubes)

1 (14.5-ounce) can diced tomatoes (puréed)

1 tablespoon onion powder (optional)

1½ teaspoons powdered black pepper

1 teaspoon powdered fennel seeds

1½ tablespoons olive oil, plus more for brushing chicken

½ cup heavy cream

1 teaspoon chopped cilantro, for garnish

Story of Tikka Masala

Rumor has it that sick of his customer's rants, a chef at an Indian restaurant in Britain tossed some tandoori chicken pieces into a tomato sauce. This dish later became popular as chicken tikka masala, one of the most loved Indian dishes all around the globe.

1. In a large bowl, add the Kashmiri red pepper powder, Ginger-Garlic Paste, corinader powder, Garam Masala, yogurt, lemon juice, red food color, and chicken and mix well. Cover the bowl and let it sit in the refrigerator for at least 1 hour.

2. Thread the chicken pieces onto the skewers. Brush lightly with oil. Grill the skewered chicken until done or place it into the oven for 15–20 minutes at a temperature of 400°F. When cooked, set the grilled chicken tikkas aside.

3. Combine the rest of the ingredients (*except* for the heavy cream and cilantro) together in a slow cooker. Cover and cook on high for 1½ hours or on low for 3 hours, letting the masala simmer into a thicker sauce.

4. During the last 45 minutes of cooking, add the heavy cream and stir in the chicken tikka. Adjust salt and add up to ¾ cup water, if necessary. Stir everything together well and continue cooking for 45 minutes.

5. Garnish with cilantro and serve hot with Simple Naan (Chapter 15) or Perfect Slow Cooker Basmati Rice (Chapter 11).

Chili Coconut Chicken (Mangalorian Murgh Gassi)

The coconut milk provides a nice balance to the red chilies.
Serve this with Perfect Slow Cooker Basmati Rice (Chapter 11).

INGREDIENTS | SERVES 4

½ teaspoon black mustard seeds

½ teaspoon cumin seeds

½ teaspoon coriander seeds

3 tablespoons vegetable oil

8 curry leaves

2 medium-size red onions, finely chopped

2 teaspoons Ginger-Garlic Paste (Chapter 2)

3 dried red chilies, roughly pounded

½ teaspoon turmeric powder

Salt, to taste

1½ pounds boneless, skinless chicken, cubed

Water, as needed

1 cup light coconut milk

Coconut Milk

Don't confuse coconut water with coconut milk. Coconut water is the liquid inside a coconut. Coconut milk is produced by steeping grated coconut in hot water and straining it. Regular coconut milk is high in saturated fat. I would advise using light coconut milk. Food with lower fat content also works great in a slow cooker.

1. In a small skillet over medium heat, dry-roast the mustard seeds, cumin seeds, and coriander seeds. When the spices release their aroma, remove from heat and let cool. In a spice grinder, grind to a coarse powder. Set aside.

2. In a large skillet, heat the oil over medium heat. Add the curry leaves and the onions; sauté for about 1 minute.

3. Add the Ginger-Garlic Paste and red chilies. Sauté over medium heat until the onions are well browned and the oil begins to separate from the sides of the onion mixture, about 8 minutes. (You can also use ½ cup Curry Paste, but the results would be slightly different because of the strong flavor of the Garam Masala in Curry Paste.)

4. Add the ground spices, turmeric powder, and salt; sauté for 1 minute.

5. Add the chicken pieces; mix well and transfer into a 3–4 quart slow cooker. You can add up to ¼ cup of water, although not necessary. Cover and cook on high for 2–3 hours, or on low for 4–6 hours, or until the chicken is cooked through.

6. During the last 30 minutes, add the coconut milk and simmer. Serve hot.

Coriander Chicken (Dhaniye Wala Murgh)

Serve this with a raita of your choice and Simple Naan (Chapter 15).

INGREDIENTS | SERVES 4–5

4 tablespoons vegetable oil

2 cloves

2 green cardamom pods

1 (1") cinnamon stick

2 teaspoons Ginger-Garlic Paste (Chapter 2)

8 skinless chicken thighs

1½ medium tomatoes, finely chopped

½ teaspoon red chili powder

Salt, to taste

2 tablespoons coriander powder

Water, as needed

½ cup plain yogurt, whipped

1 cup minced cilantro

You Can Do This, Too!

Another variation to the dish can be to add 1½ cups of Hot Cilantro Chutney (Chapter 2) to the chicken and ignore the rest of the spices.

1. In a large pan, heat the vegetable oil over medium heat. Add the cloves, cardamom, and cinnamon. When they begin to sizzle, add the Ginger-Garlic Paste and sauté for about 15 seconds.

2. Add the spice mixture, chicken, and the remaining ingredients, *except* for the yogurt and cilantro to a slow cooker. Cover and cook on high for 2½–3 hours, or on low for 5–6 hours, or until the chicken is cooked through.

3. During the last 45 minutes of cooking, add the yogurt and mix well. Cover and continue cooking.

4. Turn the heat off. Add the cilantro leaves and mix well. Put the lid back on and let it stay covered for 10 minutes before serving.

Fenugreek-Flavored Chicken (Murgh Methiwala)

A very aromatic dish, using either fresh or dried fenugreek leaves.
Serve this with the Simple Naan (Chapter 15).

INGREDIENTS | SERVES 4–5

4 tablespoons vegetable oil

2 cloves

1 green cardamom pod, bruised

1 (1") cinnamon stick

1 medium-size red onion, finely chopped

1 tablespoon Ginger-Garlic Paste (Chapter 2)

2 tablespoons dried fenugreek leaves

8 skinless chicken thighs

½ teaspoon red chili powder

½ teaspoon turmeric powder

Salt, to taste

1 cup plain yogurt, whipped

Water, as needed

1. In a large skillet, heat the vegetable oil over medium heat. Add the cloves, cardamom, and cinnamon. When they begin to sizzle, add the onions and sauté for about 2–3 minutes.

2. Add the Ginger-Garlic Paste and the dried fenugreek leaves. Sauté until the onions are well browned and the oil begins to separate from the onion mixture, about 3–4 minutes.

3. Add the chicken thighs, red chili powder, turmeric powder, and salt. Mix well. Transfer the contents to the slow cooker. Cover and cook on high for 2–3 hours, or on low for 4–5 hours, or until the chicken is cooked through, stirring occasionally.

4. During the last 30–45 minutes of cooking, stir in the yogurt. Add the water if needed. Cover and simmer until the chicken is tender and cooked through. Serve hot.

Ginger-Flavored Chicken Curry (Murgh Adraki)

Use fresh tender ginger for this recipe. Serve with plain Simple Naan (Chapter 15).

INGREDIENTS | SERVES 4–5

2 tablespoons grated gingerroot

1 teaspoon coriander powder

1 teaspoon Garam Masala Powder (Chapter 2)

½ teaspoon red chili powder

¾ cup plain yogurt, whipped

4 tablespoons vegetable oil, divided

8 skinless chicken thighs

½ teaspoon cumin seeds

1 black cardamom pod

1 bay leaf

2 medium-size fresh tomatoes, puréed

Salt, to taste

Water, as needed

Indian Cooking Oils

Indian cooking uses peanut, vegetable, mustard, sesame, and corn oil for cooking. There are two varieties of ghee that are used, *vanaspathi* (vegetable) and *usli* (clarified butter). Indian cooking does not use any animal fat or lard as a cooking medium.

1. In a large bowl or resealable plastic bag, combine the gingerroot, coriander powder, Garam Masala, red chili powder, yogurt, and 2 tablespoons of the vegetable oil; mix well. Add the chicken and coat all pieces evenly with the marinade. Set aside.

2. In a large skillet, heat the remaining 2 tablespoons of vegetable oil. Add the cumin seeds, cardamom pod, and bay leaf. When the seeds begin to sizzle, add the tomato purée.

3. Sauté over medium heat until the tomatoes are cooked and the oil begins to separate from the tomato mixture, about 3–4 minutes.

4. Add the chicken and the marinade to the tomato mixture, along with the salt. Transfer to the slow cooker. Add up to ½ cup of water. Cover and cook 2½–3 hours, or on low for 5–6 hours, or until the chicken is completely cooked and the juices run clear. Stir occasionally. If you like a thinner gravy, add some more water. Remove the black cardamom pod and bay leaf before serving. Serve hot.

Goan Chicken Curry (Goan Murgh Xcautti)

This delight from western India takes a bit of an effort to make, but the results are really rewarding.

INGREDIENTS | SERVES 4–5

2 dried red chilies

1 tablespoon white poppy seeds

1 teaspoon black mustard seeds

2 teaspoons cumin seeds

1 tablespoon coriander seeds

¼ teaspoon black peppercorns

1 (1") cinnamon stick

3 cloves

¼ cup unsweetened desiccated coconut

3 tablespoons vegetable oil

1 large red onion, minced

1 tablespoon Ginger-Garlic Paste (Chapter 2)

1½ pounds skinless, boneless chicken chunks (preferably thighs)

Salt, to taste

Water, as needed

1 tablespoon fresh lemon juice (optional)

1. In a small skillet over medium heat, dry-roast the red chilies, poppy seeds, mustard seeds, cumin seeds, coriander seeds, black peppercorns, cinnamon stick, and cloves. When the spices release their aroma, remove from heat and let cool. In a spice grinder, grind the spices, along with the coconut, to a coarse powder. Set aside.

2. In a large skillet, heat the vegetable oil over medium heat. Add the onions and sauté until well browned, about 7–8 minutes. Add the Ginger-Garlic Paste and sauté for 1 minute.

3. Add the chicken and the reserved spice powder and salt. Transfer the contents to the slow cooker. Add up to ½ cup of water if desired. Cover and cook on high for 2½–3 hours, or on low for 5–6 hours, or until the chicken is cooked through.

4. Add 1 tablespoon of lemon juice to the dish before serving, if desired. Serve hot.

Kati Roll

Perfect for a quick weeknight meal, the preparation time is short and the spices get the entire day to flavor the meat. Traditionally this dish is made with red meat, so you can easily adapt it if you want.

INGREDIENTS | SERVES 4

2 boneless, skinless chicken breasts

1 tablespoon Ginger-Garlic Paste (Chapter 2)

1 teaspoon Kashmiri lal mirch (see Lamb Roganjosh recipe in Chapter 9)

1 tablespoon coriander powder

¼ cup yogurt

1 tablespoon lemon juice

1 teaspoon Garam Masala Powder (Chapter 2)

1 teaspoon Tandoori Spice Mix (Chapter 2)

1½ teaspoons cooking oil

Salt, to taste

Water, as needed

¼ cup Hot Cilantro Chutney (Chapter 2)

5–6 whole wheat tortillas

¼ cup sliced onion

¼ cup sliced tomato

Juice of 1 lime (optional)

Pinch Chaat Masala (Chapter 2)

1. Make a few slits in each piece of chicken. Mix together the next 9 ingredients. Rub the resulting spice blend onto the chicken. Place the chicken mixture inside a slow cooker with an oiled insert. Add ¼ cup water. Cover and cook on high for 3–4 hours, or on low for 6–7 hours, or until the chicken is cooked through.

2. When cooked through, let the chicken cool enough that it can be handled with bare hands. Either pull it into pieces with a fork or cut it into smaller pieces.

3. For the roll, or wrap, smear a thin layer of Hot Cilantro Chutney on a tortilla. Then place on it some chicken, sliced onion, tomato, a squirt of lime juice, and a pinch of Chaat Masala. Make a tight wrap and cover with paper or aluminum foil. Enjoy!

Lehsun Wala Chicken (Garlic Chicken)

For this recipe you just need chicken and tons of garlic, along with some basic ingredients like lemon and whatever else you have in your spice shelf.

INGREDIENTS | SERVES 4–5

1 teaspoon grated ginger

2–3 Thai green chilies

15–17 cloves of garlic

½ tablespoon lemon juice

Salt, to taste

6–8 whole cloves (optional)

2 whole cardamom pods (optional)

3 tablespoons olive oil

1½ cups thinly sliced red onion

1 pound chicken, cut into 1–2" pieces

½ teaspoon turmeric (optional, just for color)

¼ cup yogurt

Tips

If you need to cook the chicken longer than the suggested 6–7 hours, add ¼ cup chicken broth to the slow cooker at the beginning of the cooking time. This will help keep the chicken juicy. Alternately, add half an onion.

1. Make a paste of the ginger, chilies, and about 10–12 cloves of garlic in a blender. Add the lemon juice and mix. Add a pinch of salt. Set the paste aside. Smash the rest of the garlic cloves with a knife or between your palms. Set aside.

2. If you are using cloves and cardamom, add them along with the smashed garlic in a cool skillet. Pour in the olive oil and turn the heat to medium. (Slow heating of the pan infuses the olive oil beautifully with the flavor of garlic and cloves, which will be so distinct in your chicken.)

3. When the oil is hot enough, add the onion. Let it sauté until golden. Transfer the contents, along with the ginger paste prepared earlier, to the slow cooker. Add the chicken and the turmeric into the slow cooker. Stir well. Cover and cook on high for 3–4 hours or on low for 6–7 hours.

4. During the last 45 minutes of cooking, stir in the yogurt. Adjust salt and water as necessary. Continue cooking until the chicken is cooked through. Serve hot with Perfect Slow Cooker Basmati Rice (Chapter 11) or Simple Naan (Chapter 15).

Green Chutney Wings

You can replace Hot Cilantro Chutney (Chapter 2) with Curry Paste (Chapter 3) or Tandoori Spice Mix (Chapter 2).

INGREDIENTS | SERVES 10

3 pounds chicken wings, tips removed

8 ounces thick Hot Cilantro Chutney (Chapter 2)

3 tablespoons olive oil

1 tablespoon light coconut milk

1 tablespoon minced fresh ginger

Salt, to taste

1. Place the wings into a 4-quart slow cooker.

2. Drain any extra liquid from the chutney. Chutney should be thick like a paste. In a small bowl, whisk together the chutney, oil, coconut milk, ginger, and salt. Pour the sauce over the wings. Toss the wings to coat.

3. Cook on low for 6 hours. Stir prior to serving.

Mango Duck Breast

Slow-cooked mangoes soften and create their own sauce in this easy duck dish.

INGREDIENTS | SERVES 4

2 boneless, skinless duck breasts

1 large mango, cubed

¼ cup duck stock or chicken stock

1 tablespoon ginger juice

1 tablespoon minced hot pepper

1 tablespoon minced shallot

1. Place all ingredients into a 4-quart slow cooker. Cook on low for 4 hours.

Murgh Achari (Chicken with Pickling Spices)

You can also substitute Homemade Paneer (Chapter 2), lamb, or potatoes for the chicken in this recipe—just adjust the cooking times accordingly.

INGREDIENTS | SERVES 4–5

2 tablespoons mustard oil or vegetable oil

½ teaspoon black mustard seeds

½ teaspoon wild fennel seeds (nigella seeds)

2 dried red chilies

¼ teaspoon fenugreek seeds

1 tablespoon Ginger-Garlic Paste (Chapter 2)

8 skinless chicken thighs

½ teaspoon red chili powder

¼ teaspoon turmeric powder

Salt, to taste

1 cup plain yogurt

Juice of ½ lemon

Cooking with Mustard Oil

Mustard oil is very pungent. When you are using it, make sure it's smoking hot first, then decrease the heat. It's now ready for use. Smoking the oil allows you to enjoy the taste without the pungency.

1. In a large skillet, heat the oil until almost smoking. Reduce the heat to medium. Quickly add the mustard and nigella seeds, red chilies, and fenugreek seeds. Fry for about 30 seconds or until the seeds start to change color and release their aroma.

2. Add the Ginger-Garlic Paste and sauté for another 10 seconds. Add the chicken and sauté for about 5–6 minutes.

3. Transfer the chicken to the slow cooker. Add the red chili powder, turmeric, and salt. Cover and cook on high for 2 hours or on low for 4 hours.

4. During the last 30 minutes of cooking, add the yogurt and mix well. Prop the lid open by ½" for the steam to escape.

5. Add the lemon juice and cook for 10 more minutes. Serve hot.

Murgh Musallam

Murgh musallam is one of the most famous dishes of the Lahori cuisine.
Lahore, earlier a part of India and now a part of Pakistan, gave birth to this type of cooking.
Its roots go deep into the imperial kitchen of the Mughal Empire.

INGREDIENTS | SERVES 4

2–3 big, whole Cornish hens

1 lemon, cut into quarters

4–6 cloves of garlic

1 teaspoon black peppercorn

3–4 black cardamom pods

1 teaspoon cloves

1 cup curry paste

4 tablespoons ghee

3 tomatoes, sliced thick

What Is a Cornish Game Hen?

The Cornish game hen first became available in the United States during the 1960s. Although the hen is often considered a separate kind of poultry, it is actually a small chicken.

1. Wash the hen well under water. Pat the bird dry. Stuff each cavity with lemon wedge, garlic, whole spices, and 1 tablespoon of Curry Paste.

2. Rub the outside of the bird first with ghee and then with 2 tablespoons of Curry Paste. Set aside.

3. Place the tomatoes in the bottom of the slow cooker insert. Place the hens on top of the tomatoes and pour the rest of the Curry Paste on top, followed by the remaining ghee.

4. Cook on low for 6–7 hours. Discard the skin and pour the thick sauce on top before serving. This dish goes well with hot Parathas (Chapter 15) or simple Roti (Chapter 15).

Slow Cooker Tandoori Chicken

For a crispier outer skin broil the chicken for 5–10 minutes under a broiler after cooking in a slow cooker.

INGREDIENTS | SERVE 6

¼ cup Tandoori Masala (Chapter 2)

½ cup Slow Cooker Yogurt (Chapter 3)

¼ teaspoon red coloring

1½ tablespoons Ginger-Garlic Paste (Chapter 2)

1 tablespoon Garam Masala Powder (Chapter 2)

3 tablespoons oil

Salt, to taste

1 whole chicken (washed well and skinned)

1½ cups sliced onion

1. Mix all the ingredients (*except* for the onion and chicken) together in a bowl making a thick, brightly colored marinade. Make a few incisions in the chicken and rub the marinade all over the chicken. If there is some marinade left, pour it inside the cavity of the bird. Tuck the bird tight (Place the loose ends of its legs and wings inside to prevent it from burning during the prolonged cooking process.)

2. Add the onion to the slow cooker forming a bottom layer. Place the chicken on top of the onion. Cover and cook on high for the first 1½ hours. Then reduce the heat to low and continue cooking for 4–5 hours or until the chicken is cooked through.

3. Cooking time will depend on the size of the chicken. Cut through the meatier part of the bird and if the juice comes out clear, then the chicken is cooked. Serve hot with Hot Cilantro Chutney (Chapter 2).

Slow-Roasted Chicken with Potatoes, Parsnips, and Onions

Chicken made in the slow cooker is amazingly tender. The onions add a lot of flavor with no added fat needed. You can also add a tablespoon of Curry Paste (Chapter 3) or Tandoori Masala (Chapter 2) as a substitute for the panch foran spices.

INGREDIENTS | SERVES 6

4 medium onions, sliced

1 (6-pound) roasting chicken

1 teaspoon black pepper

1½ teaspoons Panch Foran Spices (Chapter 2)

1 teaspoon salt

6 large red skin potatoes, halved

4 parsnips, diced

A Snippet about Parsnips

Parsnips have a mild flavor and a texture that is well suited to extended cooking times. Always peel off the bitter skin before cooking. If parsnips are not available, carrots are an acceptable substitute.

1. Cover the bottom of a 6–7-quart slow cooker with half of the onions.

2. Place the chicken, breast-side up, on top of the onions. Sprinkle with all the spices and salt.

3. Cover the chicken with the remaining onions.

4. Arrange the potatoes and parsnips around the chicken.

5. Cover and cook on low for 8 hours or until the chicken has an internal temperature of 165°F as measured using a food thermometer. Discard the chicken skin before serving.

Spiced Chicken in Green Curry (Murgh Hariyali)

This dish is at its best when fresh herbs are used. Serve with Garlic Rice (Chapter 11).

INGREDIENTS | SERVES 4

3 tablespoons vegetable oil

1 large onion, minced

2 teaspoons Ginger-Garlic Paste (Chapter 2)

2 green chilies, seeded and minced (optional)

4 tablespoons minced cilantro

4 tablespoons minced mint

5 tablespoons minced spinach

1½ pounds skinless, boneless chicken chunks (preferably thighs)

Salt, to taste

¼ teaspoon red chili powder

Water, as needed

½ cup heavy cream

1. In a large pan, heat the vegetable oil over medium heat. Add the onions and sauté until well browned, about 7–8 minutes. Add the Ginger-Garlic Paste and sauté for 1 minute.

2. Add the green chilies, cilantro, mint, and spinach; fry for about 4–5 minutes. Add the chicken, salt, and red chili powder. Stir well together.

3. Transfer the contents to the slow cooker. Add up to ½ cup of water if needed. Cover and cook on high for 2½–3 hours, or on low for 5–6 hours, or until the chicken is cooked through.

4. During the last 30 minutes of cooking, add the cream and continue cooking. Serve hot.

Dried Mint Chicken

Here is another dish that uses mint: Dry fresh mint (or use dried mint leaves) and crush it. Create a marinade of the mint, red chili powder, salt, pepper, and vegetable oil. Add chicken to the marinade and let it marinate for at least 4 hours. Grill or roast in an oven. Simple yet flavorful.

"Teekha" Peanut Chicken

This dish can serve either as an appetizer or main course. Add a little garam masala for extra punch.

INGREDIENTS | SERVES 6

1 pound boneless, skinless chicken breasts, cubed

2 cups broccoli florets

1 cup chicken stock

¼ cup coarsely chopped peanuts

3 tablespoons Chili-Garlic Paste (Chapter 2)

2 tablespoons minced Thai green chili

2 tablespoons minced fresh ginger

¼ cup diced onions

1. Place the chicken, broccoli, chicken stock, peanuts, Chili-Garlic Paste, chili, and ginger into a 4-quart slow cooker. Stir.

2. Cook on low for 4–5 hours or until the chicken is thoroughly cooked. Stir in the onions right before serving.

Whole Roast Chicken

Try using the same spices to roast your turkey this Thanksgiving!

INGREDIENTS | SERVES 12

3 pounds boneless, skinless chicken breasts or thighs

3 tablespoons Jamaican jerk seasoning

1 Scotch bonnet pepper, sliced

¼ cup fresh cilantro leaves

½ cup lemon juice

1 onion, chopped

1 tablespoon Ginger-Garlic Paste (Chapter 2)

1 teaspoon Kashmiri lal mirch

1 teaspoon garam masala

½ teaspoon cloves

3–4 green cardamom pods

Easy Mornings

Cut up vegetables in the evening and refrigerate them overnight. If cutting and storing meat, place it in a separate container from the vegetables to avoid cross contamination. To save even more time, you can measure out dry spices and leave them in the slow cooker insert overnight.

1. Place the chicken on the bottom of a 6–7-quart slow cooker. Pour the remaining ingredients on top. Cover and cook on low for 5 hours.

CHAPTER 9

Beef, Pork, Goat, and Lamb

Braised Pork
162

Garlic, Pepper, and Lemon Pork
Loin
162

Cardamom-Flavored Lamb
(Eliachi Gosht)
163

Extra-Hot Boneless Leg of Lamb
164

Gosht Shorba (Goat Curry)
165

Haleem
166

Hot Spiced Lamb
(Andhra Gosht Pittu)
167

Kheema and Quinoa (Quinoa
with Minced-Meat Curry)
168

Lamb Curry with Turnips
(Shalgam Wala Gosht)
169

Lamb Roganjosh
170

Lamb Vindaloo
171

Meat Belli Ram
(Belli Ram Ka Gosht)
172

Meatball Curry (Kofta Curry)
173

Mutton Do Pyaza
174

Peas and Minced-Meat Curry
(Kheema Mattar)
175

Pork Bafat
176

Pot Roast with Root Vegetables
177

Royal Lamb (Nawabi Gosht)
178

Shredded Beef for Sandwiches
179

Slow Cooker Shammi Kabab
180

Spinach Lamb Curry
(Saag Gosht)
181

Tandoori Meatballs
182

Braised Pork

This dish is perfect served sliced over rice and garnished with chopped green cilantro.

INGREDIENTS | SERVES 4

1 teaspoon ghee
1⅓ pounds pork loin
2 cloves minced garlic
1 tablespoon red pepper flakes
1 small onion, minced
1 tablespoon Ginger-Garlic Paste (Chapter 2)
½ teaspoon cinnamon
½ teaspoon ground star anise
1 tablespoon rice vinegar
Salt, to taste

1. Heat the ghee in a large nonstick skillet over medium heat. Add the pork and cook it for 2–3 minutes on each side.

2. Place the pork in a 4-quart slow cooker. Pour the remaining ingredients over the meat. Cover and cook on low 8 hours.

Garlic, Pepper, and Lemon Pork Loin

A thick paste of fresh garlic and lemon keep the pork from drying out during the long cooking time. You can also replace the garlic with honey for a sweeter taste.

INGREDIENTS | SERVES 4

1½ teaspoons black peppercorns, coarsely crushed
¼ cup lemon juice
1 tablespoon garlic paste
1 pound pork tenderloin

1. In a small bowl, mix the peppercorns, lemon juice, and garlic paste. Spread the mixture on the pork tenderloin in an even layer.

2. Place into a 3–4-quart slow cooker. Cook on low for 6 hours.

Cardamom-Flavored Lamb (Eliachi Gosht)

Fragrant cardamom pods and powder perfume this dish.
Adjust the amount of cardamom to your taste. Serve with warm Roti (Chapter 15).

INGREDIENTS | SERVES 4

¼ cup blanched almonds

1 cup water, as needed

3 tablespoons vegetable oil

1 large red onion, minced

2 serrano green chilies, seeded and minced

4 green cardamom pods, bruised

1 pound lean lamb chunks

Salt, to taste

½ cup plain yogurt

2 tablespoons cream

1 teaspoon cardamom powder

Cardamom Powder

Most stores sell this fragrant powder. Use a little at a time—it goes a long way. If you want to make your own, here is a simple recipe: Open the cardamom pods. Remove the seeds and discard the shells. In a spice grinder, grind the seeds to a fine powder. Store in an airtight jar. Approximately 8–10 cardamom pods will give about ½–1 teaspoon of cardamom powder, depending on the size.

1. In a food processor, combine the almonds with 2–3 tablespoons of water to make a thick, coarse paste. Set aside.

2. In a large pan, heat the vegetable oil over medium heat. Add the onion and sauté until golden brown, about 7–8 minutes. Add the green chilies, cardamom pods, and lamb. Sauté for about 5–8 minutes or until the lamb browns on the outside.

3. Transfer the contents to the slow cooker. Add up to ¼ cup of water. Add salt. Stir well. Cover and cook on low for 8–10 hours.

4. During the last 45 minutes of cooking add the yogurt and the almond paste. Adjust salt and water if required. Continue cooking until the lamb is cooked through and falls apart.

5. Add the cream and mix well. Simmer for about 10 minutes on high. Sprinkle with the cardamom powder and serve hot.

Extra-Hot Boneless Leg of Lamb

Lamb does surprisingly well in the slow cooker. It is nearly impossible to overcook, and every bite is meltingly tender. Add more red chili pepper if you like it extra hot!

INGREDIENTS | SERVES 12

4 pounds boneless leg of lamb
1 tablespoon ghee
1 tablespoon black pepper, coarsely crushed
1 teaspoon Goda Masala Powder (Chapter 2)
1½ teaspoons red chili pepper powder
¼ teaspoon kosher salt
¼ cup lemon juice
¼ cup water

1. Slice off any visible fat from the lamb and discard.

2. Heat the ghee in a pan over medium heat. Add the lamb and brown it on both sides. Pour the remaining ingredients on top of the lamb. Place the lamb in a 4- or 6-quart slow cooker. Cook on low for 8 hours.

3. Remove the lamb from the slow cooker. Discard the cooking liquid. Remove any remaining visible fat from the lamb. Slice the lamb prior to serving.

Healthy Cooking with Lamb

Lamb has a reputation as a somewhat fatty meat. However, buying a leaner cut, like the boneless leg where much of the fat and bone has been removed by the butcher, and slicing off any excess at home, can eliminate much of the fat. When slow cooking, the fat melts off the meat and accumulates in the bottom of the cooker where it can be easily discarded after removing the meat.

Gosht Shorba (Goat Curry)

This is one of the most common goat curry recipes cooked in the homes of India. The basic spices stay the same all around the country, with variations made depending on the region.

INGREDIENTS | SERVES 4–6

¼ cup oil or ghee

2–3 bay leaves

4–5 cloves

3–4 whole dried red chilies

1 cinnamon stick

4–5 green crushed cardamom pods

2 tablespoons Ginger-Garlic Paste (Chapter 2)

1 cup Curry Paste (Chapter 3)

Salt, to taste

2 pounds goat meat (with bones, cut into 2" pieces)

1 (10-ounce) can diced tomatoes

Water, as needed

½ cup chopped cilantro

Gosht?

Gosht is an Urdu name for goat meat. Since the Muslim community in India is the biggest consumer of goat meat, the Urdu name was slowly adapted.

1. Heat the oil in a pan over medium heat. Add all the dry whole spices. Let it cook for 1 minute until brown. Add the Ginger-Garlic Paste. Let it brown and then add the Curry Paste and salt. Cook for 1 minute until the oil starts to separate.

2. Add the goat meat. Cook for 5–10 minutes or until the outside of the meat is browned. Transfer to the slow cooker.

3. Drain the extra liquid from the canned tomatoes and pour tomatoes over the meat. Add up to 1 cup of water. Stir well. Cover and cook on high for 4–5 hours, or on low for 8 hours, or until the meat is cooked through and falls apart from the bones.

4. Garnish with chopped cilantro and serve with hot Simple Naan (Chapter 15) or any basic bread of your choice.

Haleem

This dish is particularly popular in the Muslim community and served during the Ramazaan period. It is a great fit for the slow cooker because the meat, along with the grains and lentils, is cooked on low heat for a long time resulting in a stew-like consistency.

INGREDIENTS | SERVES 6–8

1 cup chana dal (Bengal gram lentil), soaked in water for 2 hours

½ cup ghee, or oil

2½ tablespoons coriander powder

1 teaspoon turmeric powder

3 tablespoons Ginger-Garlic Paste (Chapter 2)

2 cups thinly sliced onions

2 pounds mutton (goat meat), or beef

½ pound cracked wheat, washed well with water

1 tablespoon Garam Masala Powder (Chapter 2)

1 tablespoon Thai green chili paste

Salt, to taste

2–2½ cups water

½ cup chopped cilantro

½ cup chopped mint

1–2 lemon wedges (optional)

1. Discard the lentils' soaking water and make a paste with the soaked lentils in a blender, using up to ½ cup of water to let the blades of the blender move. Set aside.

2. Heat the ghee, or oil, in a pan. Add the coriander and turmeric. As they sizzle, add the Ginger-Garlic Paste and sauté for 1 minute. As the mixture turns brown, add the onion. Cook for 5 minutes until the onion turns translucent.

3. Add the mutton or beef and cook with the spices for 5–8 minutes or until the outside of the meat is brown. Add the cracked wheat. Stir everything together. Transfer to the slow cooker.

4. Add the Garam Masala, chili paste, salt, and lentil paste. Add up to 2–2½ cups of water. Stir well. Cover and cook on high for 5–6 hours, or on low for 10–12 hours, or until the meat is cooked well enough to fall apart. Mix well.

5. Stir the final dish together well. Garnish with cilantro and mint. Add lemon juice, if desired, and serve hot.

Hot Spiced Lamb (Andhra Gosht Pittu)

Andhra Pradesh, a state in southern India, is famous for its highly spiced meats.
The garam masala adds a nice zing to the dish.

INGREDIENTS | SERVES 4

3 tablespoons vegetable oil

1½ pounds lean minced lamb

1 teaspoon grated fresh gingerroot

½ teaspoon red chili powder

1 teaspoon minced garlic

¼ teaspoon turmeric powder

1 serrano green chili, seeded and minced

½ cup water

1 large red onion, minced

2 tablespoons plain yogurt, whipped

¼ cup unsweetened desiccated coconut

Salt, to taste

½ teaspoon Garam Masala Powder (Chapter 2)

1. Pour 1 tablespoon of oil in a pan and brown the lamb over medium heat for 8–10 minutes. Transfer it to a slow cooker. Add the gingerroot, red chili, garlic, turmeric, and green chili. Add the water. Cover and cook on low setting for 8–10 hours or until the lamb is cooked through. Set aside.

2. In a large skillet, heat 2 tablespoons vegetable oil over medium heat. Add the onion and fry, stirring constantly, until well browned, about 8 minutes. Add the lamb from the slow cooker, along with the yogurt, and fry for another 4–5 minutes. Add the coconut and salt; sauté for another 5 minutes.

3. Serve hot, garnished with Garam Masala.

Green Chili Lamb Chops

Here is a really easy recipe for lamb chops: In a bowl, combine equal portions of Hot Cilantro Chutney (Chapter 2) and Mint-Cilantro Chutney (Chapter 2). Add lamb chops and coat evenly with the marinade. Marinate for about 2 hours and then cook according to your preference.

Kheema and Quinoa (Quinoa with Minced-Meat Curry)

Try this as an alternative to rice. It's a very simple dish to fix when you have some leftover kheema mattar. You can also use it with leftover stir-fried vegetables and meat dishes. Just cut back on the amount of water you use if the curry has plenty of liquid.

INGREDIENTS | SERVES 4–5

½ recipe Kheema Mattar (see recipe in this chapter)

1 cup quinoa, rinsed

1½ cups water

Quinoa Basics

Although quinoa is treated like a grain, it is actually an edible seed. It is very high in protein and contains a balanced set of essential amino acids, making it a particularly complete source of protein. Quinoa is also high in fiber, iron, and magnesium.

1. Warm up the Kheema Mattar in a small nonstick saucepan. Drain off any excess fat. Add to a 3–4-quart slow cooker along with the quinoa and water.

2. Cover and cook on low for 2 hours or until the quinoa is cooked well. Fluff with a fork before serving.

Lamb Curry with Turnips (Shalgam Wala Gosht)

Turnips are a mild vegetable, but this dish provides flavors that give them a delicious taste. Serve with Perfect Slow Cooker Basmati Rice (Chapter 11).

INGREDIENTS | SERVES 4

3 tablespoons vegetable oil

2 cloves

1 bay leaf

1 cup Curry Paste (Chapter 3)

Salt, to taste

1½ pounds boneless lean lamb chunks

1 teaspoon red chili powder

½ teaspoon turmeric powder

1½ teaspoons coriander powder

½ teaspoon Garam Masala Powder (Chapter 2)

Water, as needed

1 cup plain yogurt, whipped

2 small turnips, peeled and diced

Pressure-Cooking Meats

If you are in a hurry and want to reduce the cooking time for meats, invest in a good pressure cooker. Most Indian homes have pressure cookers. They are a boon not only for meats but for lentils as well.

1. In a deep pan, heat the vegetable oil over medium heat. Add the cloves and bay leaf. When the spices begin to sizzle, add the Curry Paste and salt. Sauté for about 1 minute or until the oil separates from the sides.

2. Add the lamb and fry for about 5–7 minutes to brown the outside of the meat, stirring constantly. If the mixture starts to stick to the sides of the pan, add 1 tablespoon of water.

3. In quick succession, add the red chili, turmeric, coriander, and Garam Masala. Transfer everything to the slow cooker.

4. Cover and cook on high 4–5 hours, or on low for 8–10 hours, or until the meat is cooked through. You can add up to 1 cup of water to make the curry thinner. Stir occasionally.

5. During the last 45 minutes of cooking, add yogurt and turnips. Cover and continue cooking until the lamb has cooked through and the turnips are soft. Serve hot.

Lamb Roganjosh

The main spice used in a roganjosh is Kashmiri lal mirch, or red pepper powder, from the northern state of Kashmir. It is not very hot, but it gives a vibrant red color to the dish. You can find it in any Indian or international food store. But if you still can't find it, just use ½ tablespoon red pepper powder.

INGREDIENTS | SERVES 4

2 tablespoons oil

1 cup onion paste (chopped onion ground in a food processor)

1 teaspoon turmeric

1 teaspoon fennel seeds

2–3 cloves

1 teaspoon cinnamon powder

1 teaspoon cumin seeds

Pinch of asafetida

1 pound boneless lamb (cut into 1–2" thickness)

3 tablespoons Ginger-Garlic Paste (Chapter 2)

1 tablespoon Kashmiri lal mirch (red pepper powder)

1 cup whole fat yogurt

1 teaspoon Garam Masala Powder (Chapter 2)

1 tablespoon ghee

1. Heat the oil in a thick-bottomed pan over medium heat. Add the onion paste and cook it until it turns a golden brown color. Turn heat to medium low. Now add the turmeric, fennel seeds, cloves, cinnamon powder, cumin seeds, and asafetida. Mix it all together.

2. Add the lamb and let it cook for 5–8 minutes or until the outside of the lamb is browned. Transfer the contents to the slow cooker.

3. Add the Ginger-Garlic Paste and Kashmiri lal mirch. Stir well along with salt. If you want a thinner gravy, you can add up to 1 cup of water. Cover and cook on high for 4–5 hours, or on low for 8 hours, or until the lamb is cooked well.

4. During the last 45 minutes of cooking, stir in the yogurt, Garam Masala, and also the ghee. Cover and continue cooking for 45 minutes until the lamb is cooked through. Serve hot over a simple vegetarian rice dish and an Indian bread on the side.

Roganjosh

Roganjosh was primarily brought to India by Mughals but was later adopted by Kashmiri pandits. The version made by the Kashmiri pandits is made with no onions and garlic because pandits wouldn't eat them. The gravy is cooked in creamy yogurt with a mixture of several spices.

Lamb Vindaloo

You can prepare this with pork or beef; adjust seasonings to taste (the cooking times will stay the same).

INGREDIENTS | SERVES 4

¾ cup rice vinegar

¼ cup water

1 teaspoon black peppercorns, roughly pounded

1 tablespoon minced garlic

2 teaspoons red chili powder

2 serrano green chilies, minced

1½ pounds boneless lean lamb, cubed

3 tablespoons vegetable oil

1 tablespoon grated gingerroot

1 large red onion, peeled and finely chopped

6 whole dried red chilies, roughly pounded

1 (1") cinnamon stick

½ teaspoon turmeric powder

Salt, to taste

Selecting Lamb

Color can be a great help when buying lamb. Younger lamb is pinkish red with a velvety texture. It should have a thin layer of white fat surrounding it. If the meat is much darker in color, it means that the lamb is older and flavored more strongly.

1. In the slow cooker insert, combine the rice vinegar, water, black peppercorns, garlic, red chili powder, and green chilies. Add the lamb and coat evenly with the marinade. Refrigerate, covered, for 1 hour.

2. In a deep pan, heat the oil over medium heat. Add the gingerroot and sauté for about 10 seconds. Add the onion and sauté for about 7–8 minutes or until golden brown.

3. Add the dried red chilies, cinnamon stick, and turmeric powder; sauté for 20 seconds.

4. Remove the lamb pieces from the marinade. Add the lamb to the pan with onions and sauté on high heat for about 10 minutes or until the lamb is browned and the oil starts to separate from the mixture.

5. Transfer the browned lamb back to the slow cooker. Mix with the marinade and salt. Cover and cook on high for 4–5 hours, or on low for 8–10 hours, or until the lamb is cooked through and tender. Serve hot.

Meat Belli Ram (Belli Ram Ka Gosht)

Belli Ram was a celebrated Indian chef from northern India.
This dish, named for him, is a delicacy served on special occasions.

INGREDIENTS | SERVES 4

2 medium-size red onions, peeled and thinly sliced

3 tablespoons Ginger-Garlic Paste (Chapter 2)

2 cloves

2 green cardamom pods, roughly pounded

1 (1") cinnamon stick

1 teaspoon red chili powder

1 cup water

Salt, to taste

2 tablespoons ghee, or vegetable oil

1 tablespoon coriander seeds, roughly pounded

1½ pounds lean boneless lamb, cut in 1" cubes

2 cups plain yogurt, whipped

Indian Lamb Curries

Most of the curries taste even better if you allow the spices to do their magic overnight. Cook the dish according to directions. Cool to room temperature. Cover and refrigerate overnight. The next day, heat the dish on high and serve.

1. In a bowl, combine the onions, Ginger-Garlic Paste, cloves, cardamom pods, cinnamon, red chili powder, ½ cup water, and salt; mix well. Set aside.

2. In a deep pan, heat the ghee over medium heat. Add the coriander seeds. When they begin to sizzle, add the lamb. Cook for 5–10 minutes or until the lamb is browned on the outside.

3. Transfer the lamb to the slow cooker. Pour the marinade over it. Cover and cook on high for 4–5 hours or on low for 8–10 hours. Add the rest of the water if the meat dries out while cooking.

4. During the last 45 minutes of cooking add yogurt. Cover and cook further on high setting. Cook until the fat begins to leave the sides of the lamb. This will depend on the leanness of your meat, about 45 minutes. Remove from heat. Serve hot.

Meatball Curry (Kofta Curry)

You can make extra meatballs and freeze them. Then, when you are ready, this recipe is a snap! Serve with Simple Naan (Chapter 15).

INGREDIENTS | SERVES 4

4 tablespoons vegetable oil

2 bay leaves

1 (1") cinnamon stick

4 cloves

4 black peppercorns

2 black cardamom pods

2 medium-size red onions, peeled and finely chopped

2 teaspoons Ginger-Garlic Paste (Chapter 2)

2 small tomatoes, finely chopped

1 teaspoon Garam Masala Powder (Chapter 2)

½ teaspoon red chili powder

¼ teaspoon turmeric powder

Salt, to taste

½ cup water

½ cup plain yogurt, whipped

1 recipe Lamb Kofta (Chapter 4)

1. In a large skillet, heat the vegetable oil over medium heat. Add the bay leaves, cinnamon stick, cloves, black peppercorns, and cardamom pods. When the spices begin to sizzle, add the onions. Stirring constantly, fry until the onions are golden brown, about 7–8 minutes. Add the Ginger-Garlic Paste and sauté for 1 minute.

2. Add the tomatoes and fry, stirring constantly, for 10 minutes or until the oil starts to separate from the mixture.

3. Add the Garam Masala, red chili powder, turmeric powder, and salt; mix well.

4. Transfer the skillet mixture (the masala) to the slow cooker. Add the water and yogurt, cover, and cook on high for 30 minutes or until the sauce comes to a boil.

5. Reduce heat to low. Add the meatballs and simmer for 35–40 minutes or until the meatballs marry well with the spices and in turn thicken the sauce. Serve hot.

Using Bay Leaves

When using bay leaves, tear them and roughly crush them. They should be quite aromatic, sweet, and pungent. Don't use more than 1 or 2 leaves, or the food will get an acrid and unpleasant taste. Always remove the bay leaves before serving—the leaf is inedible.

Mutton Do Pyaza

This is my father's recipe that he has mastered over the years. The meat and onions are slowly cooked with whole spices for hours, until they begin to fall off the bone.

INGREDIENTS | SERVES 4–5

2 tablespoons of oil

1½ tablespoons of coriander powder

1 teaspoon cumin seeds

1 stick cinnamon

2 whole black cardamom pods

1½ teaspoons whole peppercorn, coarsely crushed

2 bay leaves

3 cups thinly sliced onion

1½ pounds goat meat with bone, cut into pieces

1 tablespoon Ginger-Garlic Paste (Chapter 2)

1 cup diced tomato

Salt, to taste

Onions

You can also substitute fresh onions with 1½ cups of slow-cooked Caramelized Onions (Chapter 3). If you do, add the onions during the last 1½ hours, once the meat is almost cooked through with the spices.

1. Heat the oil in a pan over medium heat. Once it is smoking hot, add the coriander, cumin, cinnamon, black cardamom, peppercorn, and bay leaves. Cook them in oil until they turn light brown. Add the onions. Sauté 5 minutes or until they begin to sweat and turn translucent.

2. Add the meat. Cook for 5–8 minutes on high heat, stirring continuously to brown the outside. Transfer to the slow cooker.

3. Add the rest of the ingredients; mix well. Cover and cook on low for 8–10 hours or until the meat is cooked through and falls off the bone. Serve hot with Simple Naan (Chapter 15) and a simple rice dish.

Peas and Minced-Meat Curry (Kheema Mattar)

Make an extra batch and freeze it to make a casserole of ground lamb, peas, and rice at a later date.

INGREDIENTS | SERVES 4

2 tablespoons vegetable oil

¾ cup Curry Paste (Chapter 3)

Salt, to taste

2 small tomatoes, puréed

1¼ pounds minced lamb

1 teaspoon Garam Masala Powder (Chapter 2)

½ teaspoon red chili powder

¼ teaspoon turmeric powder

1 cup frozen peas, thawed

1. In a large skillet, heat the vegetable oil over medium heat. Add the Curry Paste, salt, and tomatoes. Cook for 4–5 minutes or until the tomatoes melt.

2. Add the lamb and sauté for about 2–3 minutes. Break up any lumps with the back of your spoon.

3. Drain any excess fat and transfer the contents to the slow cooker. Add the Garam Masala, red chili powder, and turmeric powder; mix well. Cover and cook on high for 3 hours or on low for 5–6 hours, stirring occasionally.

4. Add the peas and cook, covered, for another 1 hour or until the peas and lamb are cooked through. Serve hot.

Pork Bafat

Another Goan-inspired dish, this is fiery hot. Add more chilies if you like your dishes really hot!

INGREDIENTS | SERVES 4

2 tablespoons Ginger-Garlic Paste (Chapter 2)

1 teaspoon black peppercorns

4–6 cloves

1 teaspoon cumin seeds

½ teaspoon black mustard seeds

8–10 dried red chilies

⅓ cup malt vinegar

4–6 tablespoons vegetable oil

2 pounds pork, cubed

2 tablespoons tamarind pulp, soaked in ½ cup hot water for 10 minutes

1½ cups frozen pearl onions

Salt, to taste

Water, as needed

1. In a food processor, grind together the Ginger-Garlic Paste, black peppercorns, cloves, cumin seeds, mustard seeds, red chilies, and malt vinegar. Set aside.

2. In a large skillet, heat the vegetable oil over medium heat. Add the pork and brown on all sides, about 8–10 minutes. Strain excess fat and transfer the browned pork to the slow cooker.

3. Add the ground paste. Strain the tamarind; keep the liquid and discard the residue. Add the strained liquid to the pork and mix well. Add the frozen onions and salt.

4. Add ½ cup of water. Cover and cook on high for 4–5 hours, or on low for 8–10 hours, or until the pork is cooked through. Stir occasionally. Add more water if the dish becomes too dry or starts to stick. Serve hot.

Pot Roast with Root Vegetables

A variety of autumnal vegetables makes this pot roast a complete meal in one.

INGREDIENTS | SERVES 12

1 cup water

4 russet potatoes, quartered

4 carrots, cut into thirds

4 parsnips, peeled and quartered

3 beet roots, quartered

2 onions, sliced

1 celeriac, cubed

4 cloves garlic, sliced

4 pounds lean top round beef roast, excess fat removed

½ teaspoon salt

1 teaspoon red chili powder

½ teaspoon freshly ground black pepper

1 teaspoon turmeric powder

1 tablespoon Tandoori Masala (Chapter 2)

½ cup Slow Cooker Yogurt (Chapter 3)

2 tablespoons Ginger-Garlic Paste (Chapter 2)

1. Pour the water into a 6-quart slow cooker. Add the potatoes, carrots, parsnips, beetroots, onions, celeriac, and garlic. Stir.

2. Add the beef. Sprinkle with salt, red chili powder, and pepper. Cook on low for 8 hours.

3. In a mixing bowl, mix together the rest of the spices with the yogurt and Ginger-Garlic Paste. During the last hour of cooking, pour the paste over the beef. Spread it all over the beef. Cover and continue cooking.

4. Remove and slice the beef. Use a slotted spoon to serve the vegetables. Discard the cooking liquid.

Royal Lamb (Nawabi Gosht)

This typically difficult recipe is simplified here into easy, manageable steps. Serve hot with Roti (Chapter 15).

INGREDIENTS | SERVES 4

3 tablespoons ghee

1½ teaspoons fennel seeds

4 dried red chilies

1 cup packed curry paste

Salt, to taste

1½ pounds lean, bone-in lamb, cut into 1–1½" chunks

1 teaspoon Ginger-Garlic Paste (Chapter 2)

Water, as needed

½ cup yogurt, whipped

Vegetable oil, for deep-frying

4 hard-boiled eggs, peeled and quartered

¼ teaspoon Roasted Saffron (Chapter 2)

Unsalted cashews, roasted, for garnish

1. In a large skillet over medium heat, heat the ghee. Add fennel seeds and red chilies. As they sputter, add the Curry Paste and salt. Fry the paste until the oil separates, for about 2–3 minutes.

2. Add the lamb along with Ginger-Garlic Paste to the onion mixture. Fry, stirring constantly, for about 10 minutes. If the lamb sticks, add 1 tablespoon of water. Brown the lamb.

3. Transfer the contents to the slow cooker. Add up to 1 cup of water. Cover and cook on low for 8–10 hours.

4. During the last 45 minutes of cooking, add whisked yogurt. Mix well. Adjust salt and water if needed. Continue cooking until the lamb is tender and falls apart.

5. In the meantime, heat the vegetable oil in a deep pan to about 300°F. Deep-fry the eggs until crispy on the outside. Remove with a slotted spoon and place on a paper towel. Set aside.

6. Add saffron and eggs to the slow cooker. Cook, uncovered, for another 15 minutes on high. Serve garnished with unsalted roasted cashews.

Shredded Beef for Sandwiches

Due to the long cooking time, it is possible to prepare the meat late the night before serving so it will be ready to eat for lunch. Wrap some of this in Simple Naan (Chapter 15) and you are good to go!

INGREDIENTS | SERVES 16

4¼ pounds lean boneless beef roast, excess fat removed

1 onion, chopped

3 cloves garlic, chopped

1 teaspoon paprika

1 teaspoon chili powder

½ teaspoon cumin seed

½ teaspoon mustard seeds, crushed

½ teaspoon freshly ground black pepper

¼ teaspoon salt

1 tablespoon Garam Masala Powder (Chapter 2)

½ cup water

1. Place all ingredients in a 6–7-quart slow cooker. Cook on low for 10–12 hours.

2. Remove the meat from the slow cooker to a plate. Shred with a fork. Mash the contents of the slow cooker with a potato masher. Return the beef to the slow cooker and stir to distribute the ingredients evenly.

Ask the Butcher

If the beef sitting on the shelf of the local store is too fatty, ask the butcher to cut a fresh leaner cut. Then you won't have to do fat removal at home, which can be tricky depending on the cut of meat. The butcher can also suggest lean beef alternatives to fattier cuts.

Slow Cooker Shammi Kabab

This is a popular Indian snack or appetizer dish that goes well with beverages like Masala Chai (Chapter 14) or Chach (Chapter 14). A lot of time can be saved if cooked in a slow cooker.

INGREDIENTS | **SERVES 6–8**

3–4 tablespoons oil, plus more for deep-frying

1 teaspoon cumin seeds

1½ tablespoons Ginger-Garlic Paste (Chapter 2)

1 teaspoon minced green chili

2½ pounds ground pork or beef

½ teaspoon red chili powder

1 tablespoon Garam Masala Powder (Chapter 2)

1½ tablespoons coriander powder

3–4 cups water

Salt, to taste

½ cup chana dal (split Bengal gram), soaked overnight

1 cup minced onion

1 egg

½ cup bread crumbs

1. Heat the oil in a pan over medium heat. Add the cumin seeds followed by Ginger-Garlic Paste and green chili. Add the meat and cook for 10 minutes. Break lumps with the back of your spoon.

2. Drain the extra fat and transfer the sautéed meat to the slow cooker. Add all the dry spices along with 3–4 cups of water and salt. Add the soaked chana dal. Cover and cook on low for 7–8 hours.

3. Once cooked, let the meat cool a little. Then add the rest of the ingredients. Mix everything together well.

4. Divide the prepared mixture into equal parts, about 2–2½ dozen. Roll balls out of them and then press the balls between your palms to flatten them to ¼" thickness.

5. Heat oil and deep- or pan-fry the kababs according to your liking. Serve hot with your choice of chutney or raita dip.

Spinach Lamb Curry (Saag Gosht)

This dish graces menus at innumerable Indian restaurants.
Serve with Simple Naan (Chapter 15), brushed with spiced garlic butter.

INGREDIENTS | SERVES 4

½ pound frozen chopped spinach

4 tablespoons vegetable oil

1 cup, packed, Curry Paste (Chapter 3)

Salt, to taste

1 (10-ounce) can diced tomatoes, drained

1¼ pounds boneless lean lamb, cut into chunks

1 teaspoon Garam Masala Powder (Chapter 2)

½ teaspoon red chili powder

¼ teaspoon turmeric powder

½–1 cup water

½ cup plain yogurt, whipped

Spiced Butter

Brush your favorite Indian breads with spiced butter for an added *oomph*. Take a stick of butter at room temperature, add 1 teaspoon of crushed garlic and ¼ teaspoon roasted cumin; mix well. Refrigerate and use as needed.

1. Cook the spinach in boiling water until just wilted; drain. Purée in a food processor. Set aside.

2. In a large skillet, heat the vegetable oil over medium heat. Add the Curry Paste and salt. Cook for 1 minute and as the oil separates add tomatoes. Cook for 3–5 minutes.

3. Add the lamb and fry for about 10 minutes, stirring constantly. Once the lamb is browned on all sides, transfer the contents to the slow cooker.

4. Add the Garam Masala, red chili powder, turmeric powder, and salt; mix well. Add up to 1 cup of water. Cover and cook on high for 4–6 hours, or on low for 8–10 hours, or until the lamb is cooked through.

5. During the last 1½ hours of cooking, add the spinach purée. Add up to ½ cup water or to reach a consistency of your liking and continue cooking.

6. During the last 30 minutes of cooking, add the yogurt. Adjust salt if needed. Cook further till the lamb is cooked through. Serve hot.

Tandoori Meatballs

A simple meatball recipe can be used for Kofta Curry
(see recipe in this chapter) in place of Lamb Kofta (Chapter 4).

INGREDIENTS | YIELDS 4 DOZEN MEATBALLS

2 pounds ground beef

½ cup bread crumbs

1 tablespoon minced green chili

1 tablespoon Ginger-Garlic Paste (Chapter 2)

1 egg

½ cup boiled and mashed potatoes

1 cup chopped cilantro

4 tablespoons Tandoori Masala (Chapter 2)

1 tablespoon Garam Masala Powder (Chapter 2)

Salt, to taste

1 tablespoon oil

1½ cups chicken stock

1. Preheat the oven to 350°F.

2. Mix all the ingredients, except chicken stock, together in a mixing bowl. Divide into equal parts, up to 4 dozen. Roll into balls. Place in a single layer on an oiled baking sheet. Place in the oven and bake for 15 minutes.

3. Add meatballs to a 6–7-quart slow cooker. Pour the chicken stock over them.

4. Cover and cook on low for 6–8 hours or until the meatballs are cooked through. Serve hot with your choice of chutney or raita dip on the side.

CHAPTER 10

Fish

Brown Rice Curry with
Vegetables and Scallops
184

Creamy Shrimp (Malai Jhinga)
185

Fish in a Velvety Sauce
(Bengali Doi Maach)
186

Fish in Tomato Sauce
187

Goan Shrimp
188

Kashmiri Fish Curry (Kashmiri
Macchi)
189

Kerala Fish Curry (Meen Moilee)
190

Lobster in Creamy Sauce
(Lobster Ka Korma)
191

Macchi Dum Pukht
(Slow-Cooked Fish)
192

Macher Jhol
193

Mixed Seafood Dip
194

Muri Ghonto
195

Parsi Fish (Patrani Macchi)
196

Prawn Masala (Jhinga Masala)
197

Salmon in Saffron-Flavored
Curry (Zaffrani Macchi)
198

Shorshe Maach (Fish Cooked in
Hot Mustard Sauce)
199

Shrimp in Coconut Milk
(Chingri Maacher Malai Curry)
200

Shrimp Patio (Kolmino Patio)
201

Steamed Tandoori Machi
202

Tamarind Fish Curry
(Imli Wale Macchi)
203

Brown Rice Curry with Vegetables and Scallops

Serve this dish with a dry white wine.

INGREDIENTS | SERVES 6

1 large yellow onion

3 cloves garlic

1 tablespoon olive oil

1 pound baby scallops

1½ cups water

1 tablespoon Garam Masala Powder (Chapter 2)

½ teaspoon cinnamon

½ teaspoon salt

2 large potatoes

1 large zucchini

2 large carrots

1 (16-ounce) can tomatoes, liquid drained

1. Peel and chop the onion into ¼" pieces. Peel and slice the garlic paper-thin with a sharp kitchen knife.

2. Heat the olive oil in a medium-size skillet; sauté the scallops, onions, and garlic on medium-high heat until the onion is translucent and limp. The scallops should be slightly brown. Drain off the oil and place the scallops, onion, and garlic in the slow cooker.

3. Add the water, Garam Masala, cinnamon, and salt to the slow cooker; stir well. Cook covered on high for 1 hour.

4. Peel and cut the potatoes into 1" cubes. Slice the zucchini into ¼"-thick pieces. Peel and slice the carrots into ¼" pieces. Slice the tomatoes into 1" pieces, retaining the resulting juice. Add the potatoes, zucchini, and tomatoes to the slow cooker. Cook covered on low setting for 6–8 hours.

Creamy Shrimp (Malai Jhinga)

Malai, or cream, gives this dish a rich taste, and the spices bring a new dimension to a simple shrimp curry. Serve with Perfect Slow Cooker Basmati Rice (Chapter 11).

INGREDIENTS | SERVES 4

1 pound shrimp, peeled and deveined

1 teaspoon turmeric powder, divided

3 tablespoons vegetable oil

2 teaspoons Ginger-Garlic Paste (Chapter 2)

2 medium tomatoes, chopped

Water, as needed

1 teaspoon red chili powder

2 teaspoons coriander powder

Salt, to taste

4 tablespoons light cream

1. Place the shrimp in a bowl. Rub about ¾ teaspoon of the turmeric on the shrimp and set aside for about 10 minutes. Rinse them well and pat dry.

2. In a large skillet, heat the vegetable oil. Add the Ginger-Garlic Paste and sauté for about 30 seconds. Add the tomatoes, quickly mix with the paste, and transfer to the slow cooker. Cover and cook on high for 45 minutes, or on low for 1½–2 hours, or until all the tomatoes are cooked enough to melt. Add 1 tablespoon of water if the mixture appears to be sticking.

3. Add the remaining turmeric, the red chili powder, coriander powder, and salt with ½ cup water. Mix well.

4. When the sauce is ready and simmering, add the shrimp. Cook for about 15 minutes or until the shrimp are cooked through.

5. Remove from heat and add the light cream; mix well. Serve hot.

Fish in a Velvety Sauce (Bengali Doi Maach)

*For this recipe, you can use tilapia or catfish. Serve this with
Perfect Slow Cooker Basmati Rice (Chapter 11).*

INGREDIENTS | SERVES 4

4–5 catfish fillets

¾ teaspoon turmeric powder

8 tablespoons vegetable oil, divided

1 bay leaf

½ teaspoon cumin seeds

2 teaspoons Ginger-Garlic Paste (Chapter 2)

1 large red onion, minced

1 teaspoon red chili powder

2 serrano green chilies, seeded and minced

½ cup plain yogurt, whipped

Salt, to taste

Water, as needed

1. Place the catfish fillets in a bowl. Rub the fillets well with the turmeric and set aside for about 10 minutes. Rinse the fillets and pat dry.

2. In a medium-size skillet, heat 6 tablespoons of the vegetable oil over medium-high heat. Add 1 fillet at a time and fry until brown on both sides, about 5–8 minutes. Remove from heat with a slotted spoon and drain on a paper towel. Continue until all the fillets are fried. Set aside.

3. In a large skillet, heat the remaining 2 tablespoons of vegetable oil. Add the bay leaf and cumin seeds. When the spices begin to sizzle, add the Ginger-Garlic Paste and onions; sauté for about 7–8 minutes or until the onions are well browned.

4. Transfer the contents to a slow cooker. Add the red chili powder and green chilies; mix well. Add the yogurt and salt, and mix well. Add about ½ cup of water. Cover and simmer on high for 30 minutes.

5. Uncover and stir well with a whisk. Add the fish fillets, cover, and simmer for another 15 minutes. Be careful not to break the fillets when you stir. Serve hot.

Fish in Tomato Sauce

This is another dish that comes from the state of Bengal. Bangladesh, formerly a part of India, shares almost the same culinary history and practices as Bengal.

INGREDIENTS | SERVES 4–5

5–6 fish steaks or 8–10 fish fillets, cut into 2–3" pieces

1 teaspoon turmeric

Salt, to taste

¼ cup oil, plus more if deep-frying

½ teaspoon mustard seeds

½ teaspoon nigella (onion seeds)

2–3 Thai green chilies, minced

1 tablespoon ginger paste

1½ cups tomato sauce, or tomato purée

Water, if needed

Fish and Bengali Cuisine

Fish is one of the most dominant proteins in the Bengali cuisine, and fish is mainly cultivated in sweet water. Fish from sea water is neither very popular nor easily available. Any freshwater fish like bass, carp, or rohu works best for this dish, instead of fish such as salmon or mahi mahi.

1. Rub the fish with the turmeric and a little salt. Let it sit for 30 minutes.

2. Heat oil in a pan over medium-high heat. Pan-fry the fish if using fillets; if using steaks, deep-frying works better. Once browned, about 5–8 minutes, take the fish out and set aside.

3. In the remaining oil in the pan, add the mustard seeds, nigella, and green chilies. As they sputter, add the ginger paste. Cook for 10–15 seconds.

4. Add the tomato sauce. Stir everything well, scraping the sides. Transfer the contents to the slow cooker. Add salt to taste. Cover and cook on high for 1 hour, or on low for 2 hours, or until the sauce simmers down to a thicker consistency. Add up to ¾ cup of water if it gets too thick.

5. Place the fish in the slow cooker. Pour the sauce over the fish. Cover and simmer on low for another 15–20 minutes or until the fish flakes when using a fork. Serve hot over Perfect Slow Cooker Basmati Rice (Chapter 11).

Goan Shrimp

Goan food, especially the curries, is popular for its combination of tanginess, heat, and vibrance.

INGREDIENTS | SERVES 4–5

5–6 dried red chilies

1 tablespoon coriander seeds

1 teaspoon cumin seeds

4 tablespoons unsweetened grated coconut

2 tablespoons white wine vinegar

¼ cup oil

2 tablespoons Ginger-Garlic Paste (Chapter 2)

1 cup minced onion

Salt, to taste

Water, as needed

1 pound shrimp, shelled and deveined

1. Dry roast the spices and grated coconut in a pan for 3–5 minutes, stirring continuously. Cool and place them in a bowl. Pour the vinegar over them and let the spices sit in the vinegar for about 1 hour. After an hour, make a paste out of it in a blender. Set aside.

2. Heat the oil in a pan. Add the Ginger-Garlic Paste and sauté it. Add the onion and salt. Cook until the onion begins to sweat. Add the spice paste to the onion. Cook for about 1–2 minutes.

3. Transfer the spices to the slow cooker. Add 1 cup water. Adjust salt. Cover and let the sauce simmer on high for 1 hour or on low for 2 hours.

4. Add the shrimp to the simmering sauce. Mix everything well and cook further for 15–20 minutes or until the shrimp is cooked through. Serve hot over Perfect Slow Cooker Basmati Rice (Chapter 11).

Kashmiri Fish Curry (Kashmiri Macchi)

*Traditional Kashmiri cooking uses dried ginger powder and
dried red chili powder called Kashmiri lal mirch.*

INGREDIENTS | SERVES 4

4–5 whitefish fillets (such as tilapia, catfish, or cod)

¾ teaspoon turmeric powder

1 teaspoon ginger, finely ground

1 teaspoon anise seeds, roughly pounded

4 tablespoons vegetable oil

1 teaspoon red chili powder (preferably Kashmiri lal mirch)

2 teaspoons coriander powder

Salt, to taste

1 cup plain yogurt, whipped

1. Place the fish fillets in a bowl. Rub the fillets well with the turmeric, ginger, and anise seeds; set aside for about 10 minutes.

2. In a medium-size skillet, heat the vegetable oil. Add 1 fillet at a time and shallow-fry until brown on both sides, about 3–5 minutes. Remove from the skillet with a slotted spoon and drain on paper towels. Continue until all the fillets are fried. Set aside. Keep the oil.

3. In the slow cooker, pour 3–4 tablespoons of the oil used for frying the fish. Add the red chili, coriander, and salt; mix well. Add the yogurt. Cover and cook on high for 45 minutes.

4. Whisk the sauce, blending everything together well. Add the fried fish.

5. Cover and simmer on low heat until the fish is completely heated through (about 30 minutes). Serve hot.

Kerala Fish Curry (Meen Moilee)

This popular dish comes to you from the gorgeous state of Kerala on the west coast of India. Serve with Perfect Slow Cooker Basmati Rice (Chapter 11).

INGREDIENTS | SERVES 4

4–5 whitefish fillets (such as tilapia, catfish, or cod)

1 teaspoon turmeric powder, plus ¼ teaspoon for the sauce

6 tablespoons vegetable oil

½ teaspoon black mustard seeds

2 green cardamom pods, bruised

2 cloves

8 fresh curry leaves

1 large red onion, finely chopped

1 teaspoon grated fresh gingerroot

Salt, to taste

1 teaspoon red chili powder

1 teaspoon coriander powder

1 (14-ounce) can light coconut milk

1. Place the fish fillets in a bowl. Rub the fillets well with 1 teaspoon of turmeric and set aside for about 10 minutes. Rinse the fillets and pat dry.

2. In a medium-size nonstick skillet, heat 4 tablespoons of the vegetable oil. Add 1 fillet at a time and shallow-fry until brown on both sides, about 5–8 minutes. Remove from the skillet with a slotted spoon and drain on a paper towel. Continue until all the fillets are fried. Set aside.

3. In a large skillet, heat the remaining vegetable oil. Add the mustard seeds, cardamom, and cloves. As soon as they begin to sputter, add the curry leaves, onions, and gingerroot. Sauté for 7–8 minutes or until the onions are well browned.

4. Transfer the contents to the slow cooker. Add the salt, red chili, the remaining turmeric, and coriander powder. Add the coconut milk, cover, and cook on high for 45 minutes or until the coconut milk starts to simmer.

5. Add the fried fish to the coconut curry and spoon the sauce over the fish. Simmer for another 30 minutes or until the fish is completely heated through. Serve hot.

Lobster in Creamy Sauce (Lobster Ka Korma)

Keep the lobster shell and spoon the dish into the shell for a lovely presentation.

INGREDIENTS | SERVES 4

3 tablespoons unsalted cashew nuts, soaked in water for 10 minutes

2 tablespoons white poppy seeds, soaked in water for 20 minutes

2 tablespoons blanched almonds

2 teaspoons white sesame seeds

Water, as needed

3 tablespoons ghee

1 (1") cinnamon stick

1 black cardamom pod, bruised

1 small bay leaf

2 cloves

1 green cardamoms pod, bruised

1 teaspoon Ginger-Garlic Paste (Chapter 2)

2 serrano green chilies, seeded and minced

½ teaspoon red chili powder

¼ teaspoon turmeric powder

1 cup yogurt, whipped

1½ pounds cooked lobster meat

Salt, to taste

1 teaspoon Garam Masala Powder (Chapter 2)

1. Drain the cashews and poppy seeds and process or blend together with the almonds and sesame seeds using just enough water to make a thick paste. Set aside.

2. In a large skillet, heat the ghee. Add the cinnamon stick, black cardamom pod, bay leaf, cloves, and green cardamom pod. When the spices begin to sizzle, add the Ginger-Garlic Paste, green chilies, and the nut paste. It will splatter a little; add 1 tablespoon of water to stop the splattering. Fry, stirring constantly, until the oil begins to separate from the mixture.

3. In a large bowl, add the red chili, turmeric, yogurt, lobster, salt, and Garam Masala. Transfer to the slow cooker. Cook on high for 45 minutes or until the lobster is heated through and the spices have married well with it. Serve hot.

Tamarind Lime Sauce

This delicious full-bodied dipping sauce takes its inspiration from a Vietnamese sauce. Use this sauce on grilled seafood as well as grilled chicken. The honey in this sauce balances out the tanginess of the tamarind, ginger, and lime juice. In a bowl, combine 1 tablespoon of tamarind concentrate, ¼ cup ice water, 2 teaspoons lemon juice, 2 teaspoons fresh grated ginger, 2 tablespoons honey, and ½ teaspoon salt. Mix well and refrigerate until ready to use.

Macchi Dum Pukht (Slow-Cooked Fish)

Even if you are not a fan of fish, the moment you put this dish in your mouth you will turn into one! Tastes best with Simple Naan (Chapter 15).

INGREDIENTS | SERVES 6

4 fish steaks, scaled and cut into 3" pieces

1 tablespoon turmeric

Salt, to taste

¼ cup oil, preferably mustard oil

1 cup onion paste (grind onion in a food processor)

2 inches gingerroot

3 Thai green chilies

¼ cup blanched almonds, skins off

1 teaspoon Kashmiri lal mirch

1 teaspoon Garam Masala Powder (Chapter 2)

Water, as needed

½ cup yogurt

1. Rub the fish with turmeric and salt. Set aside for 30 minutes. Heat the oil in a pan and pan-fry the fish steaks until they turn golden brown on all sides, about 5–8 minutes. Set aside on a paper towel to drain the excess oil.

2. In your food processor, grind together the onions, gingerroot, chilies, and blanched almonds.

3. In the remaining oil from the fried fish, add the prepared onion, almond, and chili paste. Add salt to the paste. Cook it on the stovetop until all the water is cooked off and the onion starts to separate from the oil, about 10 minutes.

4. Transfer this masala mixture to the slow cooker. Add Kashmiri lal mirch and Garam Masala. Add up to 1½ cups of water. Cover and cook on high for 1 hour, or on low for 2 hours, or until the sauce simmers down to a thicker consistency.

5. Stir in the yogurt and carefully place the fish pieces into the sauce. Cover and cook for another 30 minutes or until the sauce is thickened to a consistency of your liking and the fish flakes with a fork.

6. Once cooked, turn the slow cooker off and let the lid stay in place for 15–20 minutes before serving.

Macher Jhol

Bengali cuisine is less spicy as compared to other Indian regional cuisines like Hyderabadi or Rajasthani. A few whole spices are used, mustard and cumin being dominant.

INGREDIENTS | SERVES 4–5

1 pound fish, cut into 3" pieces

1 teaspoon turmeric powder

1 tablespoon ginger paste (or grated)

¼ cup oil, preferably mustard

1 teaspoon mustard seeds

1 cup minced onion

1½ teaspoons cumin paste (soak cumin in water and then grind to a paste)

¾ cup potatoes, peeled and cut into cubes

1 teaspoon red chili powder

Salt, to taste

Water, as needed

1. Place the fish fillets in a bowl. Rub the fillets well with the turmeric and ginger, and set aside for about 10 minutes.

2. Heat the oil in a skillet. When smoking hot, pan-fry the fish, about 5–8 minutes. Set aside. Leave the remaining oil in the pan.

3. To the oil add the mustard seeds. As they sputter, add the onions. Cook them until they are translucent and begin to turn brown, about 5 minutes. Add the cumin paste. Cook for another 30–40 seconds. Transfer the contents to the slow cooker.

4. Add the rest of the ingredients except for the fried fish. Add up to ¾–1 cup of water. Mix well. Cover and cook on high for 1½ hours, or on low for 3 hours, or until the potatoes are fork tender.

5. Carefully place the fish in the simmering sauce inside the slow cooker. Cover and cook further for 15 minutes on high setting. Serve hot with rice.

Mixed Seafood Dip

Many stores carry frozen mixes of cooked seafood like shrimp, scallops, squid, and clams. Defrost overnight in the refrigerator before using.

INGREDIENTS | SERVES 12

8 ounces Slow Cooker Yogurt (Chapter 3)

½ cup reduced-fat cream cheese

½ cup diced green onion

⅔ cup minced cooked mixed seafood

1 teaspoon dried chopped onion

1 tablespoon minced cilantro

1 tablespoon ghee

½ teaspoon cumin seeds

1. In a medium bowl, stir together all the ingredients *except* the ghee and cumin seeds. Scrape into a 2-quart slow cooker. Cook on low for 1 hour or until heated through.

2. Heat the ghee in a tempering pan. Add the cumin seeds. When they sputter, add them to the slow cooker.

3. Stir before serving.

Little Dipper

Slice a naan into 6 pieces. Brush lightly with olive oil and sprinkle with salt and pepper. Bake at 350°F for 10 minutes or until crisp.

Muri Ghonto

This recipe comes from a dear friend who hails from the state of Bengal where fish is almost a staple. For a vegetarian version, potatoes can be substituted for fish heads. Lentils and vegetables also can be added.

INGREDIENTS | SERVES 5–6

2 medium-size fish heads

1 teaspoon turmeric, plus more for rubbing on the fish heads

Salt, to taste

2 cups parboiled rice

2–3 tablespoons cumin seeds

⅓ cup oil, preferably mustard oil

3–4 dried red chilies

3–4 cloves

2–3 bay leaves

1 stick cinnamon

1½ teaspoons Ginger-Garlic Paste (Chapter 2)

Water, as needed

Muri Ghonto

Muri/muro in Bengali means fish head, and *gonto* is just a medley of ingredients, which in this case is spices with rice and fish.

1. Rub the fish heads with turmeric and salt. Set aside for 30 minutes and then wash under cool running water. Pat dry, set aside.

2. Wash the rice under water. Drain the water; set the rice aside.

3. Soak the cumin seeds in water for 30 minutes. Make a paste with it in a blender or with the help of a mortar and pestle, adding a little water to make the process easier. Set aside.

4. Heat the oil in a pan over medium-high heat. Pan-fry the fish heads until they turn golden brown, about 5–8 minutes. Take the fish heads out and place them on a paper towel to drain the excess oil. Set aside.

5. In the remaining oil in the pan, add all the dry spices. As they sizzle, add the Ginger-Garlic Paste. As the mixture starts to brown, add the rice. Toss everything together, adding salt to taste. Transfer to the slow cooker.

6. Add the fish heads. Add 3½–4 cups of water. Cover and cook on high setting for 3 hours, or on low for 5–6 hours, or until the rice is cooked through.

7. Turn off the heat and let the contents sit in the slow cooker covered for 10 minutes. Fluff with fork. Serve hot.

Parsi Fish (Patrani Macchi)

A perfect recipe when you have lots of leftover chutney and very little time. Serve with plain white rice.

INGREDIENTS | **SERVES 4**

4 (1" thick) fish steaks, your choice of type

¾ teaspoon turmeric powder

8 tablespoons Green Chili and Coconut Chutney (Chapter 2)

1. Place the fish steaks in a bowl. Rub the steaks well with the turmeric and set aside for about 10 minutes. Rinse and pat dry.

2. Cut 4 squares of aluminum foil large enough to accommodate the steaks. Place a steak in the center of each piece of foil. Cover the fish with 2 generous tablespoons of the chutney. Fold the foil over it as if you were wrapping a present. Leave a little room for the steam to expand.

3. Place the foiled fish in the slow cooker, all touching the surface. Cover and cook on low for 2 hours or until the fish is cooked through. The timing will depend on the thickness of your steak. Serve hot.

Prawn Masala (Jhinga Masala)

This is a simple masala fish curry and can be substituted with any fish. Just adjust the cooking time accordingly.

INGREDIENTS | SERVES 4–6

3–4 tablespoons ghee

1 teaspoon black peppercorns

2–3 green cardamom pods, smashed

¾ cup Curry Paste (Chapter 3)

1 (10-ounce) can tomato sauce

Salt, to taste

Water, as needed

1½ pounds tiger prawns

¼ cup chopped cilantro

1. Heat the ghee in a tempering pan. Add the black peppercorns and cardamom. As they sizzle, add the Curry Paste. Transfer the spices to the slow cooker.

2. Add the tomato sauce and salt. Add up to 1 cup of water depending on how thick you want the gravy. Cover and cook on high for 1 hour, or on low for 2½ hours, or until the masala simmers down to a thicker sauce.

3. Add the prawns. Stir well. Cover and continue cooking for another 20–25 minutes or until the shrimp is cooked through.

4. Garnish with cilantro and serve hot with warm Simple Naan (Chapter 15) or over a rice dish.

Salmon in Saffron-Flavored Curry (Zaffrani Macchi)

"The king of the sea marries the queen of spices" is the best way to describe this dish. Serve with Simple Naan (Chapter 15).

INGREDIENTS | SERVES 4

4 tablespoons vegetable oil

1 large onion, finely chopped

1 teaspoon Ginger-Garlic Paste (Chapter 2)

½ teaspoon red chili powder

¼ teaspoon turmeric powder

2 teaspoons coriander powder

Salt, to taste

1 pound salmon, boned and cubed

½ cup plain yogurt, whipped

1 teaspoon Roasted Saffron (Chapter 2)

Saffron

Saffron is one of the most expensive luxury spices, but consider this: it takes 225,000 stigmas, picked from 75,000 violet crocuses during the 2-week fall flowering period, to produce 1 pound of saffron, which costs about $4,500 per pound.

1. In a large nonstick skillet, heat the vegetable oil. Add the onion and sauté for 3–4 minutes or until transparent. Add the Ginger-Garlic Paste and sauté for 1 minute.

2. Add the red chili powder, turmeric, coriander, and salt; mix well. Add the salmon and sauté for 3–4 minutes. Transfer to the slow cooker. Cover and cook on high for 30 minutes.

3. Whisk the yogurt until smooth. Pour it over the fish in the slow cooker. Continue cooking for another 30–45 minutes or until the fish is cooked through.

4. Add the saffron and mix well. Cook for 10 minutes. Serve hot.

Shorshe Maach (Fish Cooked in Hot Mustard Sauce)

My mother belongs to a town located on the borders of Bihar and Bengal, so her recipes are greatly influenced by the Bengali cuisine. This recipe is for one of the dishes that I grew up eating.

INGREDIENTS | SERVES 4–6

¼ cup black mustard seeds (soak in water for 30 minutes)

3–4 whole dried red chilies

2–3 green Thai chili peppers, plus more for the tempering

1½ teaspoons turmeric powder, plus 1 teaspoon

Salt, to taste

3–4 fish steaks (scales removed and cut into 3" pieces)

3–4 tablespoons mustard oil, plus more for deep frying

Water, as needed

Maach in Shorshe?

Shorshe is a Bengali name for black mustard seeds and *maach* means fish. Hot mustard sauce is the base for many of traditional Bengali curries.

1. Grind the soaked mustard seeds, red chilies, and green chili peppers into a grainy paste using a mortar and pestle or a spice grinder. Set aside.

2. Rub a mixture of 1½ teaspoons turmeric and about ½ teaspoon salt on the fish steaks. Set aside for 10–15 minutes.

3. Heat oil in a deep fryer. Deep-fry the fish about 5–8 minutes. Set aside.

4. Heat 3–4 tablespoons mustard oil in a skillet. When smoking hot, add 2–3 green chilies that have been slit. Add 1 teaspoon turmeric, salt, and up to ¾ cup of water. Bring it to a quick boil and transfer the contents to the slow cooker.

5. Place the fried fish in the slow cooker, carefully coating them with the sauce. Now pour the mustard-chili sauce on top, coating all the fish. Add another 1 cup of water. Adjust salt if required. Cover and cook on high for 1 hour, or on low for 2 hours, or until the sauce thickens and the fish flakes.

6. Serve hot over Perfect Slow Cooker Basmati Rice (Chapter 11).

Shrimp in Coconut Milk (Chingri Maacher Malai Curry)

A nice variation is to fry the shrimp first. It adds a nice crispness. Serve with steamed white rice.

INGREDIENTS | SERVES 4

1 bay leaf

1 teaspoon cumin seeds

1 (1") cinnamon stick

2 cloves

4 black peppercorns

2 tablespoons Ginger-Garlic Paste (Chapter 2)

Water, as needed

3 tablespoons vegetable oil

1 large red onion, minced

½ teaspoon turmeric powder

Salt, to taste

1 (14-ounce) can light coconut milk

1 pound shrimp, peeled and deveined

1. In a spice grinder, roughly grind the bay leaf, cumin seeds, cinnamon stick, cloves, and peppercorns. Mix it with Ginger-Garlic Paste. Add a couple teaspoons of water, if needed.

2. In a medium-size skillet, heat the vegetable oil. Add the ground spice mixture and sauté for about 1 minute. Add the onion and sauté for 7–8 minutes or until the onion is well browned.

3. Add the turmeric and salt, and mix well. Transfer the contents to the slow cooker. Add the coconut milk. Stir everything together well. Cover and cook on high for 30–40 minutes, or on low for about 1 hour, or until the sauce starts to simmer.

4. Add the shrimp. Mix well with the sauce. Cover and cook further for 15 more minutes or until the shrimp is cooked through. Prop the lid open on the side ½" to let the steam escape. Serve hot.

Shrimp Patio (Kolmino Patio)

Serve with Perfect Slow Cooker Basmati Rice (Chapter 11).
You can substitute brown sugar for jaggery if you like.

INGREDIENTS | SERVES 4

3 whole dried red chilies

2 teaspoons coriander seeds

1 teaspoon cumin seeds

1 teaspoon mustard seeds

4 fresh garlic cloves

¼ teaspoon black peppercorns

1 (1") cinnamon stick

½ teaspoon turmeric powder

½ teaspoon red chili powder

¼ cup white vinegar

Water, as needed

3 tablespoons vegetable oil

1 large red onion, minced

1½ pounds shrimp, peeled and deveined

1 tablespoon jaggery, or brown sugar

Salt, to taste

Deveining Shrimp

To devein shrimp, run the tip of a small knife down the back of the shrimp. Use the tip of the knife or your finger to pull out the vein. Make sure you rinse all the shrimp after deveining.

1. In a spice grinder, grind together the whole dried red chilies, coriander seeds, cumin seeds, mustard seeds, garlic, black peppercorns, and cinnamon, as finely as possible. Place in a glass bowl and add the turmeric, red chili powder, and vinegar; mix well. If you need more liquid, add a little water. Set aside.

2. In a large skillet, heat the vegetable oil. Add the onion and sauté for about 7–8 minutes or until the onions are well browned. Add the spice paste from Step 1 and cook for 1 minute. Set aside.

3. Add the cleaned shrimp to the slow cooker. Pour in the prepared sauce. Cover and cook on high for 30 minutes. (Shrimp cook better when cooked on high setting).

4. Add the jaggery and salt. Add about ½ cup of water. Cover and continue cooking for up to another 30 minutes or until the shrimp is cooked through.

Steamed Tandoori Machi

This recipe also works great when grilled or baked.
Steamed fish need a smaller proportion of spices though.

INGREDIENTS | SERVES 4

2 tablespoons Tandoori Masala
(Chapter 2)

1 tablespoon Ginger-Garlic Paste
(Chapter 2)

1 tablespoon lemon juice

½ teaspoon sugar

½ teaspoon salt

5–6 fish fillets (any white or oily fish
works well)

1 tablespoon olive oil

1. In a large bowl, mix together all the ingredients *except* the fish and oil.

2. Rub the spice mix on both sides of the fish fillet. Brush the fish with a little oil. Wrap each fillet inside a separate piece of aluminum foil.

3. Line the fish packets inside a slow cooker so that each fillet touches the surface. Cover and cook on low for 1½–2 hours or until the fish flakes with a fork. Serve hot with your choice of raita.

Tamarind Fish Curry (Imli Wale Macchi)

If you do not have tamarind, add a bit of lemon juice for a flavor that is similar. Serve with Perfect Slow Cooker Basmati Rice (Chapter 11).

INGREDIENTS | SERVES 4

1½ pounds whitefish, cut into chunks

¾ teaspoon and ½ teaspoon turmeric powder

2 teaspoons tamarind pulp, soaked in ¼ cup hot water for 10 minutes

3 tablespoons vegetable oil

½ teaspoon black mustard seeds

¼ teaspoon fenugreek seeds

8 fresh curry leaves

1 large onion, minced

2 serrano green chilies, seeded and minced

½ cup tomato sauce

2 dried red chilies, roughly pounded

1 teaspoon coriander seeds, roughly pounded

½ cup unsweetened desiccated coconut

Salt, to taste

1. Place the fish in a bowl. Rub well with the ¾ teaspoon turmeric and set aside for about 10 minutes. Rinse and pat dry.

2. Strain the tamarind and set the liquid aside. Discard the residue.

3. In a large skillet, heat the vegetable oil. Add the mustard seeds and fenugreek seeds. When they begin to sputter, add the curry leaves, onions, and green chilies. Sauté for 7–8 minutes or until the onions are well browned.

4. Add the tomato sauce and cook for another 2 minutes. Add the remaining ½ teaspoon turmeric, the red chilies, coriander seeds, coconut, and salt; mix well, and cook for another 30 seconds. Set aside.

5. Place the fish in the bottom of the slow cooker. Pour tamarind pulp on top followed by the prepared sauce. Adjust salt. Cover and cook on high for 2 hours, or on low for 3½–4 hours, or until the fish flakes with a fork. Serve hot.

CHAPTER 11

Rice

Andhra Vegetable
Pulao
205

Bengali Butter Rice
(Bengali Ghee Bhaat)
206

Carrots and Peas Pulao
206

South Indian Rice and
Vegetable Delight
(Bissi Bela Hulianna)
207

Calcutta (or *Kolkata*)
Biryani
208

Cumin-Scented Rice
(Jeere Wale Chawal)
209

Hyderabadi Biryani
210

Garlic Rice
(Lasuni Pulao)
211

Kabuli Chane
ke Chawal
(Rice with Chickpeas)
212

Kacchi Biryani
213

Khichdi
214

Leelva Nu Bhat
215

Lemon Rice
(Nimbu Wale Chawal)
216

Malabari Coconut Rice
(Thenga Choru)
217

Minty Rice
(Pudine Wale Chawal)
218

Perfect Slow Cooker
Basmati Rice
219

Pork Fried Rice
(Pork Wale Chawal)
220

Rice with Chutney
(Chutney Wale Chawal)
221

Ruz Bukhari
222

Saffron Rice
(Kesari Chawal)
223

Slow Cooker Chicken
Dum Biryani
224

Slow Cooker Upma
225

Spicy Shrimp Rice
(Jhinge Ki Biryani)
226

Spinach and Paneer
Pulao
227

Sprouted Moong
Bean Rice
228

Stuffed Peppers
229

Taheri
(Spicy Vegetable Pulao)
230

Tamarind Rice
(Pulihora)
231

Tomatillo Rice
232

Tomato Rice
(Tamatar Ka Pulao)
233

Turmeric Rice
(Peele Chawal)
234

White Chicken
Rice (Safeed Murgh
Ka Pulao)
235

Yogurt Rice
(Dahi Bhaat)
236

Andhra Vegetable Pulao

This is a slightly different version of Taheri (see recipe in this chapter), with just a few variance in the spices. Again, any vegetable can be used for the recipe.

INGREDIENTS | SERVES 4–6

3 tablespoons ghee, or oil

½ teaspoon cumin seeds

3–4 cloves

3 bay leaves

3 green cardamom pods

1 stick of cinnamon

2 star anise

1 tablespoon Ginger-Garlic Paste (Chapter 2)

1 medium potato (peeled and cubed)

1½ cups mixed vegetables (carrots, French beans, and peas)

1½ cups florets of cauliflower

Salt, to taste

2 cups parboiled rice

1 teaspoon Garam Masala Powder

1 teaspoon coriander powder

6 cups water

½ cup fried onions

¼ cup chopped cilantro

1. Heat the ghee in a pan. Add the cumin, cloves, bay leaves, green cardamom, cinnamon, and star anise. Cook for 30 seconds and the add the Ginger-Garlic Paste. Cook until the mixture turns pale brown in color (about 1–2 minutes). Add the vegetables. Stir and add salt. Cover and cook for 5 minutes.

2. Transfer the contents to the slow cooker. Add rice, Garam Masala, coriander powder, and water. Cover and cook on high for 2½ hours or until the rice is cooked through.

3. When the rice is cooked well, turn off the heat and let stand, covered, for about 5 minutes. Fluff with a fork and garnish with the fried onions and cilantro. Serve hot.

Bengali Butter Rice (Bengali Ghee Bhaat)

Whole spices add an amazing flavor to this aromatic and buttery rice dish. Remove the whole spices before serving.

INGREDIENTS | SERVES 4–6

2 cups parboiled rice
3 tablespoons ghee
2 bay leaves
1 (1") cinnamon stick
3–4 cloves
½ teaspoon black peppercorns
2 green cardamom pods, bruised
3 cups water
Salt, to taste

1. Wash the rice with water. Drain and set aside.

2. In a tempering pan, heat the ghee. Add bay leaves, cinnamon, cloves, peppercorns, and cardamom. When the whole spices begin to sizzle (about 1 minute), turn off the heat; set aside.

3. Add the rice to a 3–4-quart slow cooker. Add the water, salt, and the tempered spices; stir. Cover and cook on high for 2 hours or until the rice is cooked through.

4. Turn off the heat and let the rice stay covered for 5–10 minutes. Fluff with a fork before serving.

Carrots and Peas Pulao

You can vary the recipe by using any vegetables in place of the carrots and peas.

INGREDIENTS | SERVES 4–6

2 cups parboiled rice
2 tablespoons ghee
2–3 bay leaves
1 teaspoon cumin seeds
1 cup frozen peas and carrots mix
Salt, to taste
3½ cups water

1. Rinse the rice with water. Set aside.

2. Heat the ghee in a tempering pan. Add the bay leaves and cumin seeds. As they sputter, stop heating. Set aside.

3. Combine all the ingredients in a slow cooker. Mix. Cover and cook on high setting for 2 hours or until the rice is cooked through.

4. Once the rice is cooked, turn off the heat and let stand, covered, for about 5 minutes. Fluff with a fork before serving.

South Indian Rice and Vegetable Delight
(Bissi Bela Hulianna)

Don't let the long list of ingredients worry you; you can buy the spice mix premade. For example, try MTR's Bisibele Bhath Masala.

INGREDIENTS | SERVES 4

½ cup pigeon peas (toor dal)

1½ cups basmati rice

5 cups water

½ cup cauliflower florets, fresh or frozen

½ cup peas, fresh or frozen

1 tablespoon vegetable oil

1 tablespoon chana dal, or yellow split peas

¾ tablespoon split black gram, or black lentils (urad dal)

1 (1") cinnamon stick

2 cloves

2 teaspoons coriander seeds

½ teaspoon cumin seeds

½ teaspoon black mustard seeds

½ teaspoon fenugreek seeds

2 tablespoons unsweetened desiccated coconut

2 small tomatoes, finely chopped

1 tablespoon tamarind pulp, soaked in ¼ cup water for 10 minutes

½ teaspoon red chili powder

¼ teaspoon turmeric powder

Salt, to taste

Fried cashew nuts, for garnish (optional)

1. Rinse the toor dal 3 or 4 times. Rinse the rice until the water runs clear. Set aside.

2. Transfer the toor dal to a slow cooker. Add 5 cups of water. Cover and cook on high for 1 hour. Add the rice, cauliflower, and peas to the slow cooker. Cover and cook for another 1½ hours or until the rice is cooked.

3. While the rice is cooking, prepare the spice mix (or *masala*). In a medium-size skillet, heat the vegetable oil. Add the chana dal, urad dal, cinnamon, cloves, coriander, cumin, mustard seeds, and fenugreek seeds; sauté for about 1 minute or until the spices release their aroma. Remove from heat and let cool, about 6 minutes. Add the coconut. Using a spice grinder, grind this mixture into a powder. Set aside.

4. When the rice is done cooking, add the tomatoes, tamarind pulp, red chili, turmeric, and salt. Add the reserved spice mix. Stir well. Simmer until the tomatoes are soft, about 15 minutes. You can add more water at this point, if needed. (The consistency of the dish should be like thick porridge.) Serve hot, garnished with fried cashew nuts.

Calcutta (or *Kolkata*) Biryani

Kolkata biryani is a tad less spicier than its brothers and sisters; what makes it different is the use of whole potatoes. This recipe calls for fish, but it can be substituted with any other meat of choice. Adjust the cooking time accordingly.

INGREDIENTS | SERVES 6–7

1 teaspoon turmeric

Salt, to taste

1½ pounds of any oily fish, cut into 6–7 pieces

Oil, for deep-frying

2 cups thinly sliced onion

½ pound baby potatoes, whole with skin on

3 bay leaves

4–5 green cardamom pods

1 teaspoon cumin seeds

1 teaspoon cloves

1½ sticks cinnamon

3 cups basmati rice

2 tablespoons ghee

¾ cup milk

½ teaspoon Roasted Saffron (Chapter 2)

¼ cup chopped cilantro

Origin of Kolkata Biryani

This biryani is said to have originated from the royal family. When in the 1800s Nawab Wajib Ali Shah of Lucknow moved to Kolkata, he brought a recipe for royal biryani with him. It became hugely popular in Kolkata; but because the poor families couldn't afford meat, they started replacing it with potatoes. Slowly, biryani became the quintessential dish called Calcutta Biryani.

1. Liberally rub a mixture of turmeric and salt over the clean fish pieces. Set aside for 30 minutes. Heat the oil in a deep fryer and deep-fry the fish, for about 3–4 minutes. Set aside. Deep-fry the onions until they are golden and crisp, about 3–4 minutes. Set aside.

2. Poke holes in the potatoes with a skewer or fork. Take some leftover oil, about 3 tablespoons, and pan-fry the potatoes for about 5 minutes. Set aside.

3. In the meantime, boil a big pot of salted water with all the whole spices. Add the rice and bring the pot to a rolling boil for a maximum of 5 minutes. Once the rice is half cooked (about 5 minutes), drain out all the water and set the rice aside.

4. Grease the inside walls of a 5-quart slow cooker with the ghee. Add a layer of rice (about ½ of the rice). Layer about 2–3 pieces of fish and potatoes on top of the rice, followed by the browned onion and a sprinkle of milk. Repeat the process until all the ingredients are used and fish forms the top layer. (Save about 2 tablespoons milk.)

5. Mix the Roasted Saffron in the remaining 2 tablespoons milk. Poke holes through the rice and fish layering. Pour the diluted saffron (kesar) through the holes. Cover and cook on low for 3–4 hours or until the rice is cooked through.

6. Carefully mix the biryani with a wide spoon. Garnish with cilantro and serve hot.

Cumin-Scented Rice (Jeere Wale Chawal)

*To reheat the rice, simply sprinkle some water on it, cover loosely,
and heat for a few minutes in the microwave.*

INGREDIENTS | SERVES 4

2 cups basmati rice

3 tablespoons ghee, or vegetable oil

1 small red onion, peeled and thinly sliced

1 teaspoon cumin seeds

2 cloves

Salt, to taste

1 teaspoon fresh lemon juice

3 cups water

Don't Peek!

Curiosity kills the cat! When rice is cooking, covered, resist the urge to open the cover and look inside. The rice needs the steam to cook. Also, allow the rice to rest for a few minutes before you serve it. This will help the grains separate and absorb any leftover water, giving you perfect rice each time.

1. Rinse the rice with water. Drain and set aside.

2. In a deep pan, heat the ghee. Add the onion and sauté for 3–4 minutes or until the onion is soft. Add the cumin seeds, cloves, salt, lemon juice, and rice; mix well.

3. Transfer the contents to a slow cooker. Add the water and stir. Cover and cook on high for 1½ hours or until the rice is cooked through.

4. Once the rice is cooked, turn off the heat and let stand, covered, for about 10 minutes. Fluff with a fork before serving. Serve hot.

Hyderabadi Biryani

When people hear the name biryani, *Hyderabadi Biryani is what pops into every mind at first. It is one of the most popular and widely accepted varieties of biryani. It has the perfect blend of rich Mughlai cuisine and spicy Andhra Pradesh cuisine.*

INGREDIENTS | SERVES 6–7

4 cups basmati rice

2 pounds mutton

½ cup yogurt

1 teaspoon Kashmiri lal mirch (for color)

1 teaspoon red chili powder

1½ teaspoons Garam Masala Powder (Chapter 2)

Juice of 1 lemon

Salt, to taste

2 sticks of cinnamon

3–4 bay leaves

½ cup ghee, or oil

½ teaspoon turmeric powder

1 teaspoon cloves

3–4 black cardamom pods

1 teaspoon black peppercorns

3–4 whole dried red chilies

2 cups thinly sliced onion

½ teaspoon Roasted Saffron (Chapter 2)

3 tablespoons slivered almonds

3 tablespoons cashews

¼ cup golden raisins

¼ cup chopped cilantro

Kashmiri Lal Mirch

This is a variety of red chili pepper that comes from the beautiful state of Kashmir in India. This chili is widely used to add natural red color to the dishes. It has a smoky flavor to it but is not very hot.

1. Rinse rice with water; set aside. Thoroughly clean the meat under running water. Set aside.

2. In a mixing bowl, whisk in the yogurt, Kashmiri lal mirch, red chili powder, Garam Masala, lemon juice, and ½ teaspoon salt. Make a smooth paste. Mix the mutton well into the marinade and marinate for at least 1–2 hours.

3. In the meantime, heat a big pot of salted water. Add the cinnamon and bay leaves to it. Bring the rice to a rolling boil in this water. As the rice is cooked halfway through (no more than 5–8 minutes), drain the excess water and spread the rice on a wide dish, uncovered.

4. Now heat the ghee or oil in a heavy-bottom pan (saving 1 tablespoon of ghee for later). Add the dry spices. As they sizzle and give out a nice aroma, add the onion. Fry the onion until it turns light golden in color, about 7–10 minutes.

5. Add the meat and cook uncovered for 10 minutes. Add salt to taste; mix well. Cover and cook for another 10–15 minutes or until the mutton is cooked through.

6. Oil the inner surface of the slow cooker. Transfer ¼ of the meat to the slow cooker forming the bottom layer. Add half the rice forming a thick layer on top of the meat. Repeat the process, until all the meat and rice are used. Using your palm or the back of a small dish, press the layers downward packing them tightly.

7. Dissolve the saffron in ⅓ cup of warm water. Make 3–4 holes through the layering of meat and rice. Pour the dissolved saffron equally through the holes. Cover and

Hyderabadi Biryani

(continued)

cook on low for 3–4 hours or until the rice is cooked through. Halfway through the cooking process, sprinkle some water or milk on top to prevent the top layer from drying out.

8. Heat the rest of the ghee in a frying pan. Pan-fry the nuts and raisins. Set aside. When the biryani is ready, transfer it into a serving tray; sprinkle with the cilantro, roasted nuts, and raisins. Serve hot with your choice of raita.

Garlic Rice (Lasuni Pulao)

This dish is a garlic lover's delight. It is best if served immediately. Garnish with fried onions.

INGREDIENTS | SERVES 4–5

2 cups parboiled rice

3 tablespoons vegetable oil

6 fresh garlic cloves, peeled and crushed

1 serrano green chili, seeded and minced

½ cup plain yogurt, whipped

Salt, to taste

1 teaspoon Garam Masala Powder (Chapter 2)

3 cups water

1 tablespoon minced cilantro

Stronger Garlic Taste

If you want a stronger garlic taste, use a garlic press to crush the garlic. If you don't have a press, use the flat side of a large kitchen knife and press it firmly on top of the garlic. This will give you more flavor from the garlic than you will get from simply chopping it.

1. Rinse the rice with water. Drain and set aside.

2. In a deep pan, heat the vegetable oil. Add the garlic and green chili; sauté for about 20 seconds or until the garlic turns light brown.

3. Add the yogurt, salt, and Garam Masala; sauté for 1 minute. Add the rice and mix well.

4. Transfer the contents to a slow cooker. Add the water and stir. Cover and cook the rice on high for 2 hours or until the rice is cooked through.

5. Once the rice is cooked, turn off the heat and let stand, covered, for about 5 minutes. Fluff with a fork before serving and garnish with cilantro.

Kabuli Chane ke Chawal (Rice with Chickpeas)

Canned chickpeas work best for this recipe. If you like, you can also substitute canned chickpeas with the equal quantity of Chole Masala (Chapter 7).

INGREDIENTS | SERVES 4–6

1 recipe Perfect Slow Cooker Basmati Rice (Chapter 11)

1 (14-ounce) can chickpeas

1 (10-ounce) can diced tomatoes

3–4 tablespoons oil, or ghee

1 teaspoon black mustard seeds

10–12 curry leaves

1½ teaspoons minced green chili

½ cup chopped onion

Salt, to taste

¼ cup chopped cilantro

Leftover Rice

Any leftover rice can be spiced up by frying it with a few tempered spices, a couple diced vegetables or leftover meat, or just some citrus juice, such as lemon or tangy orange juice.

1. If using leftover rice, take it out of the refrigerator and let it sit on the counter for 10–15 minutes before using. Drain the liquid from the canned chickpeas and tomatoes. Set aside.

2. Heat the oil in a large pan over medium heat. Add the mustard seeds and curry leaves. As they sputter, add the green chili and onion. Sauté for 2–3 minutes. Add the tomatoes and salt. Cover and cook on medium high for 2 minutes. Add the chickpeas. Cover and cook for another 5 minutes.

3. Add Perfect Slow Cooker Basmati Rice. Toss everything together, mixing well and heating the rice in the process. Garnish with cilantro and serve hot.

Kacchi Biryani

This dish is called kacchi biryani because the meat used in this recipe is raw (kacchi in Hindi), unlike other biryani dishes where it's cooked halfway through before putting it into dum (slow cooking) dishes.

INGREDIENTS | SERVES 4–6

1½ pounds boneless, skinless chicken

¾ cup yogurt

2½ tablespoons Garam Masala Powder (Chapter 2)

2 teaspoons salt

2–3 Thai green chilies, slit

2 tablespoons ginger-garlic paste

4–5 tablespoons oil, or ghee

3 cups basmati rice

½ teaspoon cloves

4–5 black cardamom pods

2–3 star anise

1½ sticks of cinnamon

3–4 bay leaves

1 tablespoon cumin seeds

1 cup sliced fried red onion

1 cup chopped cilantro

¼ cup water

Marinating the Meat

You do not necessarily need the meat to marinate in a slow cooker recipe, but in this case, marinating it overnight brings out the best flavors.

1. Clean the meat and cut it into 1½" cubes. Add the yogurt, 1 tablespoon Garam Masala, ½ teaspoon salt, chilies, Ginger-Garlic Paste and 1 tablespoon ghee in a mixing bowl. Rub the mixture onto the chicken well. Marinate overnight or for 6–8 hours.

2. Bring a large pot of water to boil. Add 1½ teaspoons salt and the rice. Cook the rice for 7–8 minutes or until it's half cooked. Drain out the water and save the rice uncovered.

3. Heat the remaining ghee in a tempering pan. Add all the whole spices. As they splutter, turn off the heat. Set aside.

4. Now take the chicken out of the refrigerator. Carefully spoon out all the fried whole spices from the ghee. Mix the spices with the chicken. Transfer the contents to the slow cooker, forming the bottom layer.

5. Make another layer of rice on top of the chicken using about half of the rice. Follow with a layer of fried onion, cilantro, and a sprinkle of Garam Masala. Repeat the process. Using your palm or the back of a small pan, press the layers downward making them tight. This helps to trap the steam.

6. Now use the back of a wooden spoon and make 3 holes running through all the layers. Pour the saved ghee equally into the holes. Sprinkle ¼ cup water on the top.

7. Cover and cook on high for 1½ hours. Then reduce the heat to low and continue cooking for 3–4 hours or until the rice is cooked through. Serve hot with your favorite raita and Punjabi Lassi (Chapter 14) on the side.

Khichdi

There is no right or wrong when it comes to khichdi. You can add your choice of lentils, your choice of rice, and a lot of water. You just can never go wrong with a khichdi!

INGREDIENTS | SERVES 4–6

1 cup basmati rice
1 cup moong dal
½ teaspoon turmeric
Salt, to taste
Water, as needed
2 tablespoons ghee, or oil
¼ teaspoon asafetida
1 teaspoon cumin seeds
½ teaspoon cayenne pepper

Sankranti

Sankranti is a festival celebrated all across the country (this festival has other names, as well). The day is celebrated as a harvest festival and khichdi is the main dish prepared, which is then shared with family and friends.

1. Rinse the rice. Drain and set aside. Repeat the same with the moong dal.

2. Mix the rinsed rice and dal into a slow cooker. Add the turmeric and salt. Add at least 4–5 cups water. If it looks like you've added too much water, it's okay; it will just increase the cooking time. Cover and cook on high for 2½–3 hours, or on low for 5–6 hours, or until the rice and dal are cooked through. It's okay if they turn mushy.

3. Heat the oil in a tempering pan. Add the asafetida followed by cumin seeds. As they sputter, add the cayenne pepper and turn off the heat immediately. Stir in this *tadka* to the cooked khichdi in the slow cooker.

4. Once cooked, the khichdi should have the consistency of a thin porridge with mushy rice and dal. Add extra boiling water to thin it out if needed. Adjust salt accordingly. Serve hot with a dollop of Ghee (Chapter 3), a raita (see Chapter 13 for several recipes), and poppadum or pickle on the side.

Leelva Nu Bhat

Leelva is a gujrati name for broad beans, and bhat in the same language means "cooked rice". This dish hails from the western state of Gujrat.

INGREDIENTS | SERVES 4–6

2 cups parboiled rice

1 cup leelva (broad bean seeds)

3 tablespoons oil

⅛ teaspoon asafetida

½ teaspoon mustard seeds

2 green chilies, minced

½ tablespoon Chili-Garlic Paste (Chapter 2)

1½ teaspoons thinly sliced ginger

½ teaspoon turmeric

Salt, to taste

4 cups water

1. Rinse the rice with water. Strain and set aside. Soak the leelva in water for 2 hours.

2. Heat the oil in a pan over medium heat. Add the asafetida, mustard seeds, and green chilies. As they sputter, add the Chili-Garlic Paste and ginger. Fry for 30 seconds. Add the turmeric and mix well. Add the rice and mix with the spices. Add the leelva and mix.

3. Transfer the contents to a slow cooker. Add salt and 4 cups of water. Cover and cook on high for 2½ hours or until the rice and leelva are cooked through.

4. Once the rice is cooked, turn off the heat and let stand, covered, for about 5 minutes. Fluff with a fork before serving.

Lemon Rice (Nimbu Wale Chawal)

This is a great way to perk up leftover rice. Enjoy a Spiced Buttermilk (Chapter 14) drink alongside.

INGREDIENTS | SERVES 4–5

1 recipe Perfect Slow Cooker Basmati Rice (see recipe in this chapter)

3 tablespoons ghee, or vegetable oil

1 teaspoon black mustard seeds

8–10 fresh curry leaves

3 dried red chilies, broken

¼ cup unsalted peanuts

Salt, to taste

1 teaspoon turmeric powder

¼ cup fresh lemon juice

Fresh grated coconut, for garnish

1. If you are using Perfect Slow Cooker Basmati Rice that has been prepared earlier and refrigerated, warm it for a few minutes before proceeding.

2. In a large skillet, heat the ghee. Add the mustard seeds. When they begin to sputter, add in quick succession the curry leaves, red chilies, and peanuts. Sauté for 1 minute. Add the salt and turmeric; mix well.

3. Add the lemon juice. It will splatter a bit, so do this carefully. Add the rice; sauté for 1 minute, mixing well to evenly coat the rice with the spice mix. Serve hot, garnished with fresh grated coconut.

Rice and the Hindu Religion

In India, rice has a special religious significance. It is considered a symbol of fertility and prosperity. Hindu weddings use rice for many rituals. When a new bride enters her husband's home for the first time, she gently taps with her foot a small urn, containing rice, over the threshold. This signifies that the new bride will bring wealth and prosperity to the family.

Malabari Coconut Rice (Thenga Choru)

This recipe comes to you from the shores of southwestern India.
Traditionally it is served with hot, spicy curries.

INGREDIENTS | SERVES 4

2 cups parboiled rice

3 tablespoons vegetable oil

1 teaspoon black mustard seeds

2 dried red chilies, broken

1" piece fresh gingerroot, julienned

4 garlic cloves, minced

½ teaspoon turmeric powder

Salt, to taste

½ cup unsweetened desiccated coconut

½ cup light coconut milk

3 cups water

1. Rinse the rice with water. Drain and set aside.

2. In a deep pan, heat the vegetable oil. Add the mustard seeds. When they begin to sputter, add the red chilies, gingerroot, and garlic; sauté for about 30 seconds.

3. Add the turmeric, salt, and coconut. Mix well and sauté for 1 minute. Add the rice and mix well; sauté for 1 minute.

4. Transfer the contents to a slow cooker. Add the coconut milk and the water; stir. Cover and cook on high for 2½ hours or until the rice is cooked.

5. Once the rice is cooked, turn off the heat and let stand, covered, for about 5 minutes. Fluff with a fork before serving.

Minty Rice (Pudine Wale Chawal)

A vibrant and refreshing dish. You can garnish this dish with fresh grated coconut.

INGREDIENTS | SERVES 4

1 cup parboiled rice

2 tablespoons vegetable oil

2 serrano green chilies, seeded and minced

1 small red onion, peeled and finely chopped

Salt, to taste

¼ cup minced mint

½ cup plain yogurt, whipped

1½ cups water

Tips

This recipe works well in a small 3-quart slow cooker, but you can increase the quantity for a bigger slow cooker.

1. Rinse the rice with water. Drain and set aside.

2. In a deep pan over medium heat, heat the vegetable oil. Add the green chilies and onion; sauté for 3–5 minutes or until the onion is soft.

3. Add the salt and the mint; sauté for 1 minute.

4. Add the rice and mix well; sauté for about 2 minutes.

5. Transfer the contents to the slow cooker. Add the yogurt and water and stir. Cover and cook on high for approximately 1½ hours.

6. Once the rice is cooked, use a fork to fluff the rice. Serve hot with your favorite choice of curry, or just the mint rice on its own is very good.

Perfect Slow Cooker Basmati Rice

Cooking basmati rice can get a little tricky in a slow cooker, but a couple small tips and practice can take you a long way. The first trick is not to go overboard with water since very little evaporates. Second, and most important, add some grease to prevent sticking.

INGREDIENTS | SERVES 4–6

2 cups long-grain white basmati rice

3 cups water

1½ tablespoons ghee

Salt, if needed

Adding Grease

Adding some kind of grease or oil or butter or ghee can serve two purposes: first, it keeps the rice from sticking to the sides and, second, it helps keep the grains fluffy.

1. Rinse the rice with water. Immediately put it in the slow cooker, do not let it soak in water for long as it will turn mushy.

2. Add the water, ghee, and salt, if needed. Cover and cook on high for 1½ hours. Turn off the heat; check to see if the rice is cooked to your liking. If not, replace the lid and let the steam complete the rest of the cooking. Fluff the rice with a fork after 20 minutes. Serve hot with your favorite lentil soup or curry.

Pork Fried Rice (Pork Wale Chawal)

Substitute your choice of meat for this flavorful stir-fry.

INGREDIENTS | SERVES 4–5

½ recipe Perfect Slow Cooker Basmati Rice (see recipe in this chapter) or Brown Basmati Rice (Chapter 3)

2 tablespoons soya sauce

1 tablespoon white vinegar

1 teaspoon cornstarch

3 tablespoons vegetable oil

2 green onions (white and light green part only), finely chopped

1" piece fresh gingerroot, peeled and julienned

2 garlic cloves, minced

1 dried red chili, whole

¼ pound boneless pork, cut into ½" cubes

Another Indian Chinese Favorite

Visit any Indian Chinese restaurant in India and you will be served a hot green chili sauce along with your meal. This green chili vinegar sauce adds a wonderful zing to any Chinese dish; it is generally sprinkled over a dish before it is served. Here is how to prepare about ¼ cup of this sauce: In a deep pan, combine 4 minced green chilies, ¼ cup vinegar, and a pinch each of salt and sugar. Simmer on low heat for 3 minutes. Chill and serve.

1. The cooked rice needs to be cold. If you prepare it fresh for this recipe, refrigerate it for at least 2 hours prior to using it here.

2. In a small bowl, combine the soya sauce, vinegar, and cornstarch; set aside.

3. In a large nonstick skillet, heat the vegetable oil on high. Add the green onions, gingerroot, and garlic; sauté for 1 minute.

4. Add the red chili and the pork; sauté for 7–8 minutes or until the pork is cooked.

5. Give the soya sauce mixture a quick stir to recombine it, and add it to the pan. Add the cold rice and mix well. Sauté for about 2–3 minutes or until the rice has completely heated through. Serve hot.

Rice with Chutney (Chutney Wale Chawal)

You can substitute Green Chili and Coconut Chutney (Chapter 2)
for the Mint-Cilantro Chutney in this dish if you like.

INGREDIENTS | SERVES 4–6

1½ cups parboiled rice

3 tablespoons vegetable oil

1 teaspoon sesame seeds

2 serrano green chilies, seeded and minced

1 small red onion, peeled and finely chopped

Salt, to taste

½ cup Mint-Cilantro Chutney (Chapter 2)

½ cup plain yogurt, whipped

2½ cups water

Brown Rice

You can substitute brown basmati rice, if you like, for a healthier version. Follow the Brown Basmati Rice instructions explained in Chapter 3 to slow-cook a perfect brown basmati rice.

1. Rinse the rice. Drain and set aside.

2. In a deep pan, heat the vegetable oil. Add the sesame seeds, green chilies, and onion; sauté for 3–5 minutes or until the onions are soft.

3. Add the salt and the chutney; sauté for 1 minute. Add the yogurt, mix well, and cook for about 2 minutes.

4. Add the rice and mix well. Sauté for 2 minutes.

5. Transfer the contents to the slow cooker. Add the water and stir. Cover and cook on high for 2 hours or until the rice is cooked through.

6. Once the rice is cooked, turn off the heat and let stand, covered, for about 5 minutes. Fluff with a fork before serving.

Ruz Bukhari

This barely spiced form of biryani has some really strong flavors from the meat and vegetables.
It is traditionally made with goat meat, but this recipe is a variation using lamb.

INGREDIENTS | SERVES 6–8

3 cups sela basmati rice

1½ pounds lamb with bones, cut into medium-size chunks

¼ cup oil

3 cups thinly sliced onions

6 cups water

Salt, to taste

2 cups thinly slivered carrots

¼ cup golden raisins, soaked for 15 minutes

3½ tablespoons tomato purée

Sela Basmati Rice

Sela basmati is a variety of basmati rice that is milled just a little differently, giving it a slightly yellow color. It is perfect for slow-cooked rice dishes like biryani or pulao. You can find it in any Pakistani or Middle Eastern store.

1. Thoroughly wash the rice and soak it in water for 1–2 hours. Meanwhile, wash the meat thoroughly with water, squeeze out all the excess water, and let it set out in the air to dry or in the refrigerator overnight.

2. Heat the oil in a large thick-bottomed pot. When the oil is hot, add the lamb and stir well until the lamb doesn't stick to the bottom. The meat will start oozing liquid; keep cooking until all the liquid dries out, about 15–20 minutes.

3. Add the onion. Cook until the onion turns translucent. Add the water and salt to the pot. Cook till the meat is almost done but not all the way through, about 30 minutes.

4. Drain out all the water in which the rice is soaked.

5. In a 5–6-quart slow cooker, arrange a thin layer of rice. Then arrange all the meat on top of the layer of rice, followed by the carrots and then a layer of raisins. Top it all off with the remaining rice.

6. Pour the remaining broth from the meat over the layers in the slow cooker. Cover and cook for 1 hour on high.

7. Once the water starts bubbling, add the tomato purée; gently stir it in the water above the rice to mix thoroughly.

8. Cover and cook on high for 2 hours or on low for 4 hours. Keep checking, and if you feel that the rice is not cooked and the water is almost dried out, add a little more water. The finished dish should have rice with each grain separate and a slight orange color from the tomato purée. The dish is typically served with a simple salad or Dahi Kachumbar (Chapter 13).

Saffron Rice (Kesari Chawal)

This rice dish can be served alongside any spicy chicken or meat curry.

INGREDIENTS | SERVES 4

2 cups basmati rice
4 tablespoons ghee
3 green cardamom pods, bruised
4–5 cloves
1 cinnamon stick
2 black cardamom seeds, bruised
¼ cup golden raisins
¼ cup blanched almonds
Salt, to taste
3 tablespoons sugar
1 teaspoon Roasted Saffron (Chapter 2)
3 cups water

Bruising or Pounding Spices

To bruise whole spices, use a mortar and pestle, or put the spices in a plastic bag and pound them lightly with a rolling pin. Lightly bruising a spice is an age-old technique in Indian cooking. It helps to release its aroma and flavor into the dish.

1. Rinse the rice with water. Drain and set aside.

2. In a deep pan, heat the ghee over medium heat. Add the green cardamom pods, cloves, cinnamon stick, and black cardamom seeds. Cook for about 1–2 minutes.

3. Add the raisins, almonds, and salt. Stir for 1 minute. Add the rice and sauté for about 2 minutes. Add the sugar and the Roasted Saffron; mix well.

4. Transfer the contents to a slow cooker. Add 3 cups of water. Cover and cook on high for 1½ hours or until the rice is cooked through.

5. Turn off the heat. Let stand, covered, for about 5–6 minutes. Serve hot. Fluff with a fork before serving.

Slow Cooker Chicken Dum Biryani

There are countless ways you can cook biryani, but at its core biryani is just rice slow cooked with spices and meat or vegetables of choice.

INGREDIENTS | SERVES 6

3 cups basmati rice

2½ pounds chicken, cut into medium-size pieces

1 cup Slow Cooker Yogurt (Chapter 3)

½ teaspoon turmeric powder

2 tablespoons Ginger-Garlic Paste (Chapter 2)

1 teaspoon Kashmiri lal mirch, or cayenne pepper

Salt, to taste

3 tablespoons lemon juice

½ teaspoon cloves

4–5 green cardamom pods

3–4 bay leaves

¼ cup ghee, or oil

½ cup Curry Paste (Chapter 3)

2 cups sliced red onion

3 tablespoons coriander powder

1 tablespoon garam masala

Water, as needed

Dum Pukht

Dum pukht is one of the oldest and refined cooking practices in India. The food is slow-cooked by trapping the steam inside the cooking vessel and letting the steam do the cooking over a long period.

1. Wash the rice with water. Drain the excess water. Set aside. Clean the chicken 3 or 4 times with water. Set aside.

2. In a mixing bowl, mix together the Yogurt, turmeric, Ginger-Garlic Paste, Kashmiri lal mirch, ½ teaspoon salt, and lemon juice. Add the chicken; mix well. Cover with plastic wrap. Let it marinate for 6–8 hours or overnight.

3. Boil a big pot of water. Add 2–3 tablespoons salt and the whole spices into the water. Add the rice and bring to a rolling boil. Turn off the heat in about 5–7 minutes or once the rice is half cooked. Drain out the water and spread the rice on a flat dish. Do not cover the hot rice or steam might cook the rice more than necessary.

4. Heat the ghee or oil in a pan over medium-high heat. Stir in the Curry Paste. As it sizzles, add the onion. Cook until the onion is translucent. Add the coriander powder and Garam Masala. Mix well. Add the chicken. Cook for 5–7 minutes. Oil the inner surface of the slow cooker. Transfer half the chicken to the slow cooker forming the bottom layer. Add half the rice, forming a thick layer on top of the chicken. Repeat the process. Using your palm or the back of a small dish, press the layers downward packing them tightly.

5. Make 3–4 holes running through the layers. Pour 2–3 tablespoons of water over the ingredients in the slow cooker. Cover and cook on low for 4–5 hours. During the middle of the cooking process stir the biryani delicately, turning it from top to bottom using a wide spoon.

6. Once cooked, turn off the heat and let stand, covered, for about 5–10 minutes. Fluff with a fork before serving.

Slow Cooker Upma

This is a healthy, light, and refreshing breakfast dish. This is the basic recipe for upma, but you can add vegetables of your choice.

INGREDIENTS | SERVES 4–5

2½ tablespoons oil

1 teaspoon mustard seeds

½ tablespoon split urad dal (black lentils with no skin on)

2–3 whole dry red chilies

8–10 curry leaves

¼ cup finely chopped red onion

1 tablespoon sugar

2 cups semolina or Cream of Wheat

½ cup yogurt

Salt, to taste

Water, as needed

2–3 tablespoons lemon juice

1. Heat the oil in a pan. Add the mustard seeds, urad dal, red chilies, and curry leaves one after the other. As they sizzle, add the onion and fry it until it is browned. Stir in the sugar. Add the semolina.

2. Pan roast the semolina until it turns slightly golden in color and gives out a beautiful aroma, about 5–8 minutes.

3. In the meantime, whisk the yogurt smooth and set aside.

4. Heat about 3–4 cups of salted water, salty enough for your taste.

5. Once semolina is roasted, transfer it to the slow cooker. Stir in the yogurt. Add enough water to soak the semolina, approximately 3 cups. Cover and cook on high for 45 minutes or until all the water is absorbed in the slow cooker.

6. If the water in the slow cooker is gone and the semolina is not yet cooked through, add more water. Keep adding until the semolina is cooked.

7. Squeeze in a little lemon juice on top of your upma. Serve hot.

Spicy Shrimp Rice (Jhinge Ki Biryani)

Try this recipe with the seafood of your choice.
Garnish with minced cilantro. Serve this along with a shredded carrot salad.

INGREDIENTS | SERVES 4

1½ cups basmati rice
4 tablespoons vegetable oil
1 teaspoon black mustard seeds
4 fresh curry leaves
1 pound shrimp, peeled and deveined
2 tablespoons unsweetened desiccated coconut
1 teaspoon red chili powder
½ teaspoon turmeric powder
Salt, to taste
2 cups water

Did You Say Prawns?

Most Indians refer to shrimp as prawns. Indian prawns are much bigger than the shrimp found in the United States; some are as long as the palm of your hand. Use large shrimp for most of the recipes in this book, unless otherwise indicated.

1. Rinse the rice with water. Drain and set aside.

2. In a deep pan, heat the vegetable oil. Add the black mustard seeds. When they begin to sputter, add the curry leaves and shrimp; sauté for about 2–3 minutes.

3. Add the coconut, red chili, turmeric, and salt; cook for about 2 minutes.

4. Transfer all the contents in the pan to the slow cooker. Add the rice and mix well.

5. Add the water and stir. Cover and cook on high for 1½ hours.

6. Fluff with a fork before serving. Pair with your favorite raita or chutney.

Spinach and Paneer Pulao

This recipe was adapted from one of my favorite chef's recipes for Paneer Pulao.

INGREDIENTS | SERVES 4–6

1 recipe Brown Basmati Rice (Chapter 3)

1 tablespoon cooking oil

3 tablespoons ghee

1 cup cubed Homemade Paneer (Chapter 2)

2–3 cloves

½ teaspoon black peppercorns

½ teaspoon cumin seeds

3 cups chopped baby spinach

Salt, to taste

1. If using leftover Brown Basmati Rice, then pull it out of the refrigerator at least 15–20 minutes before starting to cook.

2. Heat the cooking oil along with 1 tablespoon ghee in a pan. Add the paneer cubes. Pan-fry the paneer, lightly browning it on all the sides. Take them out and set aside.

3. Add the rest of the ghee to the pan. Add the dry spices. As the spices crackle, add the spinach. Sauté for 2–3 minutes and then add the rice, fried paneer, and salt. Toss everything together well and serve hot with Cucumber Raita (Chapter 13) and hot Masala Chai (Chapter 14).

Sprouted Moong Bean Rice

You can replace moong bean sprouts with any bean sprout.
Even Bengal gram sprouts work very well with this dish.

INGREDIENTS | SERVES 4–6

2 tablespoons ghee
½ teaspoon mustard seeds
2–3 dried whole red chilies
¼ teaspoon turmeric
8–10 curry leaves
1½ cups moong bean sprouts
Salt, to taste
1 recipe Brown Basmati Rice (Chapter 3)
2–3 tablespoons lemon juice

1. Heat the ghee in a large pan on the stovetop. Add the mustard seeds, chilies, and turmeric. As they sputter, add the curry leaves. Stir in the moong bean sprouts. Stir-fry for 1 minute. Add salt; mix.

2. Add the Brown Basmati Rice. Stir well, mixing everything together. Turn off the heat. Stir in the lemon juice and serve hot.

Moong Bean and Brown Rice

Both moong bean sprouts and brown rice are very good sources of dietary fiber and have excellent nutritional value. So make sure you add them to your diet if you are watching that waist!

Stuffed Peppers

Try a mixture of green, red, orange, and yellow peppers for this dish.

INGREDIENTS | SERVES 4

4 large bell peppers

½ teaspoon red chili powder

½ teaspoon Garam Masala Powder (Chapter 2)

¼ teaspoon freshly ground black pepper

1/8 teaspoon salt

1 (15-ounce) can fire-roasted diced tomatoes with garlic

1 cup cooked Perfect Slow Cooker Basmati Rice (see recipe in this chapter)

1½ cups broccoli florets

¼ cup diced onion

½ cup water

1. Cut the tops off of each pepper to form a cap. Remove the seeds from the cap. Remove the seeds and most of the ribs inside the pepper. Place the peppers open-side up in a 4- or 6-quart slow cooker.

2. In a medium bowl, mix together the spices, tomatoes, rice, broccoli, and onion. Spoon the mixture into each pepper until they are filled to the top. Replace the cap. Pour the water into the bottom of the slow cooker.

3. Cook on low for 6 hours.

Taheri (Spicy Vegetable Pulao)

Taheri is typically a name given to vegetable biryani. You can use practically any vegetable for this recipe, and the same with spices. Both whole and ground spices work well. The spicier the better!

INGREDIENTS | SERVES 6

3–4 tablespoon ghee, or oil

½ cup soy chunks, soaked in warm water for 30 minutes

½ teaspoon cloves

3–4 green cardamom pods

2 bay leaves

½ cup curry paste

Salt, to taste

1 cup cauliflower florets

1 medium potato, cubed

¾ cup frozen carrots and peas mix

1½ cups parboiled rice

4–4½ cups water

3–4 tablespoons chopped cilantro

¼ cup mixed cashews and raisins, pan-roasted or pan-fried

1. Heat 1 tablespoon of the ghee in a pan. Squeeze out water from the soy chunks and pan-fry them for 4–5 minutes. Set aside.

2. Add the rest of the ghee or oil to the pan. Add the whole spices. As they sizzle, add the Curry Paste. Add salt. Mix together. Add the vegetables; stir everything together. Cover and cook on medium high for 5 minutes.

3. Rinse the rice with water. Drain and transfer the rice to the slow cooker. Add the rest of the ingredients to the slow cooker *except* for the cilantro, cashews, and raisins. Cover and cook on high for 2½–3 hours or until the rice is cooked well.

4. Once the rice is cooked, turn off the heat and let stand, covered, for about 5 minutes. Fluff with a fork and sprinkle with cilantro and fried cashews and raisins before serving.

Tamarind Rice (Pulihora)

This is a simpler version of a classic southern Indian dish.
Serve with Dahi Kachumbar (Chapter 13) or a simple salad for a complete meal.

INGREDIENTS | SERVES 4–5

1 recipe Perfect Slow Cooker Basmati Rice (see recipe in this chapter)

3 tablespoons vegetable oil

4 fresh curry leaves

½ teaspoon black mustard seeds

2 dried red chilies, broken

¼ cup salted roasted peanuts

1 cup Tamarind Chutney (Chapter 13)

In a Pinch?

If you are pressed for time, you can buy tamarind chutney from your local Indian grocer instead of making your own. Store-brand chutneys are quite delightful, although I would still recommend you make it fresh when you can.

1. If you are using leftover rice, warm it first in the microwave or on the stovetop. Layer the rice on a serving platter. Set aside.

2. In a medium-size skillet, heat the vegetable oil. Add the curry leaves and mustard seeds. When the mustard seeds begin to sputter, add the red chilies and peanuts; sauté for about 30 seconds.

3. Add the Tarmarind Chutney. Lower the heat and simmer for about 5 minutes or until the chutney is completely heated through.

4. Spoon the chutney mixture over the rice. Just before serving, mix together the rice and chutney.

Tomatillo Rice

*Many people do not know that tomatillos, or sour raw tomatoes,
are widely used in Indian cuisine to make sauces, or stir-fried with spices and rice.*

INGREDIENTS | SERVES 4

2 tablespoons olive oil

½ red onion, diced

½ red bell pepper, diced

2 cloves garlic, minced

Juice of 1 lime

1 cup finely chopped tomatillo

1 teaspoon minced Thai green chili

1 cup water

1 teaspoon salt

1 cup long-grain white rice

½ cup cilantro, chopped

1. Heat the olive oil in a sauté pan over medium heat. Add the onion, bell pepper, and garlic, and sauté for about 5 minutes; then transfer the mixture to a 4-quart slow cooker.

2. Add all the remaining ingredients *except* for the cilantro. Cover and cook on low for 6–8 hours. Check the rice periodically to make sure the liquid hasn't been absorbed too quickly and the rice isn't burning.

3. Stir in the cilantro before serving.

Tomatillos

Tomatillos are small green tomatoes that are used in many Latin and Southeast Asian–inspired dishes. They come with a papery husk that surrounds the edible fruit, which first must be removed.

Tomato Rice (Tamatar Ka Pulao)

This lovely red-hued rice has a mild, delicious flavor. You can serve it with a raita of your choice or Hot Cilantro Chutney (Chapter 2) or Mint-Cilantro Chutney (Chapter 2).

INGREDIENTS | SERVES 4

1½ cups parboiled rice

3 medium tomatoes

3 tablespoons vegetable oil

1 small red onion, roughly chopped

1" piece gingerroot, peeled and julienned

1½ teaspoons Garam Masala Powder (Chapter 2)

Salt, to taste

2½ cups water

Minced cilantro, for garnish

Soaking Rice

To reduce the cooking time, soak rice in cold water for about 10 minutes before cooking. Keep in mind that you should use less water to cook soaked rice than you would for dry rice. The water-to-rice ratio for soaked rice is 1½ cups of water to 1 cup of rice. Soaking helps the rice absorb water and expand well during the actual cooking process. Many people like to save the soaking water and use it for cooking later.

1. Rinse the rice with water. Drain and set aside.

2. Boil water in a large pot on the stovetop and plunge the tomatoes into the pot for 30 seconds, then pull them out and run them under cold water. Peel off the tomato skins. In a bowl, roughly mash the blanched tomatoes. Set aside.

3. In a deep pan, heat the vegetable oil. Add the onion and blanched tomatoes and sauté for 5 minutes or until soft. Add the gingerroot and the Garam Masala; mix well. Add the rice and salt; sauté for 1 minute.

4. Transfer the contents to the slow cooker. Add the water and stir to remove any rice lumps. Cover and cook on high for 2 hours or until the rice is cooked through.

5. Once the rice is cooked well, turn off the heat and let stand, covered, for about 5 minutes. Fluff with a fork and garnish with the minced cilantro. Serve hot.

Turmeric Rice (Peele Chawal)

This simple dish has a spectacular appearance because of its stunning yellow color. Serve with any hot curry of your choice.

INGREDIENTS | SERVES 4

2 cups basmati rice

2 tablespoons vegetable oil

2 serrano green chilies, seeded and minced

1 small red onion, peeled and finely chopped

Salt, to taste

1 teaspoon turmeric powder

3 cups water

Tri-Colored Rice

You can have a lot of fun with rice dishes. Prepare batches of Minty Rice, Tomato Rice, and Turmeric Rice (see the recipes in this chapter). Layer the rice or mound it on a plate for a spectacular presentation. Use the Minty Rice for a green layer, Turmeric Rice for yellow, and the Tomato Rice for a fiery red.

1. Rinse the rice at least 3 to 4 times with water. Drain and set aside.

2. In a deep pan, heat the vegetable oil. Add the green chilies and onions; sauté for 3–5 minutes or until the onions are soft.

3. Add the salt, turmeric, and rice; sauté for 1 minute.

4. Transfer to the slow cooker. Add the water and stir. Cover and cook on high for 1½ hours.

5. Fluff with a fork before serving.

White Chicken Rice (Safeed Murgh Ka Pulao)

Serve piping hot with the Yogurt Green Curry (Hariyali Kadhi) (Chapter 6).

INGREDIENTS | SERVES 4–5

3 cups parboiled rice

5½ cups water

¼ cup vegetable oil

1" piece fresh gingerroot, peeled and julienned

2 serrano green chilies, minced

1 cup finely chopped red onion

4 boneless, skinless chicken breasts, cubed

Salt, to taste

1½ teaspoons Garam Masala Powder (Chapter 2)

1 tablespoon coriander powder

1 teaspoon red chili powder

1 tablespoon minced cilantro

1 tablespoon minced mint

½ cup whole milk

1 teaspoon Roasted Saffron (Chapter 2)

1. Rinse the rice with water. Drain and set aside.

2. In a slow cooker, combine the rice with the water. Cook for 1–1½ hours on high, until the rice is almost cooked but still firm. Drain, if there's any water left, and set the rice aside.

3. In a large skillet, heat the vegetable oil. Add the gingerroot, green chilies, and red onions; sauté for 7–8 minutes or until the onions are browned.

4. Add the chicken and sauté for 8–10 minutes or until the chicken is well browned and completely cooked. Add the salt, Garam Masala, coriander, and red chili powder; mix well. Remove from heat and set aside.

5. In a 5-quart slow cooker, add a layer of rice (about ½ of the rice). Layer about ¼ of the chicken mixture over the rice. Add another layer of the rice (about 1 cup), sprinkle with 1 teaspoon each of the cilantro and mint. Add a layer of the remaining chicken mixture and then a final layer of the remaining rice. Sprinkle with the cilantro and mint. Sprinkle with the milk and Roasted Saffron.

6. Cover and cook 1½ hours on low or until the rice is completely cooked and all the liquid has been absorbed. Serve hot.

Yogurt Rice (Dahi Bhaat)

If you use leftover rice, ensure that the rice is heated first and then brought to room temperature before proceeding.

INGREDIENTS | SERVES 4–5

1 recipe Perfect Slow Cooker Basmati Rice (see recipe in this chapter)

2 cups plain yogurt, whipped

2 tablespoons ghee, or vegetable oil

1 teaspoon black mustard seeds

2 dried red chilies, roughly pounded

1 serrano green chili, seeded and minced

8 curry leaves

1" piece fresh gingerroot, peeled and julienned

1 small red onion, peeled and finely chopped

Salt, to taste

Fresh minced cilantro, for garnish

1. If you are using Perfect Slow Cooker Basmati Rice that has been prepared earlier and refrigerated, warm it for a few minutes before proceeding.

2. In a bowl, combine the warmed rice with the yogurt. Mix well and place in a serving bowl. Set aside.

3. In a small skillet, heat the ghee. Add the mustard seeds. When they begin to sputter, add in quick succession the red chilies, green chili, curry leaves, gingerroot, onion, and salt; mix well. Sauté for about 3–5 minutes or until the onions are just soft.

4. Pour this spice mixture over the rice. Garnish with the fresh cilantro and serve at room temperature.

Onions and Religion

Considered an aphrodisiac, onions are avoided by many Indian Hindus for religious reasons. Some even avoid ginger and garlic. Another sect won't eat anything that grows underground!

CHAPTER 12

Desserts

Almond Brittle (Chikki)
238

Almond Pudding
(Badam ki Kheer)
239

Brown Rice Pongal
240

Cardamom-Infused Cheesecake
241

Carrot and Cheese Pudding
(Gajar Paneer Ka Halwa)
242

Chai Pudding
243

Cheese Pudding (Paneeri Kheer)
243

Creamy Milk Pudding (Basoondi)
244

Firni with Pistachios
and Cashews
245

Gajar Ka Halwa (Carrot Pudding)
246

Garam Rabdi
(Warm Condensed Milk)
247

Ginger Poached Pears
247

Gulkand Ice Cream
248

Kalakand
249

Mango Yogurt Pudding
(Amrakhand)
250

Opo Squash Pudding
(Dudhi Ki Kheer)
250

Rice Pudding (Kheer)
251

Rose-Scented Custard
252

Saffron-Infused Rabdi
with Fresh Berries
252

Saffron Yogurt Pudding
(Kesari Shrikhand)
253

Semolina Pudding
(Sooji Ki Kheer)
253

Shahi Tukda
254

Spicy Guava Butter
255

Sweetened Yogurt (Mishti Doi)
255

Vermicelli Pudding
(Seviyan Ki Kheer)
256

Wheat Payasam
257

Almond Brittle (Chikki)

Chikki is an Indian name for nut brittle. Chikki (Indian nut brittle) is made with jaggery, or gur, which is a traditional unrefined whole cane sugar.

INGREDIENTS | YIELDS APPROXIMATELY 1½ POUNDS

2 tablespoons unsalted butter

1 pound jaggery powder

2 cups roasted, salted almonds

Tips

If you can't find jaggery powder, you can break and powder jaggery blocks, which should be easily available.

1. Butter the inner walls of a 4½-quart slow cooker. Add the jaggery powder. Cover and turn the slow cooker to high. Cook for 2 hours or on low for 3–4 hours or until it melts.

2. Coarsely crush the whole almonds in a food processor.

3. Once the jaggery in the slow cooker starts bubbling, turn the heat off, add the rest of the butter, and mix thoroughly. You should get a thick, syrupy, slightly grainy mixture.

4. Add the crushed almonds into the syrup. Mix it all together. Carefully take the slow cooker insert out and pour the whole mixture onto a buttered 9" × 13" baking sheet lined with parchment paper. Using your spatula, spread the mixture evenly on the baking sheet. Let it cool for 1 hour. Then carefully take it off the sheet and break into pieces.

Almond Pudding (Badam ki Kheer)

Serve garnished with silver foil (optional). You can add a few drops of amaretto flavoring if you like.

INGREDIENTS | SERVES 4

2 cups water
½ cup blanched almonds
½ cup unsalted cashews
4 cups whole milk
6 tablespoons sugar, or to taste

Almond Truths

Almonds are a member of the peach family. In some parts of the world, newlyweds are showered with almonds, considered a fertility charm.

1. Put the water into the slow cooker. Add the almonds and cashews to the water. Cover and turn on low. Let the water warm for 1 hour, leaving the nuts immersed.

2. Drain the almonds and cashews and transfer them to a blender. Add 1 cup of the milk and blend to a coarse paste.

3. Add the rest of the milk and sugar to the slow cooker, stir to combine. Taste and add more sugar if needed. Add the nut paste. Stir. Cover and turn it to high. Cook for approximately 2 hours (stirring every 30 minutes).

4. During the end of cooking, the pudding will start getting creamier and turn thicker. You can transfer it to a stovetop and cook for 5 minutes on medium-high heat to hasten this process. Allow to cool for about 30 minutes. Serve.

Brown Rice Pongal

Pongal is a harvest festival celebrated in the south of India and is also a sweet, rich, and creamy rice pudding. Pongal comes in two types: ven pongal (or savory), which is spicy, and sakarai pongal, which is sweet.

INGREDIENTS | SERVES 6

3–4 tablespoons ghee
2 cups brown rice
½ cup moong dal
¼ cup cashews
¼ cup raisins
3 cups milk
1 cup powdered jaggery
½ teaspoon cardamom powder
1½ cups water, as needed

1. Heat 2 tablespoons ghee in a pan over medium-high heat. Roast the rice and dal for about 5 minutes. Set aside.

2. Heat the rest of the ghee in the same pan; fry the cashews and raisins for 2–3 minutes on medium-high heat until they turn slightly golden in color. Set aside.

3. Transfer all the ingredients (*except* for the fried nuts) to a 4–5-quart slow cooker. Add ½ cup water to begin with; later you can add more, if needed. Cover and cook on low for 7–8 hours or on high for 3–4 hours.

4. Toward the end of the cooking process, check the dish to ensure it is not too dry. If needed, add some more water and cook further. In the end you should have a creamy, golden porridge-like consistency.

5. Add the fried nuts and serve hot.

Cardamom-Infused Cheesecake

Making cheesecake in the slow cooker might sound odd, but it is actually the perfect appliance for the job. The constant low heat and moist environment keeps it from drying out or cracking, even when using low-fat ingredients.

INGREDIENTS | SERVES 8

¾ cup cinnamon graham cracker crumbs

1½ tablespoons butter, melted

8 ounces reduced-fat sour cream, at room temperature

8 ounces reduced-fat cream cheese, at room temperature

⅔ cup sugar

1 egg, at room temperature

½ tablespoon cardamom powder

1½ tablespoons flour

1 tablespoon lemon juice

1 tablespoon lemon zest

Homemade Graham Cracker Crumbs

There is no need to buy packaged graham cracker crumbs; it is easy to make them at home. Break graham crackers into medium-size pieces. Place them into a food processor. Pulse until fine crumbs form. Store the crumbs in an airtight container.

1. In a small bowl, mix together the graham cracker crumbs and butter. Press into the bottom and sides of a 6" springform pan.

2. In a large bowl, mix the sour cream, cream cheese, sugar, egg, cardamom, flour, lemon juice, and zest until completely smooth. Pour into the springform pan.

3. Pour 1" of water into the bottom of a 6-quart slow cooker. Place a trivet in the bottom of the slow cooker. Place the pan onto the trivet.

4. Cook on low for 2 hours. Turn off the slow cooker and let the cheesecake steam for 1 hour and 15 minutes with the lid on. Remove the cheesecake from the slow cooker. Refrigerate 6 hours or overnight before serving.

Carrot and Cheese Pudding (Gajar Paneer Ka Halwa)

Quintessential India. Serve this warm, garnished with your choice of unsalted nuts. This dish also freezes well.

INGREDIENTS | SERVES 4

6–7 cups carrots, peeled and grated

1 (14-ounce) can sweetened condensed milk

4–5 tablespoons butter, or ghee

¼ cup raisins

¼ cup slivered almonds

¾ cup scrambled or grated Homemade Paneer (Chapter 2)

½ teaspoon cardamom powder

Banana Pudding

Very popular in western India, this nutritious pudding is quite filling. Mash a banana, add 1 cup of milk, and sugar to taste. Top with raisins and serve chilled.

1. Combine the carrots and condensed milk together in a slow cooker. Cover and cook on low for 4 hours and then prop the lid open on the side by 1". Turn the slow cooker to high and cook for 2–3 hours (stirring occasionally) or until the carrots are completely cooked.

2. Heat 1 tablespoon butter or ghee in a large pan, wok, or skillet. Pan-fry the raisins and almonds. Take them out of the pan and set aside.

3. Transfer the contents from the slow cooker into the hot pan. Cook on medium heat, stirring every 2–3 minutes for 10–15 minutes to make sure 80 percent of the liquid is evaporated.

4. Add the rest of the ghee and the Paneer to the pudding along with cardamom powder. Stir. This will make it look shiny and rich. Cook for another 4–5 minutes. Turn off the heat and serve hot.

Chai Pudding

Any tea lover would delight in this creamy tapioca pudding.

INGREDIENTS | SERVES 6

2 chai tea bags
2 cups fat-free evaporated milk
⅓ cup brown sugar
½ teaspoon cinnamon
½ teaspoon ground star anise
½ teaspoon mace
½ teaspoon ground cardamom
¼ cup small pearl tapioca
1 egg

1. In a bowl, steep the tea bags in the evaporated milk for 20 minutes. Discard the bags. Whisk in the sugar, spices, and tapioca.

2. Pour the mixture into a 2- or 4-quart slow cooker and cook on low for 1½ hours. Stir in the egg and continue to cook for 30 minutes. Let it cool and then place it into the refrigerator to slightly chill before serving.

Cheese Pudding (Paneeri Kheer)

Kheer, or pudding, is served in India during many religious ceremonies as an offering to the gods. Rice kheer, in particular, is served in some parts of western India at funerals.

INGREDIENTS | SERVES 4

1 cup Homemade Paneer, grated (Chapter 2)
3 cups whole milk
½ cup condensed milk
Sugar, if needed

1. In a large bowl, combine the Homemade Paneer, milk, and condensed milk. Mix well by hand or with a hand blender. Taste to check sweetness; add sugar if needed.

2. Transfer the mixture to a 3–4-quart slow cooker. Cover and cook on low for about 40–60 minutes (more if required), stirring every 2–3 minutes. The mixture will become creamy and have a very pale yellow color. The final consistency should be that of a thick custard.

3. Remove from heat and let cool to room temperature for about 1 hour. Then chill for at least 4 hours.

Creamy Milk Pudding (Basoondi)

Tangy and sweet cold pineapple transforms this Indian favorite into a tropical delight. The sweetened, thickened milk dessert layered over the pineapple is mouthwatering.

INGREDIENTS | SERVES 4

2 cups ricotta cheese

1 cup whole milk

1 cup heavy cream

1 cup condensed milk

Sugar, if needed

¼ teaspoon Roasted Saffron (Chapter 2)

1 (14-ounce) can crushed pineapple, drained and chilled

Vark, or Silver Foil

You will often notice Indian sweets are covered with what appears to be shining silver. It is what it appears—silver! Silver is beaten into very thin sheets and used as a decorative ingredient in desserts. It is edible and provides a majestic touch to dishes. It is not easily available—check with your Indian grocer.

1. In a medium bowl, combine the ricotta cheese, milk, heavy cream, and condensed milk. Mix well by hand or with a hand blender. Taste to check sweetness and add sugar if needed.

2. Transfer the mixture to a 3–4-quart slow cooker. Cover and cook on low for about 40 minutes, stirring frequently. The mixture will become creamy and have a very pale yellow color. The final consistency should be that of a creamy custard.

3. Remove from heat. Add the Roasted Saffron. Stir well. Cool to room temperature, about 1 hour.

4. Fold in the chilled pineapple and serve.

Firni with Pistachios and Cashews

Firni is very much like kheer (rice pudding), where you cook rice with milk, reducing it to a creamy rich texture. Only for firni, a thick paste of ground rice and cashews is used instead of whole rice. This is one of my aunt's recipes, tweaked a little to suit a slow cooker.

INGREDIENTS | SERVES 6–8

½ cup uncooked rice
½ cup cashew nuts
4 cups milk
1 cup heavy cream
1 cup condensed milk
1–2 pinches of saffron
1 teaspoon crushed cardamom seeds
½ cup chopped pistachios

1. Thoroughly clean rice with water. Mix cashews and rice together and soak in water for a couple hours. Strain all the excess water and, using a food processor or blender, make a paste of rice and cashews. (Paste should not be very smooth but rather granular so that you can feel the texture when rubbed with fingers.) Set aside.

2. In a slow cooker, combine together the milk, heavy cream, and condensed milk. Cover and cook on high for 1 hour or on low for 2 hours.

3. Add the rice and cashew paste, saffron, and crushed cardamom seeds. Cover and cook for 1½ hours on high or about 3 hours on low. Stir every 10–15 minutes until the pudding starts to thicken. If the pudding starts to thicken before the given time, turn the heat off. If you prefer a thicker and denser pudding, keep cooking.

4. Let the pudding cool. Stir occasionally to prevent it from forming a thick layer on top. Once the pudding has cooled down a little but is still warm, transfer it to serving dishes and either let it chill before serving or serve it warm. Garnish with chopped pistachios.

Gajar Ka Halwa (Carrot Pudding)

You have not tasted "real" Indian food unless you taste a good gajar ka halwa!
Prolonged slow cooking is the key to a perfect gajar halwa, and your slow cooker will make it a breeze!

INGREDIENTS | SERVES 4–6

2 pounds fat red carrots, peeled and finely grated
1 (8-ounce) can sweet condensed milk
3 tablespoons ghee
¼ cup cashews
¼ cup slivered almonds
¼ cup golden raisins
1½ teaspoons crushed cardamom seeds

1. Place the grated carrots in the slow cooker. Pour in the condensed milk. Cover and cook on low for 5 hours or until the carrots are tender but not mushy. (Toward the last 30 minutes, prop the lid open from the side about ½" for the steam to escape.)

2.. Heat the ghee in a large shallow pan on a stovetop. Once the ghee is hot, add the nuts and raisins and fry them over medium-low heat until the raisins puff and the nuts turn light golden in color, about 2–3 minutes.

3. Now add the cooked contents of the slow cooker to the hot pan. This is a crucial step. In a good halwa, carrots should be pan-fried with ghee over medium-high heat until it loses all its water and changes color from light orange to a dark brick color. Cook the mixture on the stovetop, stirring continuously for 15–20 minutes.

4. Add the crushed cardamom toward the end of the cooking time. Once cooked, let the mixture cool a little. Serve warm.

Garam Rabdi (Warm Condensed Milk)

The moment you say rabdi, it will make many Indian food lover's mouths water.
This warm condensed milk can be added to just about anything and turn it into a decadent dessert!

INGREDIENTS | SERVES 6–8

2 cups milk

2 cups heavy cream

1 cup condensed milk

¼ cup ricotta cheese (optional)

Tips

Try adding 1 cup sugar and 2–3 tablespoons of milk powder instead of condensed milk.

1. Mix the milk, heavy cream, and condensed milk in a slow cooker. Cover (propping the lid open by a couple inches) and cook on high for 4–6 hours or until it reduces to a quarter of its volume. Stir every 30 minutes.

2. Add ricotta cheese if you like it even thicker. Cook for another 20–25 minutes. In the end, rabdi should be a dense, pale-yellow-colored flowing liquid.

Ginger Poached Pears

Fresh ginger best complements pear flavor, but if you have only ground ginger,
start by adding a smaller amount and then increase it after tasting.

INGREDIENTS | SERVES 8

5 pears, peeled, cored, and cut into wedges

3 cups water

1 cup white sugar

2 tablespoons minced ginger

1 teaspoon cinnamon

1. Add all the ingredients to a 4-quart slow cooker. Cover and cook on low for 4 hours.

Gulkand Ice Cream

Here's a tip: Transfer the contents in the slow cooker to a pan over low heat on stovetop, after adding the eggs, to get better results.

INGREDIENTS | SERVES 8–10

2 cups whole milk

2 cups heavy whipping cream

4 large egg yolks

¼ cup sugar

1 teaspoon vanilla extract

5 tablespoons Gulkand (Chapter 13)

1 teaspoon rose water (optional)

½ cup coarsely chopped almonds

1. Heat the milk and cream in a slow cooker for 3 hours on low. Turn off the heat and let it sit for 1 hour.

2. In a medium bowl, whisk together the egg yolks, sugar, and vanilla extract until it's smooth.

3. Turn the slow cooker to high, whisk in the egg mixture to the milk and cream stirring continuously so that the eggs don't scramble. You can also use an electric beater to keep whisking until the mixture thickens.

4. Turn off the heat and whisk in the Gulkand and rose water if using. Let it sit for 15–20 minutes and then transfer it into the refrigerator until it cools completely.

5. After a couple hours, pour the mixture into an ice cream maker (if using) and follow the instructions of the manufacturer. Add the almonds close to the last 5 minutes when the ice cream is almost done.

6. If you do not have an ice cream maker, pour the batter into a flat 2–3" tall dish. Freeze the mixture in your freezer. Keep an eye on it and after a few hours, just before the ice cream is hard, take it out, blend it in your blender, and freezer again. Repeat the process again, and this time mix the almonds in before freezing. This process might be a little longer than using an ice cream maker, but the results are very much the same.

Kalakand

Traditionally, kalakand is made by slow-cooking sweetened milk at low heat for hours until it reduces to form granular solids. As a child, this would be one of the few desserts that was always available at home and that was never refused.

INGREDIENTS | SERVES 8–10

2 pounds ricotta cheese

1 (14-ounce) can sweetened condensed milk

½ cup sugar (optional)

½ teaspoon cardamom powder

¼ cup milk powder

¼ cup slivered almonds or pistachios

1. Mix the ricotta cheese, condensed milk, and sugar in a 4–5-quart slow cooker. Cover and cook on high for 2 hours or on low for 4 hours.

2. Uncover and stir well, scraping the sides. Put the lid on, propping it open on the side by ½". Continue cooking for another 2–3 hours on high or 4 hours on low, stirring occasionally.

3. During the last 30 minutes of cooking, add cardamom powder and milk powder. Mix well. Toward the end of cooking, when the mixture is taking its shape, excess liquid will have evaporated, oil will start to separate on the sides, and the mixture will start to thicken into a lump.

4. Take the mixture out and transfer to a flat dish, at least 9–12" long, lined with parchment paper or oiled. Spread the mixture out evenly. Sprinkle the slivered nuts over it evenly. Let it cool. Run a butter knife through it, cutting it into smaller squares or rectangles. Pop it into the refrigerator for 3–4 hours before serving cold.

Mango Yogurt Pudding (Amrakhand)

A variation on Saffron Yogurt Pudding (see recipe in this chapter), this dessert is traditionally served with Poori (Chapter 15).

INGREDIENTS | SERVES 4

2 cups Slow Cooker Yogurt (Chapter 3)
½ cup sweetened canned mango pulp
2 tablespoons sugar, or to taste

1. Place all the ingredients in a bowl and mix well. You can do this with a spatula or a handheld blender. Adjust sugar to taste. Chill for about 30 minutes, then serve.

Storing Mango Dishes

Always store dishes prepared with mangoes in nonmetallic containers, because mango can discolor metallic containers.

Opo Squash Pudding (Dudhi Ki Kheer)

*This simple pudding can be made a day in advance.
Serve warm, garnished with roasted unsalted cashews and raisins.*

INGREDIENTS | SERVES 4

2½ cups peeled and grated opo squash
1 cup whole milk
4 tablespoons milk powder
1 cup sweetened condensed milk
¼ teaspoon Roasted Saffron (Chapter 2)

1. Take a few handfuls of the opo squash at a time and squeeze out all the excess water. Place the squash in a slow cooker.

2. Add the milk, milk powder, and condensed milk to the slow cooker; mix well. Cover and cook on high for 2–3 hours, or on low for 5–6 hours, or until the squash is cooked through and becomes creamy in consistency. Stir occasionally.

3. Turn off the heat, add the Roasted Saffron, and serve warm.

Rice Pudding (Kheer)

This creamy pudding can be served hot or cold.
Serve garnished with slivered almonds or powdered cinnamon.

INGREDIENTS | SERVES 4

2 cups whole milk

1 cup sweetened condensed milk

1 cup heavy cream

¼ cup basmati rice (or small-grain rice), rinsed

1 tablespoon ghee

2–3 cloves

1 bay leaf

¼ cup coconut milk (optional)

¼ teaspoon saffron threads

½ cup slivered nuts of choice (almonds, cashews, pistachios, etc.)

Avoid Spilling Milk

Rub a little butter on the rim of the pot you are using to boil milk on the stovetop. When the milk begins to boil and reaches the buttered rim, it will settle back down and not boil over the pot.

1. Add the whole milk, condensed milk, and cream to a slow cooker. Cover and cook on high for 1 hour or on low for 2–3 hours.

2. In the meantime, soak the rice in water for 30 minutes. Drain off the water and crush the rice into smaller pieces with your hands.

3. Heat the ghee in a pan over medium heat. Add the cloves and bay leaf. Cook for 5 seconds and then add the broken rice. *Be aware; it will splatter.* Fry the rice in the ghee for 30 seconds, stirring vigorously as it can stick to the bottom of the pan. Add the contents to the cooked milk in the slow cooker.

4. Cover and cook on low for 2–3 hours or until the rice is cooked through and the milk has reduced. You will have a creamy custard-like consistency in the end. Stir frequently while cooking. (Prop the lid open by 1" to let steam escape.)

5. If you are adding coconut milk, add it now and cook for another 10 minutes on high.

6. Crush the saffron threads between your fingers and add to the rice pudding. Add the slivered nuts.

7. Remove from heat. Serve hot or cold. To serve cold, refrigerate, covered, for at least 2 hours before serving.

Rose-Scented Custard

Rose water is a common Indian ingredient that adds a vibrant, floral note to this custard.

INGREDIENTS | SERVES 10

1 tablespoon rose water
2 cups fat-free evaporated milk
5 eggs
⅓ cup sugar

1. Place all the ingredients into a large bowl. Whisk until smooth. Pour into a 4-quart slow cooker. Cook on low for 8 hours, or until the center looks set and does not jiggle. Let it cool down and then pop it into the refrigerator for 4–5 hours to chill before serving.

Saffron-Infused Rabdi with Fresh Berries

This recipe calls for raspberries and blueberries, but you can use just about any fresh berry you like.

INGREDIENTS | SERVES 6-8

2 cups milk
2 cups heavy cream
1 cup condensed milk
½ cup raspberries
½ cup blueberries
¼ cup ricotta cheese (optional)
½ teaspoon Roasted Saffron (Chapter 2)

1. Mix the milk, heavy cream, condensed milk, raspberries, and blueberries in a slow cooker. Cover (propping the lid open by a couple inches) and cook on high for 4–6 hours or until it reduces to a quarter of its volume. Stir every 30 minutes.

2. Add the ricotta cheese if you like it even thicker. Cook for another 20–25 minutes. In the end, rabdi should be a dense, pale-yellow-colored flowing liquid. Stir in Roasted Saffron.

3. Let the rabdi cool down and then you can either chill it or pour it mildly warm over fresh berries.

Saffron Yogurt Pudding (Kesari Shrikhand)

This very traditional Indian dessert is generally made with saffron or mango.

INGREDIENTS | SERVES 4

2 cups Slow Cooker Yogurt (Chapter 3)
¼ teaspoon Roasted Saffron (Chapter 2)
¼ cup sugar, or to taste

1. Place all the ingredients in a bowl and mix well. You can do this with a spatula or a handheld blender. Adjust sugar to taste. Chill for about 30 minutes, then serve.

Semolina Pudding (Sooji Ki Kheer)

Served during prayer ceremonies, this pudding is very popular. Serve it garnished with slivered almonds.

INGREDIENTS | SERVES 4

1 tablespoon ghee
½ cup semolina
3 cups milk
1 cup condensed milk
¼ teaspoon Roasted Saffron (Chapter 2)
¼ cup slivered almonds

1. In a large saucepan, heat the ghee.

2. Add the semolina and cook over low heat. Stir constantly and cook for about 15 minutes or until the semolina is golden brown. Set aside.

3. Add the milk and condensed milk to a 3–4-quart slow cooker. Stir to mix well. Cover and cook on high for 2 hours.

4. Add the roasted semolina. Continue to cook for about 30 minutes (stirring every 5 minutes) or until the semolina is cooked and the pudding is creamy and thicker in consistency, just like a pancake batter.

5. Turn off the heat. Add the Roasted Saffron and slivered almonds. Allow to cool for about 20 minutes. Serve.

Shahi Tukda

Shahi tukda is also called double ka meetha, which gets its name from milk bread (which is also known as "double roti" in local dialect, maybe because the dough used to make it rises double in size).

INGREDIENTS | SERVES 4–6

½ gallon milk
½ teaspoon saffron
1 cup condensed milk
¼ cup chopped pistachios
3 cups water
1½ cups sugar
12 slices white bread
3–4 tablespoons ghee

1. Reduce the milk in a slow cooker, cooking it on high setting. Once the milk is reduced by half, add the saffron and condensed milk. Cook on high setting for 30–45 minutes. Stir in the pistachios. Set aside to cool.

2. In a pan over medium heat, mix the water and sugar. Bring it to boil and let it simmer for about 30 minutes until it reduces to make sugar syrup. Set aside.

3. Cut the edges off the bread and then cut it into 2 triangles. Generously apply ghee to both the sides. Cook in a skillet until golden brown.

4. On a large flat dish, place the bread triangles in a single or double layer. Pour the sugar syrup over it, only enough to soak the bread. Discard any extra syrup. Once the bread has soaked the sugar syrup, pour the rabdi over it, covering the bread layer.

5. Cover the dish with a plastic wrap and let it cool in the refrigerator. Serve chilled.

Spicy Guava Butter

Guava is one of the most common and cheapest fruits available in India.
You will find a guava tree in almost every yard.

INGREDIENTS | YIELDS APPROXIMATELY 2½ CUPS

2 pounds ripe guavas, peeled and chopped
½ cup brown sugar (optional)
1 teaspoon cayenne pepper
½ teaspoon nutmeg

1. Put all the ingredients in the slow cooker. Cover and cook on low for 12–14 hours, stirring occasionally. Once done, the fruit will have reduced to a quarter of its volume. If there's more liquid than you'd like, cook the mixture on the stovetop over medium-high heat for about 8–10 minutes.

2. Spread the resulting butter over a soft whole-wheat crepe, roll it up, and serve.

Sweetened Yogurt (Mishti Doi)

This dish from the eastern Indian state of Bengal can be steamed or baked.

INGREDIENTS | SERVES 4

1 (14-ounce) can sweetened condensed milk
2 cups Slow Cooker Yogurt (Chapter 3), or plain yogurt
Pinch of cardamom powder (optional)

Nimish

Nimish is one of the most unusual and ethereal Indian desserts. It is prepared by churning boiled milk until foam forms on top. This foam is collected and served in terra cotta pots. It is believed that the milk needs to be placed outside overnight and dew formed on it for this dish to achieve perfection.

1. Preheat the oven to 275°F.

2. Blend together all the ingredients and place in an ovenproof dish. Place in the oven and bake for 40 minutes.

3. Turn off the oven and leave the dish in the oven for another 4 hours. To check for doneness, insert a toothpick into the dish; if it comes out clean, the dish is done. Refrigerate, covered, overnight.

4. Alternatively, once you blend the ingredients, place them in a small bowl. Cover with aluminum foil. Steam it in a pot of boiling water for 20 minutes or until the yogurt is set. Serve chilled.

Vermicelli Pudding (Seviyan Ki Kheer)

Roasted vermicelli is used to make this aromatic pudding.
Serve warm in decorative bowls, garnished with slivered cashews.

INGREDIENTS | SERVES 2–3

2 cups whole milk

2 tablespoons sweetened condensed milk

4 tablespoons ghee

½ cup broken vermicelli

1 tablespoon raisins

1 tablespoon slivered almonds

¼ teaspoon Roasted Saffron (Chapter 2)

1. In a slow cooker, combine the milk and condensed milk. Mix well. Cover and cook on high setting for 2 hours.

2. In the meantime, heat a medium-size nonstick pan over medium heat. Add the ghee. Add the vermicelli and sauté for 1 minute or until it turns brown. Remove from heat and set aside.

3. Add the vermicelli, raisins, and almonds to the slow cooker. Mix well and cook for another 10 minutes or until the vermicelli is soft.

4. Add the Roasted Saffron and mix well. Allow to cool to room temperature (about 30 minutes) before serving.

Wheat Payasam

Payasam is a sweet porridge that hails from the southern states of India. It can also be made with rice or several types of lentils, moong and chana dal being the most popular. Or you can use vermicelli or wheat noodles as well.

INGREDIENTS | SERVES 4–6

2 tablespoons ghee

1 cup cracked wheat

1 cup powdered jaggery, or brown sugar

1 (14-ounce) can coconut milk

½ cup heavy cream, or milk (optional)

½ cup chopped nuts and raisins (cashews, almonds, pistachios, etc.)

3–4 tablespoons grated coconut

1. Heat the ghee in a pan over medium-low heat. Add the cracked wheat. Roast for 10–15 minutes until it begins to perfume. Stop roasting. Set aside.

2. In a 4–5-quart slow cooker, add the cracked wheat, jaggery, and coconut milk. Stir well. Cover and cook on high for 2–3 hours, or on low for 4–5 hours, or until the wheat is cooked through.

3. Add the heavy cream, or milk. Cover and cook for another 20–25 minutes. In the end, the payasam should look golden brown in color with the consistency of a thin porridge.

4. Add the chopped nuts, raisins, and grated coconut. Mix. Let it cool before popping into the refrigerator. Serve chilled.

CHAPTER 13

Chutney and Raita Dips

Aam ki Launji (Raw Mango Preserve)
259

Amle ka Murabba (Gooseberries in Sugar Syrup)
259

Ananas ki Chutney (Spicy Pineapple Chutney)
260

Boondi Raita
260

Apple and Pear Chutney
261

Cilantro Chutney Raita Dip (Hari Chutney ka Raita)
262

Cucumber Mint Raita
262

Cucumber Raita
263

Dahi Kachumbar
263

Easy Peanut Sauce
264

Green Chutney Raita
264

Gulkand (Rose Petal Jam)
265

Lauki Ka Raita (Bottle Gourd Raita)
265

Homemade Hot Ketchup
266

Mango Chili Chutney
267

Mixed Fruit Raita
267

Mango-Saffron Chutney (Kairi Kesar Ki Chutney)
268

Palak Raita (Spinach and Yogurt Dip)
268

Pineapple Raita
269

Pomegranate and Mango Chutney Raita
269

Smoked Raita
270

Five-Spice Strawberry Chutney
271

Sweet and Tangy Mango Relish
272

Tamarind Chutney (Imli Ki Chutney)
272

Three-Pepper Sauce
273

Tomato and Onion Chutney
273

Tomato Chutney (Tamatar ki Chutney)
274

Vengaya Thogayal (Onion Chutney)
274

Aam ki Launji (Raw Mango Preserve)

Mango is a fruit of summer, and so when summer come, the Indian kitchen is filled with it. Mango launji is a popular preserve that is prepared all across the warm states in the country, in some form or other.

INGREDIENTS | YIELDS 2½–3 CUPS

1 tablespoon oil

1 teaspoon onion seeds (nigella)

1 teaspoon fennel seeds

3–4 whole dried red chilies

½ teaspoon caraway seeds (ajwain)

2 bay leaves

2½ pounds raw mango, peeled, deseeded, and grated

1 cup raw cane sugar, or white granulated sugar

1 teaspoon salt

¼ cup water

1. Heat oil in a tempering pan. Add all the dry spices. As they splatter, turn off the heat. Set aside.

2. Transfer all the ingredients to the slow cooker. Stir well. Cover and cook on high for 3 hours or until the mango is tender. After 3 hours, prop the lid halfway open. Stir well and cook for another 3–4 hours or until the launji turns into to a thick jam-like consistency.

3. Cool down completely before canning or storing in airtight containers in a cool, dry place.

Amle ka Murabba (Gooseberries in Sugar Syrup)

Amlas, or Indian gooseberries, are loaded with vitamins, essential oils, and many other nutrients. They are praised ever so much that they are called Amrita, or nectar from the heaven, in Hindu mythology. This particular dish is a great winter preserve and can be preserved for more than a year.

INGREDIENTS | SERVES 8–10

20–25 amlas

3 cups water

3 cups sugar

2 teaspoons coarsely crushed cardamom seeds

Spicy Tip

Add spices, such as, cinnamon, cloves, and bay leaves, to give this dish an extra punch. Or add several pickling spices to amlas, and they will make excellent pickles.

1. Wash the amlas with water. Using a fork, prick and make several superficial holes in each one and then soak them in water for 2–3 hours.

2. Take the amlas out of the water and transfer them into the slow cooker along with the rest of the ingredients. Stir everything together well to dissolve the sugar in the water. Cover and cook on low for 6–7 hours or until the amlas are fork tender.

3. Let it sit to cool down completely. Serve or store in airtight jars.

Ananas ki Chutney (Spicy Pineapple Chutney)

*Ananas is the Hindi name for pineapple. This is a simple chutney and can be
a great addition to a simple roast chicken or served as a spicy and tangy dip.*

INGREDIENTS | YIELDS APPROXIMATELY 2½ CUPS

½ cup brown sugar

6 cups pineapple, peeled, cored and chopped to ½" chunks

2 tablespoons oil

1 teaspoon fennel seeds

1 teaspoon black mustard seeds

1 tablespoon minced green chili

½ tablespoon fresh gingerroot

¼ cup chopped onion

1. Toss the sugar and pineapple together. Transfer to a slow cooker. Cover and cook on low for 3–4 hours or until the pineapple is cooked through and tender.

2. Heat the oil in a pan over medium heat. Add the fennel seeds and mustard seeds. As they splatter, add the green chili and gingerroot. Sauté for 15 seconds and then add the onion. Sauté until the onion is translucent.

3. Add the mixture to the pineapple-sugar mixture in the slow cooker. Mix well. Cover and cook further on low for 2–3 hours or until the pineapple begins to melt but still holds its shape. Serve hot or cool, depending on your taste, with hot bread or steamed rice and lentil soup.

Boondi Raita

*Boondi are tiny and light deep-fried balls made with chickpea flour. The flour is mixed
with some basic spices and then diluted with water before being dropped in hot oil.
Later, boondi can be tossed in various spices and enjoyed as a snack or can be used to make raita.*

INGREDIENTS | SERVES 6–8

3 cups Slow Cooker Yogurt (Chapter 3)

1 cup boondi

1 cup water

1 tablespoon Chaat Masala (Chapter 2)

1 tablespoon fine granulated sugar

½ teaspoon red chili flakes

Handful of chopped cilantro

Salt, to taste

1. Mix all the ingredients together and serve.

Make It Softer

For softer boondi, soak it in warm water for 5 minutes before squeezing out all the water, or add boondi to yogurt.

Apple and Pear Chutney

I use green, slightly sour apples for this recipe. That gives me a tangy and sweet chutney that goes perfectly with grilled meat, wraps, or even simple dal and rice.

INGREDIENTS | YIELDS APPROXIMATELY 3 CUPS

2 cups peeled, cored, and chopped apple

2 cups peeled, cored, and chopped pear

½ cup golden raisins

¼ cup dark brown sugar, or jaggery

1 tablespoon finely chopped ginger

½ cup water

1 tablespoon oil

½ teaspoon cumin seeds

½ teaspoon mustard seeds

½ teaspoon red pepper flakes

3–4 bay leaves

1. Place all the ingredients (*except* for the oil and dry spices) into the slow cooker. Cover and cook on low for 3–4 hours or until the fruits are cooked through and begin to blend into each other.

2. Heat the oil in a tempering pan. Add the spices and cook until they sputter, for about 1 minute. Combine this mixture with the cooked fruits in the slow cooker. Cover and cook for another 30 minutes. In the end, the chutney should be thin and syrupy. Cool down completely before storing or serving.

Choose a Different Spice

You can also add turmeric, if you like, and panch foran instead of the two whole spices, or curry leaves instead of bay leaves.

Cilantro Chutney Raita Dip (Hari Chutney ka Raita)

Green chutney made with fresh cilantro and a few other ingredients is a basic chutney recipe in Indian cooking, and so much can be done with it.

INGREDIENTS | SERVES 6

2 tablespoons Hot Cilantro Chutney (Chapter 2)

1½ cup Slow Cooker Yogurt (Chapter 3)

½ crispy sev

1. Whisk together the chutney and yogurt making a smooth paste. Sprinkle some sev on top for crunch. Serve.

Garlic Alert

Do not add garlic and tomatoes to your cilantro chutney if you are planning to freeze or mix it in yogurt.

Cucumber Mint Raita

Cucumber and mint act as a great coolant in this dip when mixed with creamy spiced yogurt. Cool cucumber raita is a staple in Indian homes during the summer.

INGREDIENTS | SERVES 8

2½ cups plain Slow Cooker Yogurt (Chapter 3)

1 cup cucumber, peeled, grated, and drained

¼ cup fresh mint leaves

½ teaspoon roasted cumin powder

1 teaspoon sugar

½ teaspoon ground black pepper

Salt, to taste

1. Whisk the yogurt in a bowl, making it smooth with no lumps.

2. Drain any extra liquid from the grated cucumber and add it to the yogurt. Crush the mint with a mortar and pestle, or just blend it in a blender. Add the rest of the ingredients. Mix well.

3. Serve as a dip for grilled naan breads and fritters or as an accompaniment with any spicy curry.

Cucumber Raita

Raita is mainly a cool yogurt-based condiment used to balance the spices and heat in Indian food.

INGREDIENTS | SERVES 3–4

1 cup finely chopped cucumber, peeled
½ cup Slow Cooker Yogurt (Chapter 3)
½ teaspoon sugar
½ teaspoon salt
1 teaspoon chaat masala
½ teaspoon red pepper powder
¼ cup chopped cilantro

1. Mix all the ingredients together and serve as a cool dip or sauce.

Dahi Kachumbar

Kachumbar is the most common form of salad served in India. Vegetables, such as onions, tomatoes, carrots, cucumbers, and so on, are chopped and thrown into a bowl with sprigs of fresh herbs, salt, and sometimes lime or lemon.

INGREDIENTS | SERVES 4–6

1½ cups Slow Cooker Yogurt (Chapter 3)
¼ cup chopped onion
½ cup chopped tomatoes
½ cup peeled and chopped cucumber
1½ teaspoons minced green chili
¼ cup chopped cilantro
Salt and pepper, to taste

1. Whisk the yogurt smooth. Stir in all the ingredients. Mix well and serve as a dip for chips and fritters or with rice or biryani.

Easy Peanut Sauce

Choose a peanut butter that is free of added flavors and is as natural as possible so that it won't distort the flavors in your dish.

INGREDIENTS | YIELDS 3 CUPS

1 cup smooth peanut butter
4 tablespoons maple syrup
½ cup sesame oil
1 teaspoon cayenne pepper
1½ teaspoons cumin
1 teaspoon garlic powder
1½ teaspoons salt
2 cups water

1. Add all ingredients *except* for the water to a blender. As you blend, slowly add the water until you reach the desired consistency.

2. Pour the sauce into a 2-quart slow cooker and cook over low heat for 1 hour.

Green Chutney Raita

Hot cilantro chutney is one of the basic condiments of Indian food. There are several ways you can make it and then a thousand ways you can use it in your food.

INGREDIENTS | YIELDS 1 CUP

¾ cup plain Slow Cooker Yogurt (Chapter 3)
1 tablespoon Hot Cilantro Chutney (Chapter 2)
1 teaspoon Chaat Masala (Chapter 2)
1 teaspoon honey
¼ teaspoon salt

1. Mix everything together and serve. This raita goes very well with rice dishes.

Tips

When making the hot cilantro chutney to be used in this recipe, do not add the garlic.

Gulkand (Rose Petal Jam)

Gulab is a Hindi name for rose. Gulkand is jam, or preserves, and is made by slow-cooking wild rose petals with sucrose for a long time, reducing the juices into a thick consistency.

INGREDIENTS | YIELDS 3 CUPS

1 pound wild rose petals
1 pound white granulated sugar
1 tablespoon rose water (optional)

Gulkand

Most popularly, *gulkand* is used in *pan* (green beetle leaves), which is used in various mouth fresheners and served after meals to aid in healthy digestion.

1. Wash the rose petals with water. Place the petals in the sun or in a convection oven to dry out the excess water.

2. Mix both the sugar and rose petals together. Add the rose water, if using. Place the mixture in a large slow cooker. Cover and cook on low for 2–3 hours (stirring a couple times) or until the rose petals wilt and get syrupy with sugar.

3. Let it cool before storing. Place in airtight containers in a cool dry place.

Lauki Ka Raita (Bottle Gourd Raita)

If raw bottle gourd is too strong a taste for you, steamed bottle gourd can also be used for this recipe.

INGREDIENTS | SERVES 4

1 cup peeled and grated bottle gourd
1 cup Slow Cooker Yogurt (Chapter 3)
1 teaspoon Chaat Masala (Chapter 2)
½ teaspoon sugar
½ teaspoon crushed black pepper
Salt, to taste

1. Bring the bottle gourd and 1½ cups of water to a boil. Turn off the heat. Drain extra liquid, leaving a tender grated bottle gourd.

2. Mix all the ingredients together and serve as a dip.

Homemade Hot Ketchup

Why buy bottled when homemade ketchup is this easy?

INGREDIENTS | SERVES 32

1 (15-ounce) can no-salt-added tomato sauce

2 teaspoons water

½ teaspoon onion powder

½ cup sugar

⅓ cup cider vinegar

¼ teaspoon sea salt

2–3 pinches nutmeg

⅛ teaspoon ground cloves

1½ teaspoons crushed hot chili peppers

Pinch freshly ground pepper

⅔ teaspoon sweet paprika

1. Add all the ingredients *except* the paprika to the slow cooker. Cover and, stirring occasionally, cook for 2–4 hours on high setting or until ketchup reaches desired consistency.

2. Turn off the slow cooker (or remove the crock from the slow cooker) and stir in the paprika. Allow the mixture to cool. Pour it in a covered container (such as a recycled ketchup bottle). Store in the refrigerator until needed.

Ketchup with a Kick

If you like zesty ketchup, you can add crushed red peppers, cayenne pepper, or salt-free chili powder along with, or instead of, the nutmeg and other seasonings. Another alternative is to use hot paprika rather than sweet paprika.

Mango Chili Chutney

Try using jaggery, which is the raw form of cane sugar, for this recipe.

INGREDIENTS | YIELDS APPROXIMATELY 2½ CUPS

1 tablespoon oil
1 teaspoon black mustard seeds
½ teaspoon cumin seeds
½ teaspoon turmeric powder
2–3 green chilies, slit
4 cups ripe mango, peeled and cubed
½ cup sugar
½ teaspoon salt
½ cup raisins
½ cup water

1. Heat the oil in a tempering pan. Add all the dry spices and green chilies. As they splatter, turn off the heat and set aside.

2. Transfer all the ingredients to the slow cooker. Cover and cook on low for 3–4 hours or until the mango is cooked through.

3. Uncover and cook on high for another 2 hours or until the mango starts to melt and form a jam- or chutney-like consistency.

4. Serve hot or cool with your favorite flatbread or as a tangy dip for chips and poppadum.

Mixed Fruit Raita

This dish can also be used as a dessert; just add agave syrup or honey instead of the spices.

INGREDIENTS | SERVES 6

¼ cup peeled and diced apple
¼ cup grapes, cut into 2
¼ cup orange, skin cleaned and cut into pieces
¼ kiwi, diced
1 cup Slow Cooker Yogurt (Chapter 3)
½ teaspoon cardamom powder
½ roasted cumin powder
¼ teaspoon cayenne pepper

1. Mix everything together. Serve.

Mango-Saffron Chutney (Kairi Kesar Ki Chutney)

Serve this on a lightly toasted bagel for a unique breakfast dish.
This chutney will keep in the refrigerator for up to 1 week.

INGREDIENTS | YIELDS 2 CUPS

2 cups green mango, peeled and grated
1 cup sugar
2 teaspoons grated gingerroot
2 dried red chilies, roughly pounded
Pinch of salt
¼ teaspoon saffron, soaked in 4 tablespoons hot water for 10 minutes

Major Grey

Patek's Major Grey Mango Chutney is a commercially made chutney, and a household name in Britain. Named after a mythical general, these chutneys are delicious and very popular in the United Kingdom.

1. In a 3–4-quart slow cooker, combine the mango and the sugar; mix well. Let it stand for about 1 hour.

2. Turn on the slow cooker. Set it to high. Cover and cook for 1½ hours, or on low for 3–4 hours, or until the mango becomes very soft and the sugar begins to turn a light brown.

3. Add the gingerroot, red chilies, and salt. Mix well.

4. Strain the saffron and discard any residue. Add the saffron-infused water and mix well. Simmer for 20 more minutes.

5. Turn off the heat and let cool for about 20 minutes. Cover and refrigerate until needed.

Palak Raita (Spinach and Yogurt Dip)

This is one of those foods that you can't stop eating, yet still not feel bad about it.
Spinach raita is refreshing and at the same time healthy and filling.

INGREDIENTS | SERVES 6

1½ cups plain Slow Cooker Yogurt (Chapter 3)
½ cup puréed raw spinach
½ teaspoon cayenne pepper
Salt, to taste

Keep the Water

You can also slightly steam or boil the spinach, then drain the extra liquid, blend, and use in the recipe.

1. Mix everything together and serve with your favorite chips.

Pineapple Raita

The refreshing sweetness of the pineapple in this recipe makes it a great treat.

INGREDIENTS | SERVES 6

2 cups Slow Cooker Yogurt (Chapter 3)

1 cup peeled, cored, and chopped pineapple

1 teaspoon agave syrup

½ teaspoon ground pepper

½ teaspoon bhuna jeera (roasted cumin seeds)

Salt, to taste

1. Mix all the ingredients together. Serve chilled with a spicy Indian meal.

Pomegranate and Mango Chutney Raita

The antioxidants and tangy flavor of the pomegranate plus the sweetness of the mango make this fruity raita especially delicious and healthy.

INGREDIENTS | SERVES 5–6

2 cups Slow Cooker Yogurt (Chapter 3)

¾ cup fresh pomegranate seeds

2½ tablespoons Mango Chili Chutney (see recipe in this chapter)

½ cup water (optional)

1. Mix all the ingredients together making the yogurt smooth. Add water, if desired. Serve as a dip for chips, over grilled meat or vegetables, or as a dressing for salads.

Smoked Raita

I learned this trick from my mother-in-law who happens to be a great cook and loves to experiment around the kitchen. This particular trick of smoking raita has been handed down for generations.

INGREDIENTS | SERVES 4–6

2 cups Slow Cooker Yogurt (Chapter 3)
Water, as needed
1 cup dry boondi
½ teaspoon roasted cumin seeds
½ teaspoon cayenne pepper
Salt, to taste
1 teaspoon sugar
½" block of charcoal
1 tablespoon ghee
¼ teaspoon asafetida

Boondi

Boondi is tiny droplets of chickpea-based batter, deep-fried in oil until the droplets turn brown and crunchy. Boondi is also easily found at Indian stores.

1. In a bowl, smooth out the yogurt by whisking it and adding about 1 cup of water to thin it out a little (add more if you like it thinner). Add the boondi, roasted cumin seeds, and cayenne pepper. Add salt and the sugar as well. Mix everything together; set aside. Keep a lid handy.

2. Light the charcoal by either placing it over a burning stovetop flame or in a grill. Now heat the ghee in a metal/steel serving spoon. The serving spoon should be deep enough to hold the hot ghee and the charcoal.

3. Add the asafetida to the hot ghee and then the burning charcoal right after. This will cause some smoke. Place the spoon inside the raita right away, in a way that the spoon is submerged in the raita, but the charcoal should not touch the raita. Cover it with a lid immediately. Let it sit for 5–10 minutes and then discard the charcoal. Serve immediately with a rice dish or a pan-fried bread.

Five-Spice Strawberry Chutney

If the slow cooker does not get the chutney thick enough,
add a packet of gelatin or pectin during the last hour of cooking.

INGREDIENTS | YIELDS APPROXIMATELY 2 CUPS

2 teaspoons olive or vegetable oil

1½ teaspoons panch foran

1 pound hulled strawberries

⅓ cup pomegranate juice

½ cup powdered jaggery, or packed brown sugar, or 1 cup sugar

Strawberry and Pomegranate

Strawberries are not a very traditional Indian fruit. Although things are changing rapidly, they still cannot be easily found in many Indian towns and cities. And the same is true for bottled pomegranate juice. But since pomegranate fruit is easily accessible, Indians are used to extracting fresh juice.

1. Heat the oil in a thick-bottom saucepan. Add the panch foran. Once it starts to pop, add the strawberries and stir it once. Transfer the contents to the slow cooker.

2. Add the pomegranate juice and the jaggery. Mix it all together. Cover and turn the heat to high. Cook for 2 hours or until the mixture comes to a boil.

3. Reduce heat to low and cook for another 4–5 hours (stirring occasionally), propping the lid open by 1" for the steam to escape.

4. To test if your chutney is done, take some in the back of your spoon and let it stay out in the air for about 10–15 minutes. Then run a finger through it. If it wrinkles, then it is done. Let it cool before serving.

Sweet and Tangy Mango Relish

This tangy dip is perfect for a cookout on a hot summer day.

INGREDIENTS | YIELDS APPROXIMATELY 2 CUPS

1 tablespoon cooking oil

2 teaspoons Panch Foran Spices (Chapter 2)

3–4 whole dried red chilies

3 cups raw mango, peeled, cored, and grated

1 cup sugar

1 teaspoon salt

1. Heat the oil in a wok. Add the Panach Foran Spices and the chilies. When they splutter, add the mango. Cook the mango in the wok with the spices for 3–5 minutes, stirring constantly.

2. Transfer the contents of the wok and the rest of the ingredients to a slow cooker. Stir well. Cover and cook on high for 2 hours, or on low for 4 hours, or until the mango changes color to golden brown and is cooked. Serve as a relish with toast or Parathas (Chapter 15).

Tamarind Chutney (Imli Ki Chutney)

If you find it hard to chop the dates, soak them in hot water for 10 minutes before chopping. This chutney will keep in the freezer for up to 6 months.

INGREDIENTS | YIELDS 2 CUPS

1 cup tamarind pulp

2 cups hot water

½ cup jaggery, or brown sugar

1 teaspoon red chili powder

Salt, to taste

½ cup dates, pitted and chopped

Storing Chutneys

Always cook and store chutneys in nonreactive pans and bowls. If cooked in other pots, the acid in the chutneys (from lemon juice, vinegar, etc.) will react to the iron, copper, and brass, giving a nasty metallic taste to the chutney.

1. In a glass bowl, soak the tamarind pulp in the hot water for 30 minutes. Strain through a fine-meshed sieve into a bowl. Discard any residue in the sieve.

2. Add the jaggery, red chili, and salt to the bowl and mix well. Add the dates and purée the entire mixture in a blender. Transfer the mixture to a small 3-quart slow cooker.

3. Cover and cook on low for 2–3 hours or until the chutney reaches a custard-like consistency. Propping the lid open on the side by 1" helps.

4. Once it's done, let cool to room temperature. Refrigerate for up to a week until needed.

Three-Pepper Sauce

Cayenne peppers are most commonly found dried and ground in the herbs and spices aisle of your grocery store.

INGREDIENTS | SERVES 4

1 (28-ounce) can diced tomatoes

2 tablespoons tomato paste

1 red bell pepper, finely diced

1 green bell pepper, finely diced

½ red onion, diced

3 cloves garlic, minced

1 teaspoon cayenne pepper

½ teaspoon sugar

½ teaspoon salt

1. Add all ingredients to a 4-quart slow cooker. Cover and cook on low heat for 6–8 hours.

Tomato and Onion Chutney

Serve this chutney with your choice of crackers or bread. It also goes very well with dosa or idly.

INGREDIENTS | YIELDS APPROXIMATELY 2 CUPS

Salt, to taste

¼ teaspoon turmeric

1 cup Caramelized Onions (Chapter 3)

2 cups chopped tomato, extra liquid drained

2 tablespoons sesame oil (or vegetable oil)

1½ teaspoons black mustard seeds

Pinch asafetida

2–3 whole dried red chilies

10–12 curry leaves

1. Add salt, turmeric, Caramelized Onions, and tomato into a 3-quart slow cooker. Cover and cook on high for 2–3 hours, or on low for 4 hours, or until the tomato is completely dissolved in the onion. Stir occasionally.

2. Once the tomato and onion are cooked well, take out the insert and stir the mixture vigorously using a fork or spoon, smoothing it out. (It will still have some chunks, which is fine.)

3. Heat the oil in a tempering pan. Add all the dry spices, curry leaves, and chilies. As they sputter transfer the tempered spices to the chutney. Mix well and serve either warm or cooled down.

Tomato Chutney (Tamatar ki Chutney)

Tomato is used in various Indian chutneys and dips in one form or the other.

INGREDIENTS | YIELDS 2 CUPS

1 tablespoon oil

2 teaspoons grated ginger

2 teaspoons green chili, cut lengthwise

2–3 bay leaves

1 teaspoon nigella

1½ pounds firm red tomatoes, cut into big chunks

2 tablespoons jaggery

1 teaspoon salt

1. Heat the oil in a tempering pan. Add the ginger, chili, bay leaves, and nigella one after the other. Cook for 5–7 seconds. Set aside.

2. Transfer all the ingredients, including the tempered spices, to the slow cooker. Mix well. Cover, leaving a slight opening for the steam to escape. Cook on high for 2 hours, or on low for 4–5 hours, or until the tomatoes are soft. Stir well and cool before serving.

Vengaya Thogayal (Onion Chutney)

Vengaya in Tamil means onion and thogayal, or thuvayal, is a name for a chutney. This is a simple yet exceptionally flavorful onion-chutney recipe, popular in the state of Tamil Nadu, in the south of India.

INGREDIENTS | YIELDS APPROXIMATELY 2 CUPS

3½ cups chopped onion

Salt, to taste

2 tablespoons split bengal gram (chana dal)

2 tablespoons split black gram (urad dal)

2 tablespoons cooking oil, preferably mustard

1 tablespoon ball of tamarind, soaked overnight in ¼ cup water

4–5 dried whole red chilies

1. Place the onion and salt in the slow cooker. Cover and cook on high for 2½–3 hours, or for 5–6 hours on low, or until the onion is wilted and turns translucent.

2. Dry roast the dals in a pan on the stovetop for a few minutes. As they begin to perfume, turn off the heat. Set aside.

3. Add the oil in a tempering pan and fry the tamarind and red chilies for 8–10 seconds. Set aside; let cool. Once cooled, grind the spices and dals in a spice grinder or with a mortar and pestle.

4. Transfer the prepared spice blend and ground dals to the slow cooker with the cooked onion. Mix well.

5. Place the resulting mixture into a food processor, blend it all together making a thick paste. Cool down and serve as a condiment.

CHAPTER 14

Beverages

Aam Pana (Raw Mango Cooler)
276

Badam Milk
(Warm Almond Milk)
277

Bajra Raab
278

Basil Tea (Tulsi Waali Chai)
278

Chach (Spiced Buttermilk)
279

Ginger Ale
279

Ginger Tea
280

Mango Lassi
280

Masala Chai
281

Mulled Wine
281

OJ Mint Punch
282

Pistachio Milk (Pista Doodh)
282

Punjabi Lassi
283

Rose Milk
283

Spiced Fruit Punch
284

Strawberry Lassi
285

Aam Pana (Raw Mango Cooler)

*Ambiya, or raw mango, is believed to be great at fighting heat,
so this drink becomes a staple in North Indian homes during the summer.*

INGREDIENTS | SERVES 4–5

2 raw mangoes
2 tablespoons fresh chopped mint leaves
1 jalapeño pepper, seeded
1½ tablespoons sugar
1½ tablespoons crushed jaggery
½ teaspoon salt
1 teaspoon toasted and ground cumin

What Does Salt Do?

Salt doesn't really give any flavor to the pana, but it helps bring out the tastes of the rest of the ingredients.

1. In a small slow cooker, put in the raw mangoes and 1½ cups of water. Cover and let the magoes cook until they are cooked through and tender.

2. Remove the mangoes from the slow cooker. Let cool and then peel off the skin. Mash the pulp, discarding the seed.

3. Crush the mint and jalapeño together into paste using a muddler or a mortar and pestle.

4. Mix everything together and add water to achieve the consistency of pana you would like. Put it in the refrigerator to chill.

Badam Milk (Warm Almond Milk)

Badam, or almond, is a nut superstar in Indian cuisine. Grind and add the paste to curries to make them rich. Mix the paste with milk. Or eat them as is. They have so many health benefits, and Indians do not want to let any of them go!

INGREDIENTS | SERVES 6–8

4½ cups milk

⅓ cup almonds, soaked in water for 4–5 hours

¼ teaspoon saffron (kesar)

½ cup sugar, adjust according to your taste

Almond Prep Work

Soak almonds for a few hours. Then peel the skin off before using.

1. Pour the milk into the slow cooker. Cover and cook on low for 1 hour.

2. In the meantime, grind the almonds and saffron together in a grinder or using a mortar and pestle. Add a little milk to make a smooth paste.

3. Transfer the almond paste and sugar to the milk in the slow cooker. Stir. Cover (but prop the lid open on the side just by ½"). Let the milk simmer on high for 1 hour or on low for 2–3 hours.

4. You can serve it either heated or chilled.

Bajra Raab

Although simple and easy to make, this beverage is a powerhouse of energy.
Perfect for those chilly winters. You can also make a savory version of raab.
Just take out the jaggery and ghee, and add salt and pepper to your taste.

INGREDIENTS | SERVES 4

4 cups buttermilk
4 tablespoons jaggery (gur)
2 tablespoons ghee
4 tablespoons millet flour

1. Heat the buttermilk in a 4-quart slow cooker set on high. Cover and cook until it comes to a boil.

2. Coarsely chop the jaggery. Mix with the ghee. Set aside.

3. Once the buttermilk comes to a boil, add the millet and the jaggery and ghee mixture. Mix it well until there are no lumps. Cover and cook on low for 30 minutes.

4. Serve warm.

Basil Tea (Tulsi Waali Chai)

Tulsi, a variety of basil, has a very sacred place in the Indian culture.
It has darker leaves and is called "holy basil." Apart from the fact that it tastes good,
basil tea has been served in India for years as a treatment for coughs, colds, and fevers.

INGREDIENTS | SERVES 8

8 cups water
6–8 black tea bags
1 cup basil leaves
Sugar (optional)
Milk (optional)
Lemon juice (optional)

1. Pour the water into the slow cooker. Add the tea bags. Cover and cook for 2 hours on high setting. Once the water starts bubbling and has turned dark in color, add the basil leaves. Cook for another 45 minutes.

2. Strain and serve. Add sugar or milk, if desired. You can also add lemon juice, but not if you use milk.

Spice It Up!

You can also add several spices to this tea, such as, cardamom, cloves, ginger, or black pepper.

Chach (Spiced Buttermilk)

Chach is a popular drink during summers. It's very light and refreshing, and aids in digestion; it is usually served at the end of a meal.

INGREDIENTS | SERVES 4–6

2 cups Slow Cooker Yogurt (Chapter 3)
½ teaspoon roasted cumin powder
½ teaspoon red chili powder
½ teaspoon rock salt
1 tablespoon Chaat Masala (Chapter 2)
1 tablespoon minced fresh mint
Salt, to taste
Water, as needed

1. In a large mixing bowl, whisk together all the ingredients *except* for the water. Whisk the yogurt mixture smooth.

2. Now add water, at least three times (6 cups) the amount of the yogurt. Transfer it to a pitcher. Add more water, if you think it necessary. Serve cold.

Ginger Ale

Forget buying ginger ale in the store! Once you've had this slow cooker version, you'll never drink store-bought again.

INGREDIENTS | SERVES 4

1 cup water
2 cups sugar
¼ cup grated ginger
1 cup lemon juice
Club soda, to taste

1. Add the water and sugar to a 3-quart slow cooker. Cover and cook on low for 4 hours. During the last hour of cooking, prop the lid open on the side by ½" for the steam to escape.

2. Turn off the heat. Add the ginger. Cover and let the water come to room temperature on its own.

3. Add the lemon juice. Strain the mixture through a strainer. Store in a tight-lidded bottle in the refrigerator.

4. Add club soda before serving.

Ginger Tea

*Ginger is said to be very good for throat infections and even nausea
or digestion problems. Often, in India, the tea served at home and at tea stalls
is cooked with gingerroot, or cardamom, or sometimes both.*

INGREDIENTS | SERVES 8–10

6 cups water

4 tablespoons loose black tea, or 10–12 black tea bags

1½ inches gingerroot, grated

¼ cup sugar, more if desired

2 cups 2% milk

1. Add the water to the slow cooker and turn the heat on high.

2. Once the water is hot, add tea, gingerroot, and sugar. Cover the lid and cook for 2 hours.

3. Open the lid, add the milk, and cook for another 20 minutes.

4. Strain and serve.

Mango Lassi

*You can easily find rose water at a grocery store or
Indian specialty store. I recommend Dabur's Red Rose Water.*

INGREDIENTS | SERVES 4

1½ cups Slow Cooker Yogurt (Chapter 3)

1 cup mango purée

1½ cups milk

¼ teaspoon rose water

1. Put everything in a blender and blend it together making a smoothie. Serve chilled.

Masala Chai

This spicy chai is soothing and comforting. Sip some on a chilly day, under a blanket on your couch!

INGREDIENTS | SERVES 8

5 cups water
2 sticks of cinnamon
1 teaspoon cloves
1 teaspoon green cardamom pods
1 tablespoon grated ginger
4 tablespoons loose black tea, or 10–12 black tea bags
¼ cup sugar
2 cups 2% milk

1. Add the water to the slow cooker and turn the heat on high.

2. Once the water is hot, add all the spices, tea, and sugar. Cover the lid and cook for 2 hours.

3. Open the lid, add the milk, and cook for another 20 minutes.

4. Strain the prepared tea through a strainer into tea mugs and serve.

Mulled Wine

Mulled wine is a perfect way to create a festive mood on those cold winter evenings. To add an extra punch, add a liquor such as brandy.

INGREDIENTS | SERVES 8

1 bottle (25.4 ounces) red wine
1 orange, peeled and sliced
8–10 cloves
¼ cup honey
½ cup raw brown sugar
3 cinnamon sticks
1 vanilla pod

1. Combine all the ingredients in a 5-quart slow cooker. On a low setting, heat for 1 hour.

2. After an hour, stir to make sure that the honey has completely dissolved. When the wine is steaming and the ingredients have been well blended, it is ready to serve.

Citrus and Spice Make Everything Nice

You can use any spices or citrus peels for this recipe. Ginger and lemon go well together too.

OJ Mint Punch

Both fresh or bottled orange juice can work for this recipe.
Strain fresh juice with a strainer to get a pulp-free juice.

INGREDIENTS | YIELDS 10 CUPS

1 cup sugar
2 green cardamom pods
4 cups orange juice
1 cup fresh mint leaves
4–5 cups ice
8 cups ginger ale

1. In a 3-quart slow cooker, combine together the sugar, cardamom, and orange juice. Cover and cook on high for 3 hours. Pop the lid open about 1", letting the steam escape and reducing the juice into a thin, flowing syrupy consistency. Strain into a jar. Store in the refrigerator or use when cool.

2. In a pitcher, add the mint leaves, ice, and 2 cups of the prepared orange juice syrup. Smash the mint with the ice using a long muddler. Add ginger ale. Stir and serve.

Pistachio Milk (Pista Doodh)

With the pistachios, this beverage packs a protein punch.

INGREDIENTS | SERVES 6–8

4½ cups of milk
½ cup sugar
½ cup shelled pistachios

1. Cook the milk and sugar together in a slow cooker on high for 2 hours.

2. Coarsely grind the pistachios. Stir them into the milk. Prop the lid open by 1" and cook for another 30–40 minutes on high. Serve hot or cold.

Pista

Pista is a Hindi name for pistachio. This recipe for pista doodh is very similar to that of almond milk, except there is no saffron and the pistachios don't need soaking.

Punjabi Lassi

This lassi is creamy and nutty, and the saffron gives it an extra touch.

INGREDIENTS | SERVES 4

12–15 almonds, soaked in water overnight
3 cups Slow Cooker Yogurt (Chapter 3)
1 cup milk
Pinch saffron
½ cup sugar
2 tablespoons crushed pistachios
½–1 cup water
½ cup thick cream (malai)

1. Peel the almonds. Coarsely crush them. Set aside.

2. Place the Yogurt, milk, saffron, sugar, pistachios, and almonds in a blender. Pulse it a couple times. Add water to your liking and pulse one more time. Make a smooth mixture.

3. Transfer to serving glasses. Spoon some cream on top and serve cold.

Rose Milk

Gulab jal, or rose water, is one of the most commonly used essences in Indian food, next to cardamom seeds and saffron.

INGREDIENTS | SERVES 6–8

4½ cups milk
⅓ cup rose syrup
½ teaspoon rose water

1. Cook the milk in a slow cooker, covered, for 3 hours on low.

2. Stir in the rose syrup and rose water. Turn off the heat. Cover the slow cooker and let sit for 10–15 minutes. Pour into serving glasses. You can also serve rose milk cold.

Rose Syrup

Rose syrup is made by simmering wild rose petals with water and sugar. Once cooked, the liquid is strained through a strainer, discarding the rose petals and any dirt.

Spiced Fruit Punch

Perfect for outdoor parties, this punch has the tangy flavor of citrus with the spicy taste of the cloves.

INGREDIENTS | SERVES 10–12

1 cup water
1½ cups sugar
½ tablespoon cloves
1 tablespoon crushed green cardamom pods
1 cup lemon juice
1 cup orange juice
Club soda, to taste

Get Fizzy with It

The amount of club soda added to the punch really depends on your taste. If you like more fizz, add more!

1. Add the water, sugar, cloves, and cardamom to a 3–4-quart slow cooker. Cover and let it simmer for 3–4 hours on low.

2. Strain the liquid through a strainer, discarding the whole spices. Add the lemon and orange juices. Stir. Let it cool before using it for the drink.

3. Add 1 part punch concentrate and 3 parts club soda (more or less to your taste). Serve with some ice.

Strawberry Lassi

You can add strawberries in any form: fresh, frozen, or sometimes I even add a preserve or Five-Spice Strawberry Chutney (Chapter 13). The chutney gives it an extra zing from the spices. Just adjust the sweetness accordingly.

INGREDIENTS | SERVES 4

2 cups fresh strawberries, or 1½ cups frozen, thawed

1½ cups Slow Cooker Yogurt (Chapter 3)

¼ cup sugar

1 cup milk

1 cup water, plus more if needed

½ teaspoon cardamom powder

1. Blend the strawberries in a blender. Strain it through a sieve, discarding the seeds.

2. Now transfer everything to a smoothie maker. Pulse a couple times. (Add some ice, if wanted). Serve chilled.

CHAPTER 15

Basic Breads of India

Dosa (Rice and Lentil Crepes)
287

Paratha (Pan-Fried Flatbread)
288

Poori (Deep-Fried Puffed Flatbread)
289

Roti/Chapatti/Fulka
290

Simple Naan
291

Dosa (Rice and Lentil Crepes)

Dosa is an Indian-style crepe or thin pancake. It is usually made by mixing rice and lentils, in a particular ratio, and then ground and fermented before making crepes out of it.

INGREDIENTS | SERVES 8–10

1½ cups parboiled rice, washed and soaked overnight

2 tablespoons semolina or poha (flattened rice)

½ cup split urad dal, washed and soaked overnight

1 tablespoon salt

Oil

1 raw potato, halved

Extra Things Needed to Make a Dosa

One raw potato, cut into two, griddle, spatula, a wet grinder (to grind rice and lentils). If you don't have a wet grinder, your blender will also work, but a wet grinder will get the batter a little smoother.

1. Grind the rices and urad dal separately into smooth, flowing batters. (Grinding the two separately and then mixing makes the batter lighter. It also helps in speeding up the fermentation process.)

2. Mix the two batters, add salt, and cover the batter. Let it ferment overnight. The lid should be tight enough to trap the temperature inside but loose enough to let a little circulation of air. So don't use an airtight container. Also, the temperature should be somewhere around 80–85°F for a proper fermentation.

3. Heat a griddle. Sprinkle water on the griddle; if the water sizzles right away, then the griddle is hot enough.

4. Spray some oil on the griddle. Rub the cut side of a potato to the pan. Now pour on a ladle of dosa batter. Starting from the center and working in an outward direction, swirl the ladle in a circular motion spreading the batter into a thin crepe.

5. When the batter is spread, after a few seconds (8–10) it will start getting dry. Spray or sprinkle oil on the dosa.

6. Give it a few more seconds and the bottom of your dosa will start getting darker and golden brown in color. This means your dosa is almost ready.

7. At this point if you want to add any filling in your dosa, you can place it in the center and fold the two sides, one over the other. The filling can be a simple potato filling or vegetables, or even minced, cooked meat. Traditionally, dosa is served with Sambhar (Chapter 6) or Green Chili and Coconut Chutney (Chapter 2).

Paratha (Pan-Fried Flatbread)

Paratha is a simple flatbread, which is at first rolled (applying oil between different layers) and then pan-fried to make it crispy on the outside while soft and layered on the inside.

INGREDIENTS | YIELDS 8–10 PIECES

1½ cups whole wheat flour
1 teaspoon salt
1 teaspoon ajwain seeds (optional)
⅓–⅔ cup water
Oil, or ghee, for frying

Types of Parathas

Other than the simple layered paratha explained here, one can also stuff the paratha with a filling or stuffing—from a simple potato filling to a vegetable or minced meat filling. One can also mix spices with the flour, knead it into a dough, and then follow the same recipe discussed here.

1. Mix all the ingredients together *except* for the oil and knead the mixture together into a dough. The trick is to slowly add water so that you have an idea of how the flour is absorbing the water.

2. When the dough is formed and you can hold it all together, transfer it to the counter or a flat dish and knead for about 4–5 minutes. The dough is ready when all the moisture is absorbed by the flour.

3. Wrap the dough in plastic wrap and let it rest for about 5–10 minutes. This will help it get even softer.

4. Take the dough out of the plastic wrap and knead it once again for just a few seconds to make it smooth. Divide the dough into smaller balls of equal size. You'll need almost 3–4 tablespoons of dough for one paratha.

5. Roll out the dough into a circle. Brush one exposed surface with oil. Hold one end of the circle and fold it over the other forming a semicircle. Now brush the exposed surface again and fold the two ends again forming a triangle.

6. Roll the triangle over a flour-dusted surface, resulting in a flattened triangle.

7. Heat a skillet. Brush ghee on both sides of the paratha and pan-fry it until both the sides have several brown spots on them and there are no uncooked spots. Serve hot with your choice of curry or chutney or raita dip (see Chapter 13 for chutney and raita recipes).

Poori (Deep-Fried Puffed Flatbread)

Poori is generally served in the festive season and goes perfectly with Vrat ka khana.

INGREDIENTS | SERVES 5–6

1½ cups whole wheat flour
1 teaspoon salt
1 teaspoon ajwain seeds (optional)
⅓–⅔ cup water
Oil, for deep frying

Kneading the Dough

The process of kneading the dough is almost the same for all the bread recipes, which is similar to roti. Dough for roti and paratha is a little softer than poori, and naan is even softer than roti.

1. Mix the flour, salt, and ajwain seeds together to make a dough. Start by adding water slowly into the bowl of flour and mix it with your hand. The trick is to slowly add water so that you have an idea of how the flour is absorbing the water.

2. When the dough is formed and you can hold it all together, transfer it to the counter or a flat dish and knead for about 4–5 minutes. The dough is ready when all the moisture is absorbed by the flour. Poori dough is just a little tougher than a roti dough.

3. Wrap the dough in plastic wrap and let it rest for about 5–10 minutes. This will help it get even softer.

4. Take the dough out of the plastic wrap and knead it once again for just a few seconds to make it smooth. Divide the dough into smaller balls of equal size. You'll need almost 1 tablespoon of dough for one poori.

5. Dust the working station and start working on one ball at a time. Using a rolling pin, try to flatten the balls into flat circles. If getting a perfect shape is difficult, just flatten the dough and use a round lid, or something similar, and cut it into round shapes. Dust the dough balls at least 2–3 times while rolling if the dough sticks to the rolling pin.

6. Roll out the dough into 3"–4" circles and then deep-fry them in the oil. Poori will puff into little balls when fried, and when both sides have turned golden brown (which will only take seconds if oil is hot enough), take them out and let excess oil drain in paper towels. Serve hot with your choice of curry or stir-fried vegetables.

Roti/Chapatti/Fulka

Roti or chapatti or fulka, whatever name you call it, is the basic or most common bread served in Indian homes almost every day. These are thin flatbreads, almost like a Mexican tortilla but softer and layered.

INGREDIENTS | SERVES 8–10

Water
3 cups flour
Flour, for dusting
Ghee (Chapter 3)

Roti Tips

Add up to ½ cup of milk to the flour while kneading to get a softer roti. If you have an electric stovetop, then use either a cooling rack or something similar to puff/roast the rotis.

1. Start by adding water slowly into the bowl of flour and mix it with your hand. The trick is to slowly add water so that you have an idea of how the flour is absorbing the water.

2. When the dough is formed and you can hold it all together, transfer it to the counter or a flat dish and knead for about 4–5 minutes. The dough is ready when all the moisture is absorbed by the flour. Wrap the dough in plastic wrap and let it rest for about 5–10 minutes. This will help it get even softer.

3. Take the dough out of the plastic wrap and knead it once again for just a few seconds to make it smooth. Divide the dough into smaller balls of equal size. You'll need almost 2 tablespoons of dough for one roti.

4. Dust the working station and start working on one ball at a time. Using a rolling pin, try to flatten the balls into flat circles. If getting a perfect shape is difficult, just flatten the dough and use a round lid, or something similar, and cut it into round shapes. Dust the dough balls at least 2–3 times while rolling if the dough sticks to the rolling pin.

5. Preheat a skillet. Place the flattened dough circle in the skillet and cook for 15–20 seconds or until you see small bubbles on the surface, and then flip it. Repeat on the other side and then transfer it to another burner for roasting. Place a cooling rack on top of the burner. This will prevent the roti from sticking to the burner. Roast the roti over open flame or direct heat from the burner. Roti will puff up in a few seconds, then flip it for the other side to get cooked as well. Remove from the heat, brush some Ghee, and serve hot.

Simple Naan

Traditionally, naan is baked in a clay oven and the char from the coal gives it its distinct flavor. You can add several flavors, such as garlic, cilantro, cumin, and so on, by either adding the ingredient to the dough or simply sprinkling it on top of the naan before cooking it.

INGREDIENTS | YIELDS 6–8 PIECES

2 cups all-purpose flour, or wheat flour
¼ teaspoon salt
¾ teaspoon baking powder
½ teaspoon baking soda
½ tablespoon sugar
½ cup warm milk
½ cup yogurt
½ tablespoon oil

Using Yeast

For a quicker recipe, use 1 tablespoon of active yeast instead of yogurt, baking soda, and baking powder. Dissolve it in warm milk with salt and sugar and follow the same process given here.

1. In a large bowl, mix all the dry ingredients together and make a well in the flour.

2. Mix the milk and yogurt together in a medium bowl and pour half of it into the flour well and slowly combine it together. There is no exact amount of liquid that should be added to the flour to make a perfect dough, so add liquid slowly and combine it all together slowly until a soft dough is made. The dough should be soft enough for you to be able to dig your finger into it without applying any pressure. If dough sticks to your hands too much, then put a little bit of oil on your hands and then punch into the dough.

3. Transfer the prepared dough to a bowl and cover the dough with a damp cloth and let it sit and rise in a warm place for at least 2 hours.

4. Dust your working board with flour, take out the dough, and knead it for about 2–3 minutes. Divide the dough into smaller balls (you should get about 8 balls).

5. Dust the board again and flatten the balls, about ½" thick and elongated to make bread. Brush 1 side with water. Heat a thick-bottom skillet or a wok with a lid. Once it's hot, place the naan wet side down and cover it with a lid. Let it cook for about 30 seconds or until you see bubbles on it.

6. Now cook the other side of the naan over direct flame of the burner with the help of tongs (alternatively you could use a broiler to roast the naan). When you see some charred brown spots, then you know that the naan is done. Serve hot with some butter smothered on top.

Glossary

Adrak lasun ka paste
Ginger-garlic paste.

Aloo tikki
Potato patties.

Buttermilk
See *Chach*.

Chaat masala
Spice blend used usually for a tangy and hot flavor.

Chach
Spiced buttermilk.

Chana dal
Split black chickpeas.

Coriander
Dried cilantro seeds:

Curry leaves
An herb used to flavor many Indian dishes. Used in both fresh and dried form. Leaves from the curry tree.

Daliya
Broken wheat.

Dosa
Rice and lentil crepes.

Ghee
Clarified butter.

Jaggery
Raw unrefined whole cane sugar.

Kashmiri lal mirch
Red chili peppers from the state of Kashmir.

Lassi
Sweetened yogurt drink.

Mishti doi
Sweetened steamed yogurt dish.

Moong dal bean
Split moong bean.

Naan
Fermented oven-baked flatbread.

Panch foran
Five whole, dry spice blend—includes fenugreek seeds, nigella, cumin, black mustard seeds, and fennel seeds.

Poha
Flattened rice.

Poori
Deep-fried flatbread.

Roti
Simple whole wheat flatbread.

Toor dal
Split pea.

Index

Note: Page numbers in **bold** indicate recipe category lists.

Adrak Lasan Ka Paste, 30
Almonds. *See* Nuts and seeds
Aloo dishes. *See* Potatoes
Appetizers, **44**–61
  Chicken Bites, 45
  Citrusy Beets, 46
  Dhaniye Waale Aloo (Potato Bites in
    Cilantro Sauce), 45
  Gingered Sweet Potatoes, 46
  Keema Pav (Indian Sloppy Joes), 47
  Lamb Kofta, 48
  Lasuni Gobhi, 49
  Masala Nuts, 50
  Papdi Chat, 50
  Pav Bhaji, 51
  Pork Tikkas (Pork Ke Tikke), 52
  Reshmi Kabab, 53
  Roasted Chickpeas, 54
  Shakarkandi (Spicy Baked Indian
    Sweet Potatoes), 54
  Slow Cooker Hara Bhara Kabab, 55
  Slow Cooker Roasted Potatoes, 56
  Spiced Fingerling Potatoes, 57
  Spice Potatoes, 56
  Sweet and Spicy Pineapple Pumpkin
    Curry, 58
  Sweet and Tangy Slow Cooker
    Almonds, 59
  Tandoori Chicken Wings, 60
  Tangy Sweet Potato Bites, 59
  Tikki Chaat, 61
Apple and Pear Chutney, 261
Asafetida (heeng), 21
Avial (Mixed Vegetables in Coconut
  Sauce), 113

Baghar or tadka (tempering), 12–13
Baigan. *See* Eggplant
Banana Pudding, 242
Basil Tea (Tulsi Waali Chai), 278
Bay leaves, using, 173

Beans. *See* Lentils, chickpeas, beans,
  and other legumes
Beef, **161**
  about: lean cuts of, 179; preparing
    in slow cooker, 24–25; pressure
    cooking, 169
  Beef Stew, 63
  Haleem, 166
  Pot Roast with Root Vegetables, 177
  Shredded Beef for Sandwiches, 179
  Slow Cooker Shammi Kabab, 180
  Tandoori Meatballs, 182
Beets
  Citrusy Beets, 46
  Easy Pickled Beets, 132
  "Roasted" Beets, 132
Bengal Gram Dal and Bottle Gourd Soup
  (Chana Dal Lauki), 84
Berries
  Amle ka Murabba (Gooseberries in
    Sugar Syrup), 259
  Five-Spice Strawberry Chutney, 271
  Saffron-Infused Rabdi with Fresh
    Berries, 252
  Strawberry Lassi, 285
Beverages, **275**–85
  Aam Pana (Raw Mango Cooler), 276
  Badam Milk (Warm Almond Milk),
    277
  Bajra Raab, 278
  Basil Tea (Tulsi Waali Chai), 278
  Chach (Spiced Buttermilk), 279
  Ginger Ale, 279
  Ginger Tea, 280
  Mango Lassi, 280
  Masala Chai, 281
  Mulled Wine, 281
  OJ Mint Punch, 282
  Pistachio Milk (Pista Doodh), 282
  Punjabi Lassi, 283
  Rose Milk, 283
  Spiced Fruit Punch, 284
  Strawberry Lassi, 285
Bhunao (sautéing), 13

Black-eyed peas. *See* Lentils, chickpeas,
  beans, and other legumes
Blender, 18
Boondi, 260, 270
Breads, **286**–91
  about: kneading dough, 289
  Dosa (Rice and Lentil Crepes), 287
  Paratha (Pan-Fried Flatbread), 288
  Poori (Deep-Fried Puffed Flatbread),
    289
  Roti/Chapatti/Fulka, 290
  Simple Naan, 291
Butter, clarified. *See* Ghee
Butter, spiced, 181, 255

Cabbage
  Bandhagobhi ki Sabji (Cabbage with
    Potatoes and Peas), 116
  Til waali Bandhagobhi (Cabbage
    with Peas, Carrots, and Sesame
    Seeds), 138
Cardamom powder, 163
Carrots
  Carrot and Cheese Pudding (Gajar
    Paneer Ka Halwa), 242
  Carrots and Peas Pulao, 206
  Dry-Spiced Carrot and Peas (Gajar
    Mattar Ki Subzi), 121
  Gajar Ka Halwa (Carrot Pudding),
    246
  Til waali Bandhagobhi (Cabbage
    with Peas, Carrots, and Sesame
    Seeds), 138
Cauliflower
  Andhra Vegetable Pulao, 205
  Cauliflower Soup, 67
  Curried Cauliflower Soup, 69
  Gobhi Aloo (Potato and Cauliflower),
    124
  Lasuni Gobhi, 49
Chaat Spice Mix (Chaat Masala), 28
Chai. *See* Beverages
Chai Masala, 29
Chana dal. *See* Lentils, chickpeas,
  beans, and other legumes

Cheese
    about: dairy dos and don'ts, 25
    Cardamom-Infused Cheesecake, 241
    Carrot and Cheese Pudding (Gajar Paneer Ka Halwa), 242
    Cheese Pudding (Paneeri Kheer), 243
    Chhurpi Soup, 68
    Homemade Paneer (Indian Cottage Cheese), 32
    Kalakand, 249
    Matar Paneer, 128
    Palak Paneer, 129
    Paneer Makhani, 130
    Spinach and Paneer Pulao, 227
    Split Pea and Cheese Curry (Paneeri Chana Dal), 103
    Split Pea Soup with Fried Paneer, 78
Chhurpi Soup, 68
Chicken. See Poultry
Chickpeas. See Lentils, chickpeas, beans, and other legumes
Chili powder, 20
Chole Masala, 119
Chutney, raita dips, and sauces, **26, 258**–74
    Aam ki Launji (Raw Mango Preserve), 259
    about: buying tamarind chutney, 231; chutney finger foods, 27; hot green chili sauce, 220; storing chutneys, 272
    Amle ka Murabba (Gooseberries in Sugar Syrup), 259
    Ananas ki Chutney (Spicy Pineapple Chutney), 260
    Apple and Pear Chutney, 261
    Boondi Raita, 260
    Cilantro Chutney Raita Dip (Hari Chutney ka Raita), 262
    Cucumber Mint Raita, 262
    Cucumber Raita, 263
    Dahi Kachumbar, 263
    Easy Peanut Sauce, 264
    Five-Spice Strawberry Chutney, 271
    Green Chili and Coconut Chutney (Hari Mirch Aur Nariel Ke Chutney), 35
    Green Chutney Raita, 264
    Gulkand (Rose Petal Jam), 265
    Homemade Hot Ketchup, 266
    Hot Cilantro Chutney, 27

    Lauki Ka Raita (Bottle Gourd Raita), 265
    Mango Chili Chutney, 267
    Mango-Saffron Chutney (Kairi Kesar Ki Chutney), 268
    Mint-Cilantro Chutney (Pudine Dhaniye Ke Chutney), 27
    Mixed Fruit Raita, 267
    Mixed Seafood Dip, 194
    Palak Raita (Spinach and Yogurt Dip), 268
    Pineapple Raita, 269
    Pomegranate and Mango Chutney Raita, 269
    Rice with Chutney (Chutney Wale Chawal), 221
    Smoked Raita, 270
    Sweet and Tangy Mango Relish, 272
    Tamarind Chutney (Imli Ki Chutney), 272
    Tamarind Lime Sauce, 191
    Three-Pepper Sauce, 273
    Tomato and Onion Chutney, 273
    Tomato Chutney (Tamatar ki Chutney), 274
    Vengaya Thogayal (Onion Chutney), 274
Cilantro chutneys, 27, 262
Citrus
    Citrusy Beets, 46
    Lemon Rice (Nimbu Wale Chawal), 216
    Mulled Wine, 281
    OJ Mint Punch, 282
    Spiced Fruit Punch, 284
Coconut
    about: coconut milk, 146
    Avial (Mixed Vegetables in Coconut Sauce), 113
    Chili Coconut Chicken (Mangalorian Murgh Gassi), 146
    Malabari Coconut Rice (Thenga Choru), 217
    Tomato Coconut Soup, 82
Coriander seeds (dhaniya), 22
Cucumber Mint Raita, 262
Cucumber Raita, 263
Cumin, 20–21, 121
Curry Paste, 39

Dairy. See also Cheese; Ghee; Yogurt
    about: avoiding spilling boiled milk, 251; dos and don'ts, 25
    desserts with. See Desserts
    drinks with. See Beverages
    Khoya (Solidified Milk), 40
Dal. See Lentils, chickpeas, beans, and other legumes
Deep-frying (talina), 13–14
Desserts, **237**–57
    about: avoiding spilling boiled milk, 251; homemade graham cracker crumbs, 241; silver foil (vark) on, 244
    Almond Brittle (Chikki), 238
    Almond Pudding (Badam ki Kheer), 239
    Banana Pudding, 242
    Brown Rice Pongal, 240
    Cardamom-Infused Cheesecake, 241
    Carrot and Cheese Pudding (Gajar Paneer Ka Halwa), 242
    Chai Pudding, 243
    Cheese Pudding (Paneeri Kheer), 243
    Creamy Milk Pudding (Basoondi), 244
    Firni with Pistachios and Cashews, 245
    Gajar Ka Halwa (Carrot Pudding), 246
    Garam Rabdi (Warm Condensed Milk), 247
    Ginger Poached Pears, 247
    Gulkand Ice Cream, 248
    Kalakand, 249
    Mango Yogurt Pudding (Amrakhand), 250
    Nimish, 255
    Opo Squash Pudding (Dudhi Ki Kheer), 250
    Rice Pudding (Kheer), 251
    Rose-Scented Custard, 252
    Saffron-Infused Rabdi with Fresh Berries, 252
    Saffron Yogurt Pudding (Kesari Shrikhand), 253
    Semolina Pudding (Sooji Ki Kheer), 253
    Shahi Tukda, 254
    Spicy Guava Butter, 255
    Sweetened Yogurt (Mishti Doi), 255

Vermicelli Pudding (Seviyan Ki Kheer), 256
Wheat Payasam, 257
Drumsticks, vegetable, 113
Drumstick Sambhar (Murungaikkai Sambhar), 89
Duck, mango breast, 153
Dum (steaming), 12
Dum pukht, 122, 224

Eggplant
  Baigan Bharta, 114
  Baigan Nu Bharta (Roasted Eggplant in Yogurt), 115
  Eggplant Cooked with Panch Foran Spices, 123
  Spiced "Baked" Eggplant, 135
  Stuffed Eggplants, 136
Eggs
  Hardboiled Eggs, 38
  Pasteurized Eggs, 43

Fish and seafood, **183**–203
  about: Bengali cuisine and, 187; deveining shrimp, 201; prawns and shrimp, 226; preparing in slow cooker, 24
  Brown Rice Curry with Vegetables and Scallops, 184
  Creamy Shrimp (Malai Jhinga), 185
  Fish in a Velvety Sauce (Bengali Doi Maach), 186
  Fish in Tomato Sauce, 187
  Goan Shrimp, 188
  Kashmiri Fish Curry (Kashmiri Macchi), 189
  Kerala Fish Curry (Meen Moilee), 190
  Macchi Dum Pukht (Slowcooked Fish), 192
  Macher Jhol, 193
  Mixed Seafood Dip, 194
  Muri Ghonto, 195
  Parsi Fish (Patrani Macchi), 196
  Prawn Masala (Jhinga Masala), 197
  Salmon in Saffron-Flavored Curry (Zaffrani Macchi), 198
  Shorshe Maach (Fish cooked in hot mustard sauce), 199
  Shrimp in Coconut Milk (Chingri Maacher Malai Curry), 200
  Shrimp Patio (Kolmino Patio), 201

Spicy Shrimp Rice (Jhinge Ki Biryani), 226
Steamed Tandoori Macchi, 202
Tamarind Fish Curry (Imli Wale Macchi), 203
Food processor, 18
Foundation recipes, **36**–43
Fruit. See also specific fruit
  Mixed Fruit Raita, 267
  Spiced Fruit Punch, 284
Frying (deep-frying), 13–14

Garam Masala Powder, 30
Garlic
  about: ginger-garlic paste, 14; Hindi name for, 49; optimizing flavor of, 211
  Chili-Garlic Paste, 29
  Garlic Rice (Lasuni Pulao), 211
  Ginger-Garlic Paste (Adrak Lasan Ka Paste), 30
Ghee, 14–15, 40
Ginger
  about: benefits of, 29; ginger-garlic paste, 14; gingerroot, 30
  Ginger Ale, 279
  Ginger-Garlic Paste (Adrak Lasan Ka Paste), 30
  Ginger Poached Pears, 247
  Ginger Tea, 280
Goat (mutton)
  about: preparing in slow cooker, 24–25; pressure cooking, 169
  Gosht Shorba (Goat Curry), 165
  Haleem, 166
  Kerala Mutton Stew, 70
  Khurdi (White Stock Soup), 71
  Mutton Do Pyaza, 174
Gobhi. See Cauliflower
Goda Masala Powder, 31
Gosht. See Goat (mutton)
Graham cracker crumbs, homemade, 241
Grilling (tandoori cooking), 13
Guava butter, spiced, 255
Gulkand. See Rose

Haleem, 166
Hariyali Kadhi, 108

Ice cream, 248
Indian cooking basics, 11–25. See also Spices
  about: overview of, 11
  essential ingredients, 14–15
  essential techniques, 12–14
  tools, 18–19
Ingredients. See also Spices; specific main ingredients

Jackfruit, in Kathal Do Pyaza, 126

Kababs, 53, 55, 180
Kati Roll, 151
Keema Pav (Indian Sloppy Joes), 47
Ketchup, homemade hot, 266
Kheema and Quinoa (Quinoa with Minced Meat Curry), 168
Khichdi, 214
Khoya (Solidified Milk), 40

Lamb, **161**
  about: curries, 172; healthy cooking tips, 164; preparing in slow cooker, 24–25; pressure cooking, 169; selecting, 171
  Cardamom-Flavored Lamb (Eliachi Gosht), 163
  Extra Hot Boneless Leg of Lamb, 164
  Green Chili Lamb Chops, 167
  Hot Spiced Lamb (Andhra Gosht Pittu), 167
  Keema Pav (Indian Sloppy Joes), 47
  Kheema and Quinoa (Quinoa with Minced Meat Curry), 168
  Lamb Curry with Turnips (Shalgam Wala Gosht), 169
  Lamb Kofta, 48
  Lamb Roganjosh, 170
  Lamb Soup, 72
  Lamb Vindaloo, 171
  Meatball Curry (Kofta Curry), 173
  Meat Belli Ram (Belli Ram Ka Gosht), 172
  Peas and Minced-Meat Curry (Kheema Mattar), 175
  Royal Lamb (Nawabi Gosht), 178
  Spinach Lamb Curry (Saag Gosht), 181
Lasuni. See Garlic

Lentils, chickpeas, beans, and other legumes, **83**–108. *See also* Peas
  about: moong bean sprouts and brown rice, 228; preparing in slow cooker, 23; reducing dal cooking time, 92; removing gas-forming compounds, 101; rinsing and cooking, 96, 101; soaking overnight, 23
  Bengal Gram Dal and Bottle Gourd Soup (Chana Dal Lauki), 84
  Black Bean Soup, 64
  Black-Eyed Peas Curry (Tarewale Lobhiya), 85
  Chole Masala, 119
  Creamy Red Lentils (Masoor Ki Dal), 86
  Curried Black-Eyed Peas, 119
  Curried Chana Dal, 87
  Dal Makhanai (Slow Cooked Beans with Spices and Cream), 88
  Dosa (Rice and Lentil Crepes), 287
  Drumstick Sambhar (Murungaikkai Sambhar), 89
  The Five-Lentil Delight (Paanch Dalo Ka Sangam), 105
  Gujarati Yellow Mung Beans (Peele Moong Ki Dal), 90
  Kabuli Chane ke Chawal (Rice with Chickpeas), 212
  Khichdi, 214
  Leelva Nu Bhat, 215
  Lentil Chili, 91
  Maharastrian Pigeon Pea Curry (Ambat Varan), 92
  Mung Ki Dal Palak (Split Mung Beans Cooked with Spinach), 93
  Puneri Dal, 95
  Punjabi Kadhi Pakoda (Chickpea Fritters in Yogurt Sauce), 94
  Rajma Masala, 96, 132
  Rasam, 97
  Restaurant-Style Dal Fry, 98
  Roasted Chickpeas, 54
  Sambhar, 99
  Simple Chickpea Sandal, 100
  Simple Mung Bean Curry (Tadka Dal), 101
  Slow Cooker Hara Bhara Kabab, 55
  Split Black Lentil Soup (Urad Dal), 102

Split Pea Soup with Fried Paneer, 78
Sprouted Moong Bean Rice, 228
Tadka Tomato Dal, 104
Tomato Rasam, 106
Lobster in Creamy Sauce (Lobster Ka Korma), 191

Makhani Masala, 41
Malai Kofta, 127
Mango
  Amchoor (Mango Powder), 28
  Aam ki Launji (Raw Mango Preserve), 259
  Aam Pana (Raw Mango Cooler), 276
  Mango Chili Chutney, 267
  Mango Duck Breast, 153
  Mango Lassi, 280
  Mango-Saffron Chutney (Kairi Kesar Ki Chutney), 268
  Mango Yogurt Pudding (Amrakhand), 250
  Pomegranate and Mango Chutney Raita, 269
  Sweet and Tangy Mango Relish, 272
Marinating, 13, 25
Meats. *See also specific meats*
  about: pressure cooking, 169; slow cooking, 24–25
  Kheema and Quinoa (Quinoa with Minced Meat Curry), 169
  Meatball Curry (Kofta Curry), 173
  Meat Belli Ram (Belli Ram Ka Gosht), 172
  Peas and Minced-Meat Curry (Kheema Mattar), 175
Milk. *See* Beverages; Cheese; Dairy; Desserts; Ghee
Mint
  Cucumber Mint Raita, 262
  Minty Rice (Pudine Wale Chawal), 218
  OJ Mint Punch, 282
Mint-Cilantro Chutney (Pudine Dhaniye Ke Chutney), 27
Mung Ki Dal Palak, 93
Murgh. *See* Poultry
Mushrooms, in Royal Mushrooms with Cashew Nut Sauce (Nawabi Guchhi), 133
Mustard greens, slow cooked, 134
Mustard oil, 154

Mustard seeds (Sarson), 21–22
Mutton. *See* Goat (mutton)

Nuts and seeds
  about: sesame seeds, 138
  Almond Brittle (Chikki), 238
  Almond Pudding (Badam ki Kheer), 239
  Badam Milk (Warm Almond Milk), 277
  Cashew Nut Sauce, 133
  Easy Peanut Sauce, 264
  Firni with Pistachios and Cashews, 245
  Masala Nuts, 50
  Pistachio Milk (Pista Doodh), 282
  Punjabi Lassi, 283
  Sweet and Tangy Slow Cooker Almonds, 59
  Til waali Bandhagobhi (Cabbage with Peas, Carrots, and Sesame Seeds), 138

Oils, 14–15, 149, 154
Onions
  about: religion and, 236
  Caramelized Onions, 38
  Tomato and Onion Chutney, 273
  Vengaya Thogayal (Onion Chutney), 274

Palak. *See* Spinach
Panch Foran Spices, 31, 123
Paneer. *See* Cheese
Pans, 18
Parsnips, 157, 177
Pav Bhaji Masala, 33
Peanut sauce, 264
Pears
  Apple and Pear Chutney, 261
  Ginger Poached Pears, 247
Peas. *See also* Lentils, chickpeas, beans, and other legumes
  Aloo Matar Masala, 110
  Bandhagobhi ki Sabji (Cabbage with Potatoes and Peas), 116
  Carrots and Peas Pulao, 206
  Dry-Spiced Carrot and Peas (Gajar Mattar Ki Subzi), 121
  Matar Paneer, 128
  Papdi Chat, 50

Pav Bhaji, 51
Peas and Minced-Meat Curry
    (Kheema Mattar), 175
Split Pea and Cheese Curry (Paneeri
    Chana Dal), 103
Til waali Bandhagobhi (Cabbage
    with Peas, Carrots, and Sesame
    Seeds), 138
Peppers
    about: green chilies, 148; Kashmiri lal
        mirch, 210
    Bell Pepper and Vegetables Cooked
        with Fennel Seeds, 117
    Chili Pepper Curry (Mirchi Ka Salan),
        118
    chutneys with. See Chutney, raita
        dips, and sauces
    Roasted Red Bell Pepper Soup, 76
    Stuffed Peppers, 229
    Three-Pepper Sauce, 273
Pineapple
    Ananas ki Chutney (Spicy Pineapple
        Chutney), 260
    Pineapple Raita, 269
    Sweet and Spicy Pineapple Pumpkin
        Curry, 58
Pomegranate
    about, 271
    Pomegranate and Mango Chutney
        Raita, 269
Pork, 161
    about: preparing in slow cooker,
        24–25; pressure cooking, 169
    Braised Pork, 162
    Garlic, Pepper, and Lemon Pork Loin,
        162
    Pork Bafat, 176
    Pork Fried Rice (Pork Wale Chawal),
        220
    Pork Tikkas (Pork Ke Tikke), 52
    Slow Cooker Shammi Kabab, 180
Potatoes
    about: cooking quicker, 57
    Aloo Matar Masala, 110
    Aloo Methi (Potatoes Cooked in
        Fenugreek Leaves), 111
    Aloo Saag ki Sabji (Potato and
        Spinach Cooked with Red Chili),
        112
    Bandhagobhi ki Sabji (Cabbage with
        Potatoes and Peas), 116

Chicken Curry with Red Potatoes, 142
Dhaniye Waale Aloo (Potato Bites in
    Cilantro Sauce), 45
Dum Aloo, 122
Gobhi Aloo (Potato and Cauliflower),
    124
Jeera Aloo (Cumin-Scented
    Potatoes), 125
Papdi Chat, 50
Pav Bhaji, 51
Slow Cooker Roasted Potatoes, 56
Spiced Fingerling Potatoes, 57
Spice Potatoes, 56
Tamatar Aloo (Curried Potato with
    Tomato Sauce), 137
Tikki Chaat, 61
Poultry, 139–60
    about: cooking thighs, 77; Cornish
        game hens, 155
    Almond-Flavored Chicken (Badaami
        Murgh), 140
    Butter Chicken (Chicken Makhani),
        141
    Chicken Bites, 45
    Chicken Braised in Beer, 142
    Chicken Curry with Red Potatoes, 142
    Chicken in a Creamy Sauce (Murgh
        Korma), 143
    Chicken Makhani, 144
    Chicken Tikka Masala, 145
    Chili Coconut Chicken (Mangalorian
        Murgh Gassi), 146
    Coriander Chicken (Dhaniye Wala
        Murgh), 147
    Dried Mint Chicken, 158
    Fenugreek-Flavored Chicken (Murgh
        Methiwala), 148
    Ginger-Flavored Chicken Curry
        (Murgh Adraki), 149
    Goan Chicken Curry (Goan Murgh
        Xcautti), 150
    Green Chutney Wings, 153
    Kacchi Biryani, 213
    Kati Roll, 151
    Lehsun Wala Chicken (Garlic
        Chicken), 152
    Mango Duck Breast, 153
    Mulligatawny Soup, 73
    Murgh Achari (Chicken with Pickling
        Spices), 154
    Murghi ka Shorba (Chicken Soup), 74

Murgh Musallam, 155
Reshmi Kabab, 53
Slow Cooker Chicken Dum Biryani,
    224
Slow Cooker Tandoori Chicken, 156
Slow-Roasted Chicken with Potatoes,
    Parsnips, and Onions, 157
Spiced Chicken in Green Curry
    (Murgh Hariyali), 158
Spicy Chicken Stew, 77
Tandoori Chicken Wings, 60
"Teekha" Peanut Chicken, 159
White Chicken Rice (Safeed Murgh
    Ka Pulao), 235
Whole Roast Chicken, 160
Pumpkin, in Sweet and Spicy Pineapple
    Pumpkin Curry, 58

Quinoa, in Kheema and Quinoa, 168

Raita. See Chutney, raita dips, and
    sauces; Yogurt
Rajma Masala, 96, 132
Rasam, 97, 106
Rasam powder, 33
Rice, 204–36
    about: adding grease/oil to, 219;
        cooking, 209; Hindu religion and,
        216; leftovers, 212; moong bean
        sprouts and brown rice, 228;
        sela basmati, 222; soaking, 233;
        substituting brown rice for basmati,
        221; tri-colored, 234
    Andhra Vegetable Pulao, 205
    Bengali Butter Rice (Bengali Ghee
        Bhaat), 206
    Brown Basmati Rice, 37
    Brown Rice Curry with Vegetables
        and Scallops, 184
    Brown Rice Pongal, 240
    Calcutta (or Kolkata) Biryani, 208
    Carrots and Peas Pulao, 206
    Cumin-Scented Rice (Jeere wale
        Chawal), 209
    Dosa (Rice and Lentil Crepes), 287
    Firni with Pistachios and Cashews,
        245
    Garlic Rice (Lasuni Pulao), 211
    Hyderabadi Biryani, 210–11
    Kabuli Chane ke Chawal (Rice with
        Chickpeas), 212

Rice—*continued*
  Kacchi Biryani, 213
  Khichdi, 214
  Leelva Nu Bhat, 215
  Lemon Rice (Nimbu Wale Chawal), 216
  Malabari Coconut Rice (Thenga Choru), 217
  Minty Rice (Pudine Wale Chawal), 218
  Perfect Slow Cooker Basmati Rice, 219
  Perfect Slow Cooker White Rice, 37
  Pork Fried Rice (Pork Wale Chawal), 220
  Rice Pudding (Kheer), 251
  Rice with Chutney (Chutney Wale Chawal), 221
  Ruz Bukhari, 222
  Saffron Rice (Kesari Chawal), 223
  Slow Cooker Chicken Dum Biryani, 224
  Slow Cooker Upma, 225
  South Indian Rice and Vegetable Delight (Bissi Bela Hulianna), 207
  Spicy Shrimp Rice (Jhinge Ki Biryani), 226
  Spinach and Paneer Pulao, 227
  Sprouted Moong Bean Rice, 228
  Stuffed Peppers, 229
  Taheri (Spicy Vegetable Pulao), 230
  Tamarind Rice (Pulihora), 231
  Tomatillo Rice, 232
  Tomato Rice (Tamatar Ka Pulao), 233
  Turmeric Rice (Peele Chawal), 234
  White Chicken Rice (Safeed Murgh Ka Pulao), 235
  Yogurt Rice (Dahi Bhaat), 235
Roasted Saffron (Kesar), 34
Rose
  Gulkand (Rose Petal Jam), 265
  Gulkand Ice Cream, 248
  Rose Milk, 283
  Rose-Scented Custard, 252
  Rose Syrup, 283

Saffron
  about, 198
  Mango-Saffron Chutney (Kairi Kesar Ki Chutney), 268
  Roasted Saffron (Kesar), 34

Saffron-Infused Rabdi with Fresh Berries, 252
Saffron Rice (Kesari Chawal), 223
Saffron Yogurt Pudding (Kesari Shrikhand), 253
Salads
  Citrusy Beets, 46
  Dahi Kachumbar, 263
Sambhar, 99
Sambhar Masala, 35
Sankranti, 214
Sauces. *See* Chutney, raita dips, and sauces
Sautéing (bhunao), 13
Seafood. *See* Fish and seafood
Shortcuts, 24
Shrimp. *See* Fish and seafood
Slow cooker
  adapting recipes for, 23
  improvising, 24
  meat preparation and, 24–25
  taking shortcuts, 24
Soups and stews, **62–82**
  Beef Stew, 63
  Bengal Gram Dal and Bottle Gourd Soup (Chana Dal Lauki), 84
  Black Bean Soup, 64
  Bottle Gourd Stew (Lauki Ka Stew), 65
  Butternut Squash Soup with Cilantro Chutney, 66
  Cauliflower Soup, 67
  Chhurpi Soup, 68
  Curried Cauliflower Soup, 69
  dals. *See* Lentils, chickpeas, beans, and other legumes
  Dudhi Ni Tarkari (Squash Soup), 69
  Kerala Mutton Stew, 70
  Khurdi (White Stock Soup), 71
  Lentil Chili, 91
  Mulligatawny Soup, 73
  Murghi ka Shorba (Chicken Soup), 74
  Palak ka Soup (Spinach Soup), 75
  Rasam, 97
  Roasted Red Bell Pepper Soup, 76
  Sambhar, 99
  Spicy Chicken Stew, 77
  Split Black Lentil Soup (Urad Dal), 102
  Split Pea Soup with Fried Paneer, 78

Sweet and Sour Bottle Gourd Soup, 79
Tamatar ka Soup, 80
Tomato Basil Soup, 81
Tomato Coconut Soup, 82
Tomato Rasam, 106
Souring agents, 15
Soy chunks, curried, 120
Spiced butter, 181
Spices, **26**
  about: asafetida (heeng), 21, 108; basics, 14; bruising or pounding, 223; cardamom powder, 163; chili powder, 20; combining, 16; cooking with, 15–17; coriander seeds (Dhaniya), 22; cumin, 20–21, 121; fenugreek seeds, 112; ginger-garlic paste, 14; grinding, 18, 29; to keep on hand, 17, 19–23; marinating, 13, 25; as medicine, 121; mustard seeds (sarson), 21–22; Panch Foran Spices, 31, 123; preparation guidelines, 16–17; souring agents and, 15; storing, 18; tenderizers and, 15; thickening agents and, 15; turmeric, 19–20, 121, 131; typical spice box (masaledani), 19–23
  Amchoor (Mango Powder), 28
  Chaat Spice Mix (Chaat Masala), 28
  Chai Masala, 29
  Chili-Garlic Paste, 29
  Curry Paste, 39
  Ginger-Garlic Paste (Adrak Lasan Ka Paste), 30
  Goda Masala Powder, 31
  Lamb Soup, 72
  Makhani Masala, 41
  Panch Foran Spices, 31
  Pav Bhaji Masala, 33
  Rasam Powder, 33
  Roasted Saffron (Kesar), 34
  Sambhar Masala, 35
  Tandoori Spice Mix (Tandoori Masala), 34
  Warm Spice Mix (Garam Masala Powder), 30
Spinach
  about: fennel and cloves in, 129
  Aloo Saag ki Sabji (Potato and Spinach Cooked with Red Chili), 112

Mung Ki Dal Palak (Split Mung Beans Cooked with Spinach), 93
Palak ka Soup (Spinach Soup), 75
Palak Paneer, 129
Palak Raita (Spinach and Yogurt Dip), 268
Slow Cooker Hara Bhara Kabab, 55
Spinach and Paneer Pulao, 227
Spinach Lamb Curry (Saag Gosht), 181
Yogurt Green Curry (Hariyali Kadhi), 108
Squash
    Acorn Squash with Fenugreek Seeds and Garlic, 110
    Bottle Gourd Stew (Lauki Ka Stew), 65
    Butternut Squash Soup with Cilantro Chutney, 66
    Dudhi Ni Tarkari (Squash Soup), 69
    Lauki Ka Raita (Bottle Gourd Raita), 265
    Opo Squash Pudding (Dudhi Ki Kheer), 250
    Sweet and Sour Bottle Gourd Soup, 79
Steaming (dum), 12
Strawberries. See Berries
Sweet potatoes
    about: yams, 46
    Gingered Sweet Potatoes, 46
    Shakarkandi (Spicy Baked Indian Sweet Potatoes), 54
    Tangy Sweet Potato Bites, 59

Tadka or baghar (tempering), 12–13
Talina (deep-frying), 13–14
Tamarind
    Tamarind Chutney (Imli Ki Chutney), 272
    Tamarind Rice (Pulihora), 231
Tandoori cooking (grilling), 13
Tandoori Spice Mix (Tandoori Masala), 34
Tea. See Beverages
Techniques, 12–14, 122
Tempeh
    Indian Curry Tempeh, 124
    Tempeh in Coconut Cream, 121
Tempering (tadka or baghar), 12–13
Tenderizers, 15

Thickening agents, 15
Tikka masala, about, 145
Tomatillo Rice, 232
Tomatoes
    Fish in Tomato Sauce, 187
    Homemade Hot Ketchup, 266
    Tadka Tomato Dal, 104
    Tamatar Aloo (Curried Potato with Tomato Sauce), 137
    Tamatar ka Soup, 80
    Tomato and Onion Chutney, 273
    Tomato Basil Soup, 81
    Tomato Chutney (Tamatar ki Chutney), 274
    Tomato Coconut Soup, 82
    Tomato Rasam, 106
    Tomato Rice (Tamatar Ka Pulao), 233
Tools, 18–19
Turmeric, 19–20, 121, 131

Vegetables. See also specific vegetables
    Andhra Vegetable Pulao, 205
    Avial (Mixed Vegetables in Coconut Sauce), 113
    Dahi Kachumbar, 263
    Pav Bhaji, 51
    Sambhar, 99
    South Indian Rice and Vegetable Delight (Bissi Bela Hulianna), 207
    Taheri (Spicy Vegetable Pulao), 230
    Vegetable Kadhi, 107
Vegetarian dishes, **109–38**
    Acorn Squash with Fenugreek Seeds and Garlic, 110
    Aloo Matar Masala, 110
    Aloo Methi (Potatoes Cooked in Fenugreek Leaves), 111
    Aloo Saag ki Sabji (Potato and Spinach Cooked with Red Chili), 112
    Avial (Mixed Vegetables in Coconut Sauce), 113
    Baigan Bharta, 114
    Baigan Nu Bharta (Roasted Eggplant in Yogurt), 115
    Bandhagobhi ki Sabji (Cabbage with Potatoes and Peas), 116
    Bell Pepper and Vegetables Cooked with Fennel Seeds, 117
    Chili Pepper Curry (Mirchi Ka Salan), 118
    Chole Masala, 119

Curried Soy Chunks, 120
Dry-Spiced Carrot and Peas (Gajar Mattar Ki Subzi), 121
Dum Aloo, 122
Eggplant Cooked with Panch Foran Spices, 123
Gobhi Aloo (Potato and Cauliflower), 124
Indian Curry Tempeh, 124
Jeera Aloo (Cumin-Scented Potatoes), 125
Kathal Do Pyaza, 126
Malai Kofta, 127
Matar Paneer, 128
Palak Paneer, 129
Paneer Makhani, 130
Potato Curry (Assami Ril Do), 131
Rajma Masala, 132
"Roasted" Beets, 132
Royal Mushrooms with Cashew Nut Sauce (Nawabi Guchhi), 133
Slow Cooked Mustard Greens (Sarson ka Saag), 134
Spiced "Baked" Eggplant, 135
Stuffed Eggplants, 136
Tamatar Aloo (Curried Potato with Tomato Sauce), 137
Tempeh in Coconut Cream, 121
Til waali Bandhagobhi (Cabbage with Peas, Carrots, and Sesame Seeds), 138

Wheat Payasam, 257
Wine, mulled, 281

Yogurt
    Mango Lassi, 280
    Mixed Seafood Dip, 194
    Punjabi Kadhi Pakoda (Chickpea Fritters in Yogurt Sauce), 94
    Punjabi Lassi, 283
    raitas with. See Chutney, raita dips, and sauces
    Saffron Yogurt Pudding (Kesari Shrikhand), 253
    Slow Cooker Yogurt, 42
    Strawberry Lassi, 285
    Sweetened Yogurt (Mishti Doi), 255
    Yogurt Green Curry (Hariyali Kadhi), 108
    Yogurt Rice (Dahi Bhaat), 235

We Have

EVERYTHING®

on Anything!

With more than 19 million copies sold, the Everything® series has become one of America's favorite resources for solving problems, learning new skills, and organizing lives. Our brand is not only recognizable—it's also welcomed.

The series is a hand-in-hand partner for people who are ready to tackle new subjects—like you!

For more information on the Everything® series, please visit *www.adamsmedia.com*

The Everything® list spans a wide range of subjects, with more than 500 titles covering 25 different categories:

Business	History	Reference
Careers	Home Improvement	Religion
Children's Storybooks	Everything Kids	Self-Help
Computers	Languages	Sports & Fitness
Cooking	Music	Travel
Crafts and Hobbies	New Age	Wedding
Education/Schools	Parenting	Writing
Games and Puzzles	Personal Finance	
Health	Pets	